THE NEW ECONOMY AND APEC

Asia-Pacific Economic Cooperation

APEC Economic Committee

October 2001

Published by the APEC Secretariat
438 Alexandra Road#14-00 Alexandra Point
Singapore 119958
Tel: (65) 2761880
Fax: (65) 2761775
E-mail: info@mail.apecsec.org.sg
Website: http://www.apecsec.org.sg
© 2001 APEC Secretariat

Reprinted by
The Institute for International Economics
1750 Massachusetts Avenue, NW
Washington, DC 20036-1903
Tel: (202)328-9000
Fax: (202) 659-3225
Web site: http://www.iie.com

APEC #201-EC-01.2
ISBN 981-04-5057-5

FOREWORD

The 2000 APEC Leaders' Declaration laid out a vision to capture the full economic and social benefits of the emerging New Economy. With a view to achieving this goal our Leaders instructed Ministers to expand and develop the agenda to create an environment for strengthening market structures; institutions and infrastructure investment; technology development; and building both human capacity and entrepreneurship development. In response to this instruction, the APEC Economic Committee agreed to put into the work program for 2001 the New Economy project at its February 2001 meeting.

The EC's work in New Economy project is focused on bringing the benefits of the New Economy to all members in a balanced way. Five member economies—Australia, Canada, Japan, Chinese Taipei and the U.S. are leading this project. As a first step to moving forward the project, the U.S. submitted the report titled *New Economy and APEC*. The initial outline of the report was discussed with members of the New Economy Task Force in April in Beijing. Building on the Beijing meeting and collaboration with APEC economies through numerous preliminary drafts, the Committee adopted and published this study for presentation to APEC Ministers meeting in Shanghai in October 2001. The key messages for the study are conveyed to APEC Leaders as well.

The report provides a framework for identifying a set of economic policies essential to maximizing economic productivity in the evolving environment. However, it does not prescribe the specific steps or pathways for achieving these policy outcomes. Furthermore, it does not suggest any obligations for or require commitments from members. Rather it presents, qualitatively and quantitatively, evidence to support attention to a set of policy priorities, relates those priorities to productivity and hence prosperity, and leaves it to policymakers whether and how to pursue such priorities as weighed against other concerns and approaches.

The Committee membership is in agreement on the value of sending forth this analytical effort as a framework for considering the New Economy challenges before us—and the goal of enhanced productivity as the key to our prosperity. We retain a diversity of views on the weight given to the policy variables assessed in the Report. By identifying a framework for discussion today, this effort provides opportunity for each APEC economy to study and employ, or rather study and rule out, the factors considered herein.

I appreciate very much the contributions of APEC economies to this report, especially to the case studies and their comments on the report itself. I believe the result is an outstanding study and provides a valuable toolbox for clarifying our understanding of this complex topic as we move ahead. My special thanks go to the U.S. and its research team, led by Dr Catherine Mann and Dr Daniel Rosen from the Institute for International Economics (IIE) who wrote this invaluable report. Thanks are also due to Mr Charles Jose, Director (Program) at the APEC Secretariat, who has taken responsibility for publishing the study.

Kyungtae Lee

Chair, APEC Economic Committee

Seoul, October 2001

THE NEW ECONOMY AND APEC

Table of Contents

I. Executive Summary

Overview of the Project

From Brunei …

This Report from the APEC Economic Committee responds to the "Action Agenda for the New Economy' announced by APEC leaders at their meeting in Brunei in November 2000 and starts the task of underpinning the theme of "Meeting New Challenges in the New Century" for the 2001 year with China at the helm.

Leaders in Brunei noted

> There is no doubt that the revolution in information and communication technology is dramatically boosting the development of a global economy. It carries with it unprecedented opportunities in a *new style of economy with new forms of markets, higher levels of productivity and new demands for knowledge, entrepreneurship and innovation.*

In their Declaration, Leaders noted that

> The Action Agenda includes ways to promote *the right policy environment … and build capacity ….*

The Leaders Action Agenda of 2000 built on earlier work within APEC and in particular on a report by the Economic Committee 'Towards Knowledge-Based Economies in APEC". That report analyzed the characteristics of a knowledge-based economy (KBE) in terms of four key dimensions: innovation system, human resource development, information and communications technology infrastructure, and business environment.

…to Shanghai

The themes for China (Meeting New Challenges in the New Century: Achieving Common Prosperity Through Participation and Cooperation, with sub-themes: Sharing the Benefits of the New Economy and Globalization; Advancing Trade and Investment; and Promoting Sustained Economic Growth.)

> *"transcend the traditional boundary* between trade and investment liberalization and facilitation, and economic and technical cooperation ….to revive the momentum of progress *in APEC's core mission of trade and investment liberalization …to foster a favorable macro-economic environment for the sustainable growth of the regional economy."*[1]

---

[1] See Leaders' Brunei Declaration; italics added.

Following the urging of the Leader's statements, the goal of this Report is to focus more explicitly on what, in the Leader's own words, constitutes the "right policy environment" to yield the "higher productivity" of the "new style of economy" where policies "transcend the traditional boundaries".

Accordingly, this Report 'The New Economy and APEC' goes forward from the KBE report of 2000 to examine what structural policies underpin a "knowledge-based economy". But, importantly, it goes one step beyond the individual members of APEC by considering what might be the implications for the forum as a whole of the potential divergence of productivity and economic growth that comes with differential paces of structural reform among the APEC membership. In making this analysis, it uses the lens of economists as advisors to policy-makers, recognizing that policymakers face many, and sometimes competing, views and factors for their consideration.

Summary Objectives of the Report and Basic Outline of Method

At the February 2001 meeting, the Economic Committee agreed to put into the work program for 2001 the preparation of a Report led by the US government on the New Economy and APEC. The initial outline of the Report was discussed with members of the sub-committee in April in Beijing, and initial findings were presented to Senior Officials in Shenzhen. The Report reviews existing research, develops new empirical analysis, and distills case studies written explicitly for this project by official and private sector representatives of the members of APEC.

The Report addresses four questions:

- What are the fundamental underpinnings of the "New Economy"?

- What evidence is there, at the macro level on benefits to growth and at the micro level of the challenges of transformation, which can assist in the domestic political discussion about policy reform and structural adjustment?

- What are the implications, particularly in terms of trade competitiveness and digital divides, of the different paces of policy reform in pursuit of the New Economy?

- What conclusions, both for economies and for the institution of APEC, can be drawn from the foregoing discussion?

With respect to empirical research, the Report both reviews existing empirical research as well as develops new analysis. It reviews existing empirical analyses of the macroeconomic benefits of putting in place the prerequisites for achieving the productivity enhancing outcomes of the New Economy; these analyses focus on the gains to GDP of trade and investment liberalization. In addition, the Report undertakes new microeconomic and sector-level analysis of the implications of the New Economy for international trade competitiveness. Specifically the Report considers the relationships between the pace of transformation of an industry sector, the sector-level trade patterns of an economy, and its policy environment.

Finally, the Report distills common themes from 16 case studies from 12 members of APEC prepared for this Report. Nominally following a "template," these mini case studies come from both official APEC sources as well as independent researchers and address how businesses, civil society, and governments are being transformed by the technologies of the New Economy—or are being held back from that transformation by the state of the domestic and international policy environments.

A New Emphasis on Transformation

What underpins the New Economy? In recent years, the rise in globalization and usage of information and communications technologies (ICTs) precipitated what was likened to a new economic paradigm dubbed "The New Economy." The initial euphoria over the Internet and ICTs subsided to a more reasonable level of expectation more recently and some demurred that the New Economy was simply a fad. The quantitative and qualitative assessment contained in this Report shows that the potential for *transformation* that is the hallmark of the New Economy remains substantial, and that policy underpinnings are needed to support and universalize the value of the technologies.

So, the New Economy is all about *transformation.* The definition of the New Economy stipulates that structural policy reforms make networked technologies immensely valuable for generating productivity. The *outcome* of this mix of policy and technology is transformation in the way markets, firms and individuals operate and make decisions. The transformation is *toward* more productive use of scarce resources, be they money, inputs like steel, lumber or water, or hours of labor. This is important and challenging for policymakers, in part because adjusting to a new way of doing things often entails displacement of old ways of doing things – displacement of people and vested corporate interests that is.

This transformation is continuous. The only thing constant in a New Economy is more constant improvement. Productivity rises because unproductive activities are more easily identified and harder to justify and perpetuate in the presence of greater awareness. But often human nature and certainly bureaucratic nature longs for permanence, for present and future conditions that will not change. This has never been possible, though some think that the past offered such security.

The reader will notice that several factors are not the focus of the analysis. Perhaps most notable is human resource development (HRD), which is not among the cardinal policy domains the Report identifies for securing the transformations of the New Economy. There is much work underway in APEC and other forums on HRD, both general and targeted to technologies as well as to the New Economy. While it is clear that the four domains of policy are *necessary, albeit not sufficient* for the New Economy to emerge, there is little or no analysis to ensure that policymakers understand the role for structural economic policies in determining relative productivity growth (manifested, for example, in the digital divide) and to support APEC as an institution to help its members pursue policy reforms, to the extent that they so desire. Consequently, this Report focuses on structural reforms, where the consequences of inattention are increasingly costly.

Summary of Analytical Conclusions:

The body of this Report provides analysis – analysis of research, of case studies and of data – for a sole purpose: to help policymakers in APEC economies better deal with the complicated challenges of the New Economy productivity paradigm which is causing shifts in relative comparative advantage in the region. This Summary provides a quick look at specific implications of the research for each of four policy domains. The overarching conclusion is much more that the sum of those findings however.

Overall, the Report finds that structural policy reform leads to transformation of firms and individuals, and markets too. This transformation, meaning significant changes in the activities of firms, governments, and individuals leads to greater economic productivity. Productivity is the source of prosperity, which implies that a shortfall of structural policy reforms can stunt the process of transformation, stymie productivity growth, and limit prosperity.

The research concludes that the differential in propensity to undertake such reforms can easily exacerbate the developmental divides already observed among APEC members today. In light of this chain of relationships, the Report concludes that while understandable given the hype over high technology manufacturing in recent years, the strategy of focusing of technology indicators, instead of policy indicators, as guideposts to the New Economy is misleading and possibly dangerous. Numerous examples, especially in the case studies, serve to demonstrate the consequences of over-reliance on technology goals to the exclusion of understanding the causal role of structural policy reform.

Yet, despite the larger and overarching conclusion about the role of transformation, no analysis can offer an exact conclusion for each economy on how much reform might be necessary to achieve some notion of "sufficient" because sovereign factors are relevant. Because the APEC members differ along many dimensions—development, culture, economic orientation-- there can be no "one-size-fits all" strategy for progress towards the desired goal.

That said, the analysis in this Report points to a framework of four policy domains crucial to underpinning the New Economy environment of transformation, higher productivity growth, and economic well-being. These are:

- Fiscal policy and the fiscal activities of government;

- Banking and financial market policy;

- Trade and cross-border investment policies; and

- Pro-competitive market policy and legal environment.

The research focuses on these four policy domains because:

- Specific structural policies are needed to achieve the KBE characteristics and subsequent New Economy outcome;

- Increased complexity, dynamism, and synergies among structural policies in the New Economy argue that these policies are better addressed together than in a piece-meal fashion;

- The forces of the New Economy affect how structural policies work to transform an economy, thus warranting a fresh review of those policies.

The specific conclusions for each policy domain flow from impediments and challenges gleaned from research both for this Report and elsewhere, as well as analysis of the case studies prepared for this Report. Several conclusions are crosscutting, which reminds us that in the New Economy the inter-relationships among policies are tighter and policy authorities and implementing bureaucracies often overlap.

This research suggests that certain policy reforms will be required in order to achieve the broadest economic benefits of the New Economy. However, policymakers face many challenges and must weigh many factors when making decisions. As written from the perspective of economists, the analysis suggests that these reforms are *required* in order to maximize the economic development potential of the New Economy. The analysis cannot say, nor does the Report try to say, that a policymaker must or should be required to undertake any specific reform. But, it is clear that choosing to undertake reform (or not) is a causal step with implications for development and the so-called digital divide. Therefore, the conclusions in this Report should not be viewed as binding on decision-makers, beyond the rational interpretation of the results of the research and analysis contained herein.

Spanning the four domains:

The New Economy presents many cross-cutting challenges and affects the conduct and performance of many policy-making agencies.

In many economies a political decision to create super-ministerial responsibility for crosscutting New Economy developments is needed. Research suggests that synergies among policies are enhanced by the forces of the New Economy, yet policies tend to be "stove-piped" within the bureaucracy of policymaking (meaning that each narrowly focused team tries to keep policy making to its self). Moreover, research suggests that access, use, and diffusion of New Economy benefits can be enhanced through public-private partnerships, particularly when domestic funds for such activities are limited. Giving the New Economy an elevated position at the bureaucratic table will promote crosscutting reforms and enable effective public-private alliances.

- New Economy does not obtain in economies where an open, frank and transparent stocktaking of policies is impossible. Policy reform and wise dispersal of limited funds for policy transformation would be aided by a more open cataloging and assessment of progress toward reforms in the four policy domains. Capacity building should reflect the imperative of making coherent progress on all policy domains concurrently. Aid agencies and organizations within and outside the APEC region might consider whether their outlays support reform in the policy domains that this Report illuminates.

- The New Economy is all about transformation. Policies that ensure that the domestic environment is conducive to transformation and that individuals and businesses can take advantage of new opportunities are crucial. It is a big task to review these policies of adjustment—indeed worthy of another report. But this Report recognizes that policies to promote domestic adjustment are complementary and mutually supportive to policies that support the New Economy.

Within the domain of trade and cross-border investment:

The productivity gains promised by the New Economy depend in part on effective participation with the global economy. The technologies that underpin the New Economy have global origins and global reach. Therefore, policies of trade and cross-border investment have immediate importance.

- Research suggests that reform and liberalization, particularly of services (telecommunications, financial sector, and distribution and logistics), are key to gaining the benefits of the New Economy. The absence of a multilateral trade round has undermined the climate for further collective liberalization in recent years. The findings in this study suggest that *if* APEC were looking to help prevent the widening of the productivity-related digital divide in the region, *then* promoting broader services liberalization and reform would be the best way. Were APEC to endorse wrapping WTO's "built-in agenda" for agriculture and services into a broader agenda for a New Round that includes complete liberalization of manufactures and extensive liberalization of cross-border investment, it would equal or surpass the value APEC provided in catalyzing the Information Technology Agreement.[2]

- Within APEC, because the incomplete fulfillment of existing commitments challenges further liberalization, the APEC forum should extend the institutionalization of transparency, monitoring, and assessment of commitments (e.g. e-IAPs and more extensive review as broached by members at SOM II/2001), which would support further liberalization. This is a specific example of the policy catalog and stock-taking noted in general above.

---

[2] The Report repeatedly argues for the reform and liberalization of services in this Report. This is not to imply that services are more important than goods in the New Economy. Rather, this emphasis reflects the fact that the benefits of open goods trade are already being realized in the world economy to a great, though incomplete, extent, whereas services opening is more incomplete.

Within the domain of banking and financial policies:

The New Economy is all about transforming the activities of governments, consumers, and firms. Financing new activities and new firms, and withdrawing funds from inefficient activities, are key to the process of transformation, as demonstrated in this Report using both empirical and anecdotal methods.

- Research suggests that poor supervisory oversight and lack of financial skills undermine the conduct and performance of the financial system and hold back New Economy transformation. To ameliorate these conditions, economies should develop on-going relationships with established supervisory training and exchange mechanisms (IMF, WB and central bank-to-central bank).[3]

- Research suggests that best practice in finance rebounds to benefit all users of financial transactions (that is, the whole economy benefits when the financial system works well). Thin non-bank financial markets (bond, stock, and venture) stymie the New Economy, particularly holding-back new firms. Transparent public listing requirements, along with strong accounting standards will help deepen financial markets. Economies should give priority attention to, in an orderly way, liberalizing barriers to cross-border financial transactions and institutions to bring in best practice.[4]

Within the domain of pro-competitive market policy and legal regime:

The New Economy depends on transparency, transformation, and greater dispersion of information. Legal regimes and competition policy are essential to ensure that corrupt, unfair, or anti-competitive practices do not imperil the benefits. Rules are important to guide behavior, but they must preserve the private sector's incentives to innovate.

- Research suggests that competition-policy regimes must work internationally for the network benefits of the New Economy to avail. APEC members should discuss how the APEC Principles to Enhance Competition Policy and Regulatory Reform operate in marketplace of the New Economy where more and more transactions cross international borders.

- Research suggests that legal reforms comprise both letter and spirit. Economies pursuing reforms should look to international forums (such as UNCITRAL, OECD, Hague) for legal precedent and legislative language, but policy must also support an overall climate

---

[3] A proposed *APEC Financial Institute* could be a focal point to ensure that all APEC members have training in these critical aspects of the New Economy. Some members do not see the importance of limited APEC resources being directed toward such an endeavor. Others have worried that it could crowd out efforts to develop other training capacity, perhaps through the Bank for International Settlements or Asian Development Bank. It is clear that the matter of financial regulatory capacity is sufficiently critical to justify resource allocation and sufficiently huge to permit multiple capacity building efforts.

[4] This is consistent with the recommendation reached in the Finance Ministers Process of APEC following the 1997-1998 Asian-Pacific financial crises.

of the "rule of law" where transparency of law is crucial, the belief that the law applies equally to all and will be enforced.

- The New Economy uses information intensively and more transactions are made at arms length and in real time. A culture of fraud and uncertainty is inconsistent with the New Economy—both stymieing its development to the extent that people feel insecure as well as being exposed by the greater transparency of information. Policymakers should consider how best to support the development of an environment of trust and certainty.

Within the domain of fiscal policy and fiscal activities of government:

Governments are big economic players in many economies, and they have big budgets. Governments can lead the way and pave the way for using the technologies of the New Economy, or they can hinder the transformation by both public and private sectors.

- Research suggests that government agencies can enjoy the same type of productivity gains from the New Economy that businesses do. Getting this expertise into the government agencies is the issue. Building on the elements of e-APEC, E-government teams that are composed of foreign, domestic, and government entities can bring productivity enhancing ICTs as well as transformation into members' government operations.

- Research suggests that governments should be more careful in their economic activities in the New Economy. High-return government spending in areas where the market fails are even more critical, given the need to *support* transformation in the New Economy, because the productivity gains to be achieved are greater. Conversely, low-return government spending on economic intervention where no market failure exists *stymies* transformation, and must be very critically assessed given the increased opportunity costs of that spending. Reform to eliminate unproductive spending or spending that forestalls transformation has added benefits, in that it enhances the fiscal balances, allows the lowering taxes, or allows increased spending on social needs. It frees up human talent previously absorbed into uncompetitive enterprises as well.

- Research reveals that the New Economy transactions will affect how tax regimes work—both in terms of types of taxes used (direct and indirect) as well as in terms of tax administration. While the future direction for tax regimes is quite complex, economies pursing the New Economy today should quantify the extent and nature of tax evasion, which is often an impediment to bringing economic activities on-line in the New Economy and which, at the present time, reduces the resources available for the valuable activities of government.

The New Economy productivity premium is quite real, and it is the product of domestic economic policies that are more than access to technology per se and that are critically complementary to HRD. Therefore, a re-emphasis and re-analysis of policy reform is called for. If the upside allure of higher growth is not sufficient to motivate policymakers to reform, then acknowledging the downside risk of lost comparative advantage relative to more actively adjusting neighbors certainly should be. The political and human challenges that accompany economic development are daunting. The hope is that this Report will provide the analytical foundation to build consensus on the scope and nature of the policy underpinnings of the New Economy so that all in the region can benefit from the New Economy.

II. The Fundamentals:
Definition and Policy Underpinnings of the New Economy

Since their Vancouver meeting in 1997 when Leaders stated, "We agree that electronic commerce is one of the most important technological breakthroughs of this decade," APEC economies have steadily integrated electronic commerce, the Internet, knowledge-based economy, and now, the New Economy into their lexicon.

The APEC Task Force on Electronic Commerce produced the "Blueprint for Action on Electronic Commerce," and a comprehensive background report in 1998. The Steering Group on E-commerce was constituted under the Senior Officials Meeting Task Force and charged with reporting annually to Senior Officials on e-commerce activities within APEC. Using the E-Commerce Readiness Guide, economy governments and businesses can assess the preparedness of their economy to participate in e-commerce activities, thereby setting the stage for a discussion of policy direction. In 2000, the Economic Committee forwarded recommendations to Ministers to support development of knowledge-based economies in APEC. The Collective Action Programs can now be up-loaded for review at the APEC Secretariat's web-site, and the e-IAP Initiative will include individual action plans and annual summaries, thereby encouraging transparency and peer review.

At Brunei in 2000, Leaders recognized both the potential benefits of the New Economy as well as the requirements: "[A]n appropriate policy framework that encourages: strengthening the functioning of markets; openness to trade and investment; innovation and new enterprises; sound macroeconomic policy; education and lifelong learning; and the enabling role of information and telecommunications infrastructure."

Even before assuming the Chairmanship of APEC in 2001, China indicated its commitment to extend and further substantiate the focus on the New Economy under its tenure. The United States was a key proponent of this work in recent years, and has sought to contribute as much as possible to China's efforts to address this theme. To this end the present Report was requested, a request which was amplified by Chinese APEC officials, leading to the invitation by the Economic Committee to submit this Report.

What is the "New Economy"?

In the APEC region, as elsewhere, policymakers are searching for a definition of the "New Economy". Why the need for consensus and why the sense of urgency? Policymakers want consensus because the term New Economy is used in so many ways that they cannot assess its value or whether they should embrace it. Many policymakers believe that a clearer and agreed-upon definition would help prioritize domestic and multilateral reforms. The urgency comes because the New Economy could bring higher economic growth; and indeed in the United States, where the paradigm is most well developed, trend output and productivity have grown faster, employment has been higher, and inflation lower than resource fundamentals and income levels were thought to permit. Economies are afraid of missing out on benefits—

or worse, falling *behind* in relative terms if their neighbors start to pull ahead with faster trend growth.

A definition offers no shortcut strategy for reform, but it is the correct starting point for deeper analysis of what the New Economy is and upon what it depends. We will argue that there is a danger that the term will become synonymous with only the technology part of the story, or the notion that technology can solve all development challenges, or that riskless growth can be achieved. That would be unfortunate, because the paradigm is real and does indeed present new opportunities for prosperity, though in many respects the New Economy rests on traditional policy foundations.

In the spirit of Brunei, we offer the following definition as a point of departure for further analysis:

> The New Economy is an economic paradigm. It is distinguished by the combination of structural policies and networked information and communication technologies. This mix increases the value of information available to individuals, firms, markets and governments, allowing each to act more efficiently, raising the return to knowledge skills, and demanding flexibility. The resulting transformation of activities yields higher overall productivity and economic well-being.

Whereas the technology part of the New Economy is new and is a key driver of productivity growth, it is the transformation of economic activity in response to the forces of the New Economy that generates the greatest gain. Therefore, this definition subordinates technology to the economic policy environment. What ICTs do —computers, the Internet, e-mail, electronic commerce – is substantially increase information. But it is the economic environment created by policies that provides opportunity and motive to actually *use* the information. The response by firms, individuals, and governments to opportunity and motive is *transformation,* as we shall describe empirically and anecdotally.[5] The ability and tendency to transform is intimately related to structural policy reform, hence the definition and focus.

ICTs matched with the policy reforms that make them usable yields a dynamic, competitive, innovative marketplace, wherein skilled people are needed to take advantage of new opportunities and transform what firms do in the economy. To some extent, ICTs embed skills, and in this sense can make people and firms more productive even when they are not highly skilled. But, a related but separate quality demanded by the New Economy is flexibility particularly associated with the use and diffusion of technologies throughout an economy. In an environment of transformation inability and unwillingness to change increasingly is untenable. Since skills are increasingly correlated with flexibility, human resource development is key.

---

[5] We could go so far as to say that an economy 100% made up of technology exporters but with little use of that technology at home to transform the marketplace is *not* a New Economy, whereas an economy with no high-tech manufacturing, let alone exports, but robust import of and use of ICTs for transforming the domestic economy *is* the forces of the New Economy at work.

While acknowledging the importance of human resource development, this study focuses on the non-human resource *structural policies* to increase an economy's productive capacity. Many reports have been written on human resource development policies. In APEC alone, the Knowledge Based Economy (KBE) study produced last year, some of the forthcoming two-year projects associated with this one-year project (all under the umbrella of the "New Economy and APEC"), and other task forces within APEC are explicitly focused on it. Consequently, we will not compete with that work here.

Moreover, it is the responsibility of policymakers to focus on getting the structural policy dimension right *so that* the conditions for robust human resource development will be in place. Without good structural policies, skilled and flexible people will migrate to environments where their abilities are allowed to shine. Without good structural policies that create a robust domestic environment, domestic firms will see little value in investing in human resource development. Without good structural policies that underpin solid economic growth, the government will be starved for financial resources to support human resource development. Thus human resource development and human resource deployment depend on the structural policy fundamentals that create a dynamic environment.

In this regard, from the OECD:

> Policies that engage ICT, human capital, innovation and entrepreneurship ... are likely to bear the most fruit over the longer terms. But to have any chance of succeeding in these areas, government must ensure that the fundamentals –macroeconomic stability, openness and competition, as well as economic and social institutions—are working.[6]

As important as they are as the foundation of strong economic performance, the policy fundamentals that will be discussed are not ends in themselves, but rather give rise to intermediate characteristics such as the four that were the focus of the *Knowledge Based Economy* (KBE) study presented in 2000 for APEC Ministers. We turn first to review these intermediate characteristics, before digging deeper to the fundamental structural policies that underpin them.

The Knowledge-Based Economy and the New Economy

In 2000 the APEC Economic Committee, in partnership with organizations in member economies, analyzed the underpinnings of the knowledge-based economy (KBE). This work concluded that four dimensions characterize KBEs and are largely responsible for the strong economic performance of some economies over the last few decades. The absence of one or more of these factors, the report concluded, explained cases of lower levels of economic development over the period. The four dimensions deduced are that (from the KBE report summary):

---

[6] OECD (2001), The New Economy; Beyond the Hype Executive Summary, pp. 8. Emphasis added.

- Pervasive innovation and technological change, supported by an effective national innovation system (i.e. a network of institutions in the public and private sector whose activities and interactions initiate, import, modify, and diffuse new technologies and practices).

- Pervasive human resource development , in which education and training are of high standard, widespread and continue "throughout a person's working life (and even beyond)".

- Efficient infrastructure, operating particularly in information and communications technology (ICT), which allows citizens and businesses to readily and affordably access pertinent information from around the world.

- A business environment (i.e. the economic and legal policies of government, and the mix of enterprises operating in the economy) supportive of enterprise and innovation.

The KBE report distinguished KBEs, on the one hand, from other economies that:

> [S]imply [have] a thriving "New Economy " or "information economy" somehow separate from a stagnant 'old economy'. In a truly knowledge-based economy, all sectors have become knowledge-intensive, not just those usually called "high technology".

Our definition of the New Economy is compatible with the KBE concept. The four dimensions of KBE success are necessary conditions for the New Economy as well. Indeed they could be used as proxies for whether an economy is successfully creating an environment in which the transformation of activities by individuals, business, governments, and markets will yield maximum sustainable growth. If the business environment is not supportive of innovation, it is fair to say the New Economy will not eventuate.

The KBE study permitted APEC economies to analyze themselves in terms of the characteristics that are associated with high sustainable growth. It did not explicitly broach the subject of *what* fundamental policies precipitate the desired characteristics. By taking this approach the KBE report facilitated debate on the nature and desirability of "mega-phenomena" such as an environment of innovation, human resource development, infrastructure performance, and facilitating business environment.

This Report pushes the analysis deeper than the four *characteristics of the KBE*, to focus on achieving the *New Economy outcome* of higher productivity growth and on minimizing the exacerbation of a digital divide which could result from too shy a discussion of policy. At the core of the push of the Report:

- First, it is not enough to recognize the importance innovation systems (dimension 1) or infrastructure performance (dimension 3) or business environment (dimension 4). Rather, specific structural policies are needed to achieve the KBE characteristics and subsequent New Economy outcome. For example, if a KBE is characterized by innovation, one must ask, "What factors give rise to innovation?" If the answer is, "Efficient financial intermediation," then one must ask what policies promote this outcome. Or, if a facilitating business environment is key, one must ask, "Do domestic regulations stand in the way of creating this environment?"

- Second, the increasing complexity and dynamism of the New Economy (in which economic transactions are bundles of goods and services) implies that the set of structural policies is better addressed together than in a piece-meal fashion. For example, if competitive markets are key to improving the performance of ICT infrastructures, then pro-competitive domestic policies and trade and cross-border investment liberalization both need to be working toward that goal. Pursuing policy reforms simultaneously yields positive synergies among them.

- Third, the forces of the New Economy affect how fundamental policies work to transform an economy. For example, technological advances may alter the strategy for achieving competitive outcomes in communications; for example, cable modems can erode the power of the domestic telecommunications monopoly faster than privatization could, making pro-competitive regulation a more prominent ingredient for a healthy outcome than it may have been the case previously. Or, faster information flow and electronic trading have altered the formula for exchange rate and international capital flow regimes. Or the New Economy affects the ability of a government to raise revenues by making more transactions services or digital products.

While policymaking uncertainties and debates remain, many (if not most) of the fundamental policies underpinning prosperity are clearer with the New Economy, not murkier. Therefore, this Report presents to APEC members the opportunity to address and discuss in a direct manner the basic policies themselves, now that the members have agreed on the intermediate conditions and have a common resolve to drive the determinants of regional economic development when possible, rather than be driven by them. A discussion of policy allows members to go beyond stating what everyone wants (e.g., an environment of innovation), to addressing how to achieve the goals. As Zhu Rongji said at the commencement of the Chinese National People's Congress in March 2001: "We have already reached the point where we cannot further develop the economy without making structural adjustments." He went on to specify policy postures needed for structural adjustment. Each economy in the APEC forum can benefit from a similarly frank discussion of the underlying policies conducive to maximizing growth, as indeed, some of them have in the context of the APEC E-Commerce Readiness Guide.

This Report does not *demand* policy reforms. Policymakers may abstain from growth-enhancing policies – no matter the reason, which is a sovereign affair, and which may under some circumstances make sense. But, that should not keep us from clarifying what set of policies leads to the most economically productive outcome – not least because that will help us forecast the severity of widening economic disparity due to a divergence of policy choices made today, allowing us to better plan the policy response to the consequences.

What Are the Policy Fundamentals?

Key to the New Economy paradigm of economic growth, where it has been observed, is a fundamental set of policies that maximize sustainable growth through dynamic and full use of resources. The policy set presented here generated growth well before the recent high-technology boom and bust; although ICTs magnify the synergies among these prerequisites and the benefits that accrue from them. As to how any policymaker should respond to this set of fundamental policies, an economy's policy history influences what reforms are most pressing—the New Economy does not burst upon a neutral scene in any economy. But, there is much to learn from the experiences of the member economies about what reforms work and in what sequence.

Four policy domains offer a useful framework for classifying policies that are crucial to creating an environment in which networked information and communications technologies can transform the activities of governments, consumers, and firms, yielding overall higher productivity growth and economic well-being. Efficient and effective *fiscal policy and fiscal activities* direct public expenditures toward high-return activities and implements efficient, progressive, and broad-based tax regimes that support private sector incentives for growth. High performance *banks and financial markets* operating with sound prudential supervision yield market-determined interest rates and allocate resources toward investments with higher rates of returns (including through venture methods). Liberalized *trade and cross-border investment* augment competition, bring in best-practices, and promote efficient production based on comparative advantage. *Pro-competitive regulation, and clear legal environment,* within a fabric of rule of law encourages flexible entry and exit of firms and workers which support business innovation, employment, and growth.

This is not a new framework and these are not new policy domains—why revisit this terrain? What specifics underlie these general policy statements, why are these domains so important for the development of the New Economy, and how can the synergies between and among them help to create the environment conducive to the New Economy?

Fiscal Policy and Fiscal Activities:

Government is like a big business. Even where streamlined, it has a large labor force, is a big spender, and interacts in many ways with its citizens, business, and economy. Therefore ensuring that administrative costs are low, procurement is efficient, taxes are collected efficiently, and communication is transparent are increasingly important, particularly in the New Economy environment where information and networked relationships have greater value. It goes without saying that poorly allocated or politically driven fiscal spending and inefficient tax policies bloat the government as well as have a deleterious impact on both macroeconomic environment and microeconomic incentives.

The technologies of the New Economy both increase the premium on efficient government as well as help enable it. Just as private firms are changing the way they do business, networked ICTs will change how government performs its core functions, including raising tax revenues, procuring goods and services, informing the public and providing for their needs.

Some policymakers are concerned that their tax bases will be undermined by non-transparent digital transactions (such as down-loaded software), increased intra-company transactions (such as through build-to-order inventory control mechanisms) and cross-border service-based flows via ICTs (such as business and professional services). Research so far indicates that lost revenue on domestic transactions is fractional and that the potential loss from increased digitization of cross-border transactions also is small.[7] Good old-fashioned tax evasion should be the bigger concern of policymakers right now.

However, as the New Economy becomes more pervasive, tax regimes that depend on indirect taxes such as value-added taxes and direct tax regimes that depend on determining so-called permanent establishment for the international apportionment of tax revenues will come under greater stress. This is because the New Economy has more numerous transactions; of greater information, service, or digital content; that take place more seamlessly across international borders. The response by policymakers is to recognize that the problem is not so much now, but in the future, which gives them time to evaluate how their tax systems should evolve in light of the new economic environment.[8]

Policymakers can take action right now, though, to proactively embrace the New Economy within the activities of government and gain efficiencies in procurement, administration, and service delivery. An "e-government team" can help. An e-government team is a "systems integrator" which rotates through the agencies of government and is comprised of global consultants (who have experience with different economies and technologies), local private sector firms (who know the local situation and marketplace) and people from within the specific agency of government (who rotate on to the team and then back to the agency after the agency goes on-line).[9]

Finally, successful e-government is a litmus test for the domestic services infrastructures and their international linkages. If the government cannot present information to its citizens, or process tax payments through the financial system, or get procurement through the distribution system, then most probably neither can the private sector.

---

[7] Efforts to measure the potential loss of tax revenue are difficult because of dynamic response. For the US, Austan Goolsbee and John Zittrain, "Evaluating the Costs and Benefits of Taxing Internet Commerce," *National Tax Journal*, vol 52 no. 3, September 1999, pp 413-428 calculate a loss over the next few years of less than 2 percent of sales tax revenues. For the full range of economies around the world, Susan Teltscher, "Revenue Implications of Electronic Commerce: Issues of Interest to Developing Countries," mimeo, UNCTAD, April 2000, also finds loss of tax revenues of less than 1 percent overall, although the figure is higher for some economies.

[8] For an extended discussion of how networked information technologies will affect the activities of government as well a further references of international study groups, see Chapter 6 "Government Operations: Tax Regimes and Administration, and Services in Global Electronic Commerce: A Policy Primer (2000) Catherine L. Mann, Sue E. Eckert, and Sarah Cleeland Knight, Washington, DC.

[9] For further discussion of e-government teams and systems integration, see Catherine L. Mann, (2001) "E-Government in Developing Countries: Galvanizing the Sense of Urgency About Global Electronic Commerce," manuscript prepared for the Commonwealth Secretariat Volume on E-Government, forthcoming.

Banking and Financial Structure:

An efficient and sound financial structure is critical for growth and development. An economy's financial system intermediates between savers and investors and helps allocate and discipline capital. The financial system also is the conduit for monetary policy, which affects the overall level of macroeconomic activity in the economy. Research makes clear that finance and development go hand in hand, particularly when the legal environment is clear. A deeper financial system populated with a variety of bank and non-bank financial institutions is both associated with and leads to higher levels of income. This type of financial environment is also more resilient to downturns and economic volatility.[10]

Competition, both from home and from abroad, increases the range of financial activities and improves the disciplining role of the financial market in allocating capital. Evidence suggests that domestic financial institutions do remain active in the home marketplace even when that market is opened to foreign competition because of their unique knowledge of the domestic marketplace.[11] Thus, liberalization to allow foreign competition does not eliminate the domestic financial sector but instead often enhances the range of financial services and price and performance of service providers. Because of the pivotal role in the whole economy played by a robust financial sector, policymakers should want to avoid policies that protect poorly run domestic financial sectors which will operate at the expense of the whole economy.

With the New Economy, performance of banks and other financial institutions and the financial skills of the people in these institutions are key. Allocating capital to new ventures, cutting-off capital to activities that are no longer viable, and working with businesses to transform their operations to make them viable requires both technology and people. Moreover, financial institutions have to be well supervised, resilient in the face of change, and able to see new opportunities as they arise. The networked ICTs of the New Economy can create databases of information and best practice, but knowledgeable people are needed to analyze and interpret this information. But don't stop the chain of reasoning there—the overall policy environment must support these bankers and financiers as they act on the information to make loans and take risks on new ventures. Thus, the synergies among the four policy domains.[12]

---

[10]Beck, Thorsten, Ross Levine, and Norman Loayza (1999) "Finance and the Sources of Growth," Policy Research Working Paper 2057, Washington: World Bank . Levine, Ross, Norman Loayza and Thorsten Beck (1999) "Financial Intermediation and Growth: Causality and Causes," Policy Research Working Paper 2059, Washington: World Bank and World Bank, Finance for Growth: Policy Choices in a Volatile World, A Policy Research Report.

[11]Demirguc-Kunt, Asli and Ross Levine (1999) "Bank based and Market based Financial Systems: Cross Country Comparisons. Policy Research Working Paper 2143. Washington: World Bank.

[12] Notably for some of the APEC members, it is not enough to simply fix the existing "bad-loan problem" at domestic institutions. People must be trained to spot new ventures that will turn into profitable business for the financial institutions. These risk takers must be allowed to make those bets. For more discussion of the difference between writing off bad loans and making good new loans, and the skills and institutional structure that is needed, see Catherine L. Mann (2000) "Korea and the Brave New World of Finance," Joint US-Korea Academic Studies, vol 10, pp. 55-68.

How do people learn how to be bankers and supervisors? Meaningful participation in the local market by foreign financial institutions that already have these capabilities will affect technology and knowledge transfers so necessary to improve domestic institutions. The partnership between international institutions with technology and best practice and local institutions with local expertise and market sense ensures that domestic firms and the domestic economy reap the fruits of the New Economy. More formal training mechanisms sponsored by development institutions can play a key role in bringing knowledge of the international private sector and official supervisory sector to the region's members, but on the job experience is critical.

Sometimes domestic reforms by themselves are insufficient to achieve a more effective financial environment. For example, domestic financial cartels can penetrate deep into the fabric of non-bank economic activities and consumer relationships and be very resistant to change. In order to boost the reform process, policymakers can turn to the technologies underpinning the New Economy for help. For example, networked ICTs enables the delivery across the border of some financial services, for example, insurance and mutual fund investments, without requiring commercial presence. Allowing these transactions (even if they have not been specifically scheduled by GATS commitments) can assist policymakers in creating a deep financial sector when domestic reform alone does not go far enough to increase competition and improve performance of the financial sector. Of course, this cross-border provision must adhere to prudential regulations and needs to be mindful of macroeconomic considerations, but the point is that trade and cross-border investment policies affect banking and financial market policies and can work in a complementary way to improve financial market and overall macroeconomic performance —once again emphasizing synergies among the four policy domains.

Trade and cross-border investment policies:

The benefits of openness to trade and to cross-border investment need no introduction. There is no question but that innovation is faster and firms stronger in a competitive business environment. Research discussed in Section III suggests that the nature of cross-border competition is different from domestic competition, so that large domestic markets are not sufficient to hone the competitive edge. Therefore, international engagement is a key underpinning of productivity growth. In the New Economy environment, cross-border investment plays an enhanced role by facilitating technology transfer that improves access to key technologies which can allow "leap-frogging" of stages of industrial development.

The New Economy paradigm puts greater emphasis on cross-border linkages. The nature of the production process (comprising both manufacturing and services) is becoming increasingly fragmented and globalized. Multinational firms and strategic business alliances communicate, get price quotes, submit bids, transfer data, offer customer service, produce product designs, code software, and basically *do business* using networked ICTs in the international arena. Past policies that focused on gaining a foothold on the global production ladder (through export processing zones for example) will no longer suffice. [13] Economies

---

[13] See evidence in Section III on the relationship between hi-tech exports and productivity growth on this point.

that do not have a complementary domestic environment conducive to using ICTs will be marginalized from the globalized production process and global economy, at increasingly great cost to their citizens.

However, for the full range of productivity benefits associated with the New Economy to accrue, domestic use and diffusion of networked ICTs is key. How does global engagement through trade and cross-border investment facilitate domestic use and diffusion? Costly technology products (such as PCs), high and metered telecommunication rates, inefficient financial systems, and cumbersome delivery systems are primary obstacles to a New Economy based on information and transformation. These areas are ones where domestic policy reforms can be complemented by a strategy of international openness. [14]

APEC members were the first to recognize that liberalization of trade and cross-border investment in technology products could jump-start productivity growth at home. The Information Technology Agreement is the exemplar of the role that APEC can play in pushing to the multilateral forum of the World Trade Organization an agreement that has both domestic and international consequences.

Communications systems simply are critical and evidence shows that foreign direct investment can play a very important role in improving the competitive climate in even the smallest economies. [15] Going beyond the Basic Telecoms Agreement in the context of an overall new Round of multilateral trade negotiations will enable broader access in the domestic marketplace. [16]

A supportive *financial payments infrastructure* is crucial to achieve the cost reductions promised by technology-based commerce. As discussed more completely in the section on banking and financial markets, cross-border liberalization along with appropriate regulation and supervision will help bring international best-practice as well as global technologies to bear to improve the functioning of the domestic financial sector.

Finally, *delivery logistics* (including customs) round out the set of service infrastructures that are key support structures for the New Economy. Government policies have a direct impact in

---

[14] For a more complete discussion of trade and investment liberalization in the context of the WTO, see Catherine L. Mann and Sarah Cleeland Knight (2000) "Electronic Commerce in the WTO," in Jeffrey Schott, ed. The WTO After Seattle, Washington DC: Institute for International Economics, and Catherine L. Mann (2000), "Electronic Commerce and the WTO: What's In IT for the Developing Countries?" World Bank WTO Handbook.

[15] See references in section "Privatization, Competition, and Regulation" in Chapter 3, "Infrastructure: Communication Systems" in Global Electronic Commerce, op cit. pp. 50-52. See OECD (2001), LOCAL ACCESS PRICING AND E-COMMERCE Working Party on Telecommunication and Information Services Policies, DSTI/ICCP/TISP(2000)1/FINAL,23 May 2001,. And George R. G. Clarke, "Bridging the Digital Divide: How Enterprise Ownership and Foreign Competition Affect Internet Access in Eastern Europe and Central Asia," Working Paper 2629, Washington: World Bank, July 2001.

[16] For a discussion of what this might entail, see OECD (1999) A REVIEW OF MARKET OPENNESS AND TRADE IN TELECOMMUNICATIONS , Working Party on Telecommunication and Information Services Policies, DSTI/ICCP/TISP(99)5/FINAL, 20 September 1999

these areas; and government has the principal task of raising the efficiency and transparency of customs operations. But policymakers will be assisted by the capital, competition, and technologies that come with liberalization of cross-border investment.[17]

In addition to being key to the New Economy, these three service sectors—telecommunications, financial transactions and institutions, and distribution logistics—are at the heart of on-gong international services negotiations, as well as being covered by bilateral agreements. There is much to do to move away from the illiberal status-quo situation that is contained in the GATS schedules and APEC members should use their collected voice to push for a new Round that will negotiate both goods and services.[18]

Competition policy and legal regimes:

The rule of law and pro-competitive policies including appropriate and independent regulatory authorities, transparent and non-onerous business rules, flexible labor markets, and ease of entry and exit of firms, including through mergers and takeovers, are fundamental to creating the New Economy environment characterized by innovation, quality infrastructure, and hospitable business environment.[19]

For key infrastructures, such as telecommunications and distribution and delivery, the research is quite clear on the importance of the private sector, independent regulation, and foreign participation in yielding a high-quality, fairly-priced, and technologically up-to-date infrastructure backbone. The New Economy puts a premium on this backbone, since the benefits of business efforts can be undercut by inefficient and costly infrastructures.

The global nature of New Economy transactions means that domestic pro-competitive regulatory authorities can butt up against the jurisdiction of policymakers in another economy. Realistically and rightly, different economies balance the interests of consumers and businesses differently when considering whether and how policymakers should intervene to affect market structure and conduct. APEC is a forum where policymakers can discuss these issues, bringing differences in views and approaches into the open. Doing so would move the international dialogue forward.

---

[17] See Antonio Estache, "Privatization and Regulation of Transport Industries in the 1990s: Successes....and Bugs to Fix for the Next Mile," Working Paper 2248, Washington: World Bank, November 1, 1999. In addition, much of the work of APEC's trade facilitation projects, paperless trading initiative, and customs standardization, as well as business travel card are directed as improving the logistics aspect of trade.

[18] See Catherine L. Mann (2000), "Electronic Commerce in Developing Countries: Issues for Domestic Policy and WTO Negotiations," IIE Working Paper 00-3 March.

[19] For a full discussion, with a precursor to the New Economy, in Edward M. Graham and J. David Richardson eds. (1997), Global Competition Policy, Institute for International Economics: Washington DC. For analysis more specific to developing economies, see Ian Alexander and Antonio Estache, "Infrastructure Restructuring and Regulation: Building a Base for Sustainable Growth," Working Paper 2415, Washington: World Bank, August 1, 2000; and Mark Dutz and Aydin Hayri, "Does More Intense Competition Lead to Higher Growth?," Working Paper 2320, Washington:World Bank, 2000. With regard to the role for mergers and takeovers, see in particular Bassanini, et al, OECD Economic Department, "Knowledge, Technology and Economic Growth: Recent Evidence from OECD Countries", Brussels, May 2000.

With respect to the legal environment, it goes without saying that private sector innovation and business dynamism depends on assurance that property rights are respected and adjudication of disputes prompt. However, it is also clear that simply writing new laws is insufficient. The "rule of law" is even more crucial, implying a commitment on the part of business, government, and citizens to the legal process.

International bodies are working to write model laws that economies can use as a starting point for their own efforts: for example, the OECD, UNCITRAL, and the Hague. However, in the New Economy, certainty of rules must be balanced against dynamism of technology. Laws must define objectives and be technology neutral. Laws should focus on guiding behavior while preserving the private sector's incentives to meet the objectives of the law.[20]

The increasingly globalized environment of New Economy transactions and actors means that the legal environment of a specific economy must consider whether it is internationally interoperable. Homogeneity of law is not required, but if laws are not internationally workable, domestic firms will not have global reach and domestic consumers will be cut off from the benefits of international markets. Both will undermine the potential benefits of the New Economy that derive from global engagement.

Synergies among policy domains:

This set of growth-fostering economic policies is not new, and precedes the New Economy paradigm. However, the New Economy tightens the inter-relationships among these policies.

- For example, capital deepening, particularly in the form of ICTs and networks, is an essential ingredient of the New Economy. So, macroeconomic mismanagement (for example, through the inflation tax from inefficient or mis-directed fiscal policies or through high interest rates caused by poor banking systems or directed credit policies) is much more costly to economic growth.

- Or, another example, the New Economy depends on a private sector responding quickly and flexibly to changes in technology, information, and the marketplace. So, excessive government intervention (for example, through "picking winners" in business, supporting large companies or monopolies, and restricting trade and investment) slows the development of the New Economy.

- Or, another example, network externalities are a key source of the New Economy benefits; so, limiting global connectedness (e.g. with domestic standards different from global ones, or limitation on domestic or cross-border information exchange) will reduce the benefits to be had from all other domestic reforms.

To reiterate the earlier point, capable human resources is distinct from the policy set we focus on here, but also important. The diffusion of benefits is influenced by flexibility and skills.

---

[20] See Catherine L. Mann (2001), "International Internet Governance: Oh What A Tangled Web We Could Weave," Georgetown Journal of International Affairs, forthcoming.

People who can use ICTs to create and promote growth may benefit even more than those who enjoy the new products and jobs that are the fruits of the ICT innovations. Well-distributed prosperity depends on some willing to take risks and others able to respond to change.

Conclusion

In sum, not only does the New Economy paradigm not provide an alternative to the difficult undertaking of policy reforms for structural adjustment and development, it favors comprehensive progress on the full range of policies—picking and choosing in piecemeal fashion is less and less rewarding. Once the set of policies is understood implementation is the next step. The benefits of the New Economy depend on *managing the political economy of policy reform in the domestic arena above all else.*

Managing the reform process is deeply challenging. The risks from embracing new policies quickly, with the potential for disruption to the economy and citizenry, must be weighed against the costs of not engaging fully in reform. The New Economy does not diminish the right of choice for policy makers but it does make more transparent the outcome when the choice is made (for political, cultural, or security reasons – it does not really matter) to diverge from growth-oriented policy. Meanwhile, adopting a "culture of transformation" – which is essentially what joining the New Economy means – may pose a challenge to the national identity of a society, which requires leadership and wisdom.[21] This we know: it can be done, and will be done by at least some in APEC, as elsewhere.

The next two sections of this Report present tools for policymakers forging policy reform at home in view of the New Economy. Section III presents evidence on changes to trend productivity (and hence economic growth) made possible with new technology operating within a facilitating environment and with diffusion throughout the economy. Evidence from the US, Australia, and Europe is compared and contrasted to interpret the different ways that economies can gain from the forces of the New Economy. Second, using modeling techniques, it highlights the aggregate macroeconomic gains reformers can achieve as the outcome of policy reforms. Section IV uses examples from APEC economies to sketch pictures of how business, civil groups and government have been able to more fully engage in the New Economy as a function of policy reform, or been held back by failure to reform.

Looking ahead, the remainder of the Report will draw out the implications of this evidence for the APEC region, considering in particular trade competitiveness and other aspects of the so-called "digital divide" (Section V). Section VI summarizes the challenges and impediments to reform and offers recommendations and conclusions. Annexes contain the mini-case studies from APEC members, detailed analysis of trade competitiveness and references.

---

[21] Economists may well ignore this, but politicians cannot. We are guilty as charged, but it is nevertheless important to provide the politicians with the ammunition of mere economic costs and benefits.

III. The Evidence: Benefits and Challenges of the New Economy

Introduction

The dramatic growth of the Internet and electronic commerce since the mid-1990s has been matched by and fueled by the hype. Some see the fall of stock markets in advanced economies – especially the United States and particularly in the stocks of technology companies – as a sign that the New Economy was an illusion. As a result the urgency to emulate the experience that changed underlying economic performance in the US and some other economies such as Finland and Australia has subsided in some places.

But, in the New Economy (and throughout the established "old economy" activities as well) entrepreneurs are creating new markets. Established companies are restructuring with new strategies of production, marketing, and sales. Consumers are interacting with businesses in new ways and across more borders. Delaying reforms that will enable these transformations in an economy comes at a price. Delay should not be an accident of inertia or ignorance, but rather a conscious policy choice for which policymakers take responsibility.

This section provides three analytical perspectives on the benefits and challenges of policy reform to achieve the growth-oriented New Economy paradigm, in an effort to help policymakers sort the confusing mix of opportunity and exaggeration. These are:

- The key role of information in transforming activities.

- Analysis of evidence from advanced economies on the relative importance of use and diffusion of information technology into society to enhance productivity and growth, including an overview of the dot-com bust.

- Econometric modeling of the aggregate benefits to be anticipated from diffusion of information technology and the policies that underpin that for both individual economies and the global economy.

Supplementing this more macro view is Section IV, which analyzes and distills "mini" case studies of companies, governments, and civil society within APEC of the benefits and challenges of New Economy opportunities.

Information and Transformation; Dot-Com Bust, But Not the New Economy

Declines in technology stocks around the world are a vindication for those who see little or nothing new in the New Economy. However, this reversal of fortune is driven, appropriately, by the fundamentals of any market, old or new: Data revealed weakness in demand, falling growth, and absence of profits (in the case of dot-coms) or unrealized (and unreasonable) expectations in the case of everyone else. That is, the business cycle (and its reflection in macroeconomic aspects such as inflation, output, and employment ups and downs) has not been eliminated just because of the New Economy, but some investors thought so and bid stocks (technology and the rest) up based on that belief.

Beyond the cyclical culling of the early crop of New Economy applications and firms, and the unrealistic expectations of a continuous increase in the rate of profitability for many other firms, sustainable and profound technological changes are taking place that will continue to lift productivity among "old economy" firms, create whole new sectors and markets for consumer and business users, and reduce misallocation of resources and man-hours in the world economy.

There is a common thread to what changes behavior across so many levels (individual, firm, government, and market) in the New Economy—networked information. Modern economic theory relies on some "stylized assumptions" to teach how economic transactions are supposed to work. The very first is the assumption of perfect information. Assuming perfect information makes it easier to see how an individual's action is in his or her economic interest, why firms buy one or another input when the price changes, or how changes in interest rates affect the macroeconomy. While this assumption does not reflect reality, it is more helpful in understanding economic and policy behavior and relationships. In the New Economy, the use of ICTs at multiple levels of society brings the economy closer to that assumption of perfect information, especially when that technology is networked to connect everyone together in real time. The network and ICTs allow more information to flow, which dramatically changes the bounds of what individuals and firms can do, and vastly increases how efficiently they can do it.

Enhancing the efficiency of business-to-business transactions and restructuring firms to take advantage of the increased information available contributes most powerfully to the benefits of the New Economy. Starting with simple analysis of their operations inside the boundaries of the firm and then radically re-engineering the relationships between and among firms, information is changing the production and use of resources within an economy and between economies.

On a real-time basis, national and multinational firms monitor information flow to decide whether to shift production, change product focus, and identify merger or acquisition targets. Suppliers must now accommodate the technology-intensive, more transparent, and faster pace or lose their position on the global value-chain of production. Job functions change as well: A purchasing manager can now solicit and compare bids from suppliers worldwide without leaving his desk and without spending weeks on the phone, freeing up his time for different and more productive activities.

Greater information and quicker response can increase individual volatility, although the volatility of whole markets is less obvious. But, both demand greater resiliency by all participants—individuals, financial intermediaries, firms, and governments. More information must be used wisely in order to reap its full range of benefits, which makes clear why there is a premium on policy reforms that contribute to the effective use of information.

For macro policymakers, the benefits of the New Economy paradigm are the better choices and behavior that come with more information and transparency. Public revenue authorities should be able to curtail tax evasion, reduce administrative costs and thereby either use budgetary resources for specific needs or reduce rates of taxation. A clearer view of which poverty reduction programs are effective may be achieved through the diffusion of ICT, allowing policymakers to better target their programs to achieve results at lower cost. Finally, greater transparency in the New Economy means citizens can demand and receive superior government services for their tax dollars. Thus government must be more responsive in the New Economy paradigm, because the cost of providing services will be better known, the results more visible, and analysis of the performance of governments compared to others more pervasive.

These fundamental and pervasive changes in the way individuals, firms, governments, and markets work are why the ICTs themselves are the obvious and simple part of the New Economy, but they are not the only, nor even the key, ingredient to its fundamental benefits.

Evidence on Productivity Growth and the Use and Diffusion of ICTs

Policy makers and economists have always cared about productivity. Rising productivity is critical to long-term economic growth without inflation. Rising labor productivity is an important source of rising real wages and family income. But what are the sources of productivity growth, and can we observe a change in trend right now in some economies? Two members of APEC—the US and Australia—offer examples that highlight the roles for information and communication technologies, structural policies, and competitive and flexible markets for products as well as workers.

In the last half of the 1990s, both the United States and Australia have enjoyed a surge in employment and non-inflationary income growth. The US continues its longest period of economic expansion ever recorded: GDP growth averaged more than 4 percent per year from 1995 to 2000. [22] Australia enjoyed 13 consecutive quarters of GDP growth in excess of 4 percent during the 1990s – the longest period of such rapid growth on record. [23] Do common characteristics underpin the economic performance?

In the most recent *Economic Report of the President*, the US Council of Economic Advisers (CEA) noted that between 1995 and 1999 fully one-third of American output growth came from increased *spending* on information technology. About one half of the increase in labor productivity came from capital *spending* on information and communications technologies (hardware and software). For Australia, about one-third of the increase in Australian labor

---

[22] US Council of Economic Advisers (2001) The Economic Report of the President, Government Printing Office: Washinton.
[23] Australian Treasury. www.budget.gov. au/papers/

productivity came from spending on information and communications technologies.[24] These impressive figures are what other policymakers want to emulate.

There are some important similarities between the United States and Australia, but some important differences as well. The key similarity is that, for both economies, about one-half of the increase in labor productivity came not from spending on ICTs, but on using them. In the future, it is this multi-factor or total-factor productivity (MFP or TFP) that will most enrich these economies, far more than simply buying more hardware and software. What is TFP? TFP reflects doing things differently in a business, in order to get more output out of the same or fewer inputs (capital, equipment, labor) – in other words, it is a proxy for transforming, restructuring, and reorienting the activities of the individual and/or business.

A key difference between the US and Australia also is insightful. The US is a major producer of ICTs and Australia is not. That is, Australia raised its TFP not through domestic production of ICTs, but by importing and then using them. Taken together, the similarity and the difference imply that the more important driver of the benefits to be gained in the New Economy--and the driver that is available to all economies--is not ICT sales or ICT production, but how individuals, firms, markets and governments use those technologies, especially in a networked environment.

Review of the Literature: The US experience precipitates research ...

During the second half of the 1990s, US economic activity was sustained and relatively faster than that of other industrial economies, but without any apparent increase in inflation. The US experience generated some urgency in the research community to answer the question about sources of productivity growth so that policymakers in other economies could follow a similar path to growth, if in fact such a path exists and could be gleaned from an investigation of the US.

Accordingly, researchers have undertaken an extensive examination of US data and conclude, in one way or another, that investment in high-technology equipment is a key source (but not the only source) of the increase in labor productivity growth and in multi-factor productivity growth. Despite the similar focus and approach of researchers, there is not full agreement on the manner or extent to which this investment might percolate through the economy to affect overall measures of productivity growth. And, there is incomplete agreement as to the permanence of the observed increase in productivity growth over the last five years. However, more and more researchers are coming to the conclusion that the increases in productivity growth are real and will be sustained.

Some authors suggest that a change in the pace of innovation in semi-conductor chips is key, so that a slowing in the pace of innovation could jeopardize the trend increase in productivity

---

[24] Gruen, David, "Australia's Strong Productivity Growth: Will It Be Sustained?" RBA Bulletin, February 2001. (Table 1)

growth.[25] Others find that capital investment is the key instigator, which suggests that the productivity gains could be mostly a cyclical event and subside as interest-rates and the business cycle position change.[26] Others suggest that the capital deepening via computer equipment (that is, raising the share of ICT in the production of goods and services) represents a step-up and permanent change in capital structure for firms inside and outside the sectors that actually produce this type of capital equipment; thus the step-up in trend productivity will not be reversed.[27]

Finally—and perhaps most importantly—a new round of research has focused on the complementary changes in organizational behavior within the firm that is needed to fully benefit from the capital investment in the ICTs. Workers' activities have to change, and how their activities within the firm have to change when ICTs enter the firm. When these organization changes are undertaken (which is not always the case in any firm), the combination of ICT investment and behavioral changes yields a more durable increase in trend labor and multi-factor productivity growth. These changes in organizational behavior are often more difficult to achieve and can take longer to take root compared with simply buying computers (a point that we will see in the mini-case studies from APEC).[28]

...and raises similar questions for other economies

Researchers have been applying similar methods to data for other economies to see if ICTs have been as important for growth there. The general outcome of this research is that the US experience generally has not been replicated—Australia being an exception among APEC members. Examining research on other economies instructs on the ingredients necessary to mirror the US performance.

Simply describing the situation in other economies is challenging because of data needs.[29] But, once data are assembled, most research finds that the US behavior of productivity growth (labor or multi-factor) has not (yet) been replicated in other economies, although there is evidence of the process underway in Canada and Australia (among APEC members) and in

---

[25] Jorgenson, Dale W. (2001)."Information Technology and the U.S. Economy," *The American Economic Review.*

[26] See Gordon, Robert. (2000). "Does the "New Economy" Measure Up to the Great Inventions of the Past?," *Journal of Economic Perspectives*, vol 14 no.4, Fall 49-74. Even Gordon admits in his latest analysis that much of the "cyclical" component captured by his time-varying parameter is sustainable.

[27] Oliner, Stephen D., and Sichel, Daniel E. (2000). "Computers and Productivity,"*The Journal of Economic Perspectives.* Stiroh, Kevin J. (2001). New and Old Economics in the "New Economy". Federal Reserve Bank, New York (9 April). Nordhaus, William D. 2001. *Productivity Growth and the new Economy*. NBER Working Paper Series 8096. Cambridge, MA: National Bureau of Economic Research.

[28] Council of Economic Advisers, (2001) US Economic Report of the President. Government Printing Office: Washington. Dunne, Timothy, Lucia, Foster, Haltiwanger, John, and Troske, Kenneth. (2000) *Wage and Productivity Dispersion in the U.S. Manufacturing: The Role of Computer Investment.* NBER Working Paper Series 7465. Cambridge, MA: National Bureau of Economic Research.
Brynjolfsson, Erik, and Hitt, Lorin M. (2000). Beyond Computation: Information Technology, Organizational Transformation and Business Performance, *The Journal of Economic Perspectives*

[29] Scarpetta, Stefano, Bassanini, Andrea, Pilat, Dirk, and Schreyer, Paul. (2000). *Economic Growth in the OECD Area: Recent Trends at the Aggregate and Sectoral Level.* Economics Department Working Papers No. 248. Paris, France: OECD. (/ DSTI/IND/STP/ICCP (2000)1)

the Nordic economies and Ireland.[30] The reasons why the behavior of productivity in most of the rest of the world differs from the US remains elusive, but possibilities focus on measurement differences, nature of capital deepening (e.g. investment in different types of capital), flexibility of labor markets, and trade patterns.

On measurement issues, some pundits initially surmised that the US use of hedonic price indexes to deflate some of the categories of information and communications technologies must account for some of the difference in performance. More careful examination revealed that this methodological difference is not a key source of the difference in productivity growth.[31]

Capital investment *in total* is not the source either. Looking at capital investment alone, or capital-labor ratios, there is little evidence that there is insufficient capital in the production process in other industrial economies.[32] But, focusing in on the *ICT sector* reveals more differentiation. Domestic production (e.g. size) of the ICT sector is relatively small in the EU economies and in Australia compared to the US. [33] Investing in ICT capital and adding it into the production process (e.g. capital deepening via ICT) has been lower in the EU, but about the same for Australia. [34] What is key, looking at the US and Australian data, is that *diffused use* of ICTs are key for productivity growth. On balance, the lower share of ICTs in the capital investment of firms in most other economies (which precipitates the transformation of the production process overall) is likely the main reason for their relatively lack-luster performance to date.

Whether firms in other industrial economies will follow the US and Australian pattern and significantly increase capital investment via ICTs is another question. First, capital-labor ratios are, if anything, higher in most non-US industrial economies. Raising capital intensity further via more investment in ICTs might not make sense. Moreover, one must ask whether an economy's financial market structure (in conjunction with accounting rules and corporate governance) can facilitate a change in the composition of capital. Thus banking and financial structure and the policies that underpin banking and financial structure appear to be important factors underlying the ability of an economy to transform its physical capital structure.

---

[30] OECD (2001), The New Economy: Beyond the Hype, Executive Summary.

[31] Gust, Christopher, and Marquez, Jaime. 2000. *Productivity Developments Abroad.* Federal Reserve Bulletin (October). Schreyer, Paul (2001). *Computer Price Indices and International Growth and Productivity Comparisons.* Paris, France: OECD.

[32] Scarpetta, Stefano, Bassanini, Andrea, Pilat, Dirk, and Schreyer, Paul. 2000.op. cit.

[33] For EU see Roeger, Werner. 2001. *The Contribution of Information and Communication Technologies to Growth in Europe and the US: A Macroeconomic Analysis.* Economic Papers No. 147. Brussels: European Commission. See Gruen, David, "Australia's Strong Productivity Growth: Will It Be Sustained?" RBA Bulletin, February 2001. (Table 1) for Australia.

[34] Gust, Christopher, and Marquez, Jaime. Op. cit. Schreyer, Paul. 2000. The Contribution of Information and Communication Technology to Output Growth: A Study of the G7 Countries. STI Working Paper Series 2000/2. Paris, France: OECD. Elmeskov, Jørgen, and Scarpetta, Stefano. 2000. New Sources for Economic Growth in Europe? Paper presented at "The New Millennium-Time for an Economic Paradigm, Oesterreichische NationalBank, Vienna (15-16 June). Gruen, David, "Australia's Strong Productivity Growth: Will It Be Sustained?" op. cit.

At least as important, evidence from the US and Australia points to changes in work organization and methods, which impact the labor market. Most authors, in comparing the US and Australia with other industrial economies, conclude that the industrial economies that employ less ICT capital must have a less complementary environment for the needed changes in organizational behavior within firms and resource reallocations across plants that appear to be a key component of the US and Australian experience.[35] The OECD as well has found a positive correlation between ICT investments and adoption of new workplace practices.[36] While these analyses do not prove the point, it appears that policies that allow flexible entry and exit of firms and movement of labor around the economy are key for the New Economy successes that have not been emulated or replicated elsewhere.[37]

ICTs are the fad now, but research on productivity growth goes back a long way.

The current spate of research, much of which has focused on the US and on the role for ICT capital per se, should be placed within the rich and extensive literature that investigates more broadly the trends and cyclical dynamics of labor productivity and multi-factor productivity. Researchers have investigated how the level of productivity is affected by resource reallocation across industries, R&D spending, capital deepening, and trade patterns.[38] This previous research has implications for the recommendations on innovation systems in the KBE report.

Initially, much of this work used long time series, focusing on aggregate data on productivity for an economy.[39] More recently, however, researchers have focused on increasing the range of included variables, and using shorter time series but more disaggregated industry or even firm-level data.[40]

---

[35] Gust, Christopher, and Marquez, Jaime. 2000. op. cit. Bassanini, Andrea, Scarpetta, Stefano, and Visco, Ignazio. 2000. *Knowledge, Technology and Economic Growth: Recent Evidence from OECD Countries.* Economics Department Working Paper Series No. 259. Paris, France: OECD. See Gruen op. cit. for Australia Treasury, op. cit. For a different view on the EU see Roeger, Werner. 2001. op. cit.

[36] OECD (2001) The New Economy: Beyond the Hype (Executive Summary), esp. pp 15-17 and Figure 6.

[37] See generally OECD (2001), The New Economy: Beyond the Hype.

[38] Navaretti, Giorgio Barba, and Tarr, David G. 2000. International Knowledge Flows and Economic Performance: A Review of the Evidence. *The World Bank Economic Review* 14, No. 1: 1-15.

[39] Basu, Susanto (1996), "Procyclical Productivity: Increasing Returns or Cyclical Utilization," Quarterly Journal of Economics, August , p.719-751. Basu, Susanto and John Fernald (1997), "Aggregate Productivity and Aggregate Technology," manuscript, Federal Reserve Board, February. Bils, Mark (1992), "Measuring Returns to Scale from Shift Practices in Manufacturing," manuscript, University of Rochester. Burnside, Craig, Martin Eichenbaum, and Sergio Rebelo (1995), "Capital Utilization and Returns to Scale," in B. Bernanke and J. Rothenberg, eds., NBER Macroeconomics Annual. Burnside, Craig, Martin Eichenbaum, and Sergio Rebelo (1996), "Sectoral Solow Residuals," European Economic Review, p 861-869. Caballero, Ricardo J. and Richard K. Lyons (1992), "External Effects in U.S. Procyclical Productivity," Journal of Monetary Economics, vol 29, pp 209-226. Shapiro, Mathew (1996), "Macroeconomic Implications of Variations in the Workweek of Capital," BPEA vol2, p.79-119. Solow, Robert M. (1957), "Technological Change and the Aggregate Production Function," Review of Economics and Statistics, vol 39, p 312-320.

[40] Dunne, Timothy, Lucia, Foster, Haltiwanger, John, and Troske, Kenneth. 2000. , op. cit. Bresnahan, Timothy F., Brynjolfsson, Erik, and Hitt, Lorin M. 1999, op. cit. Bartelsman, Eric (1990), "R&D Spending and Manufacturing Productivity: An Empirical Analysis," FEDS Working Paper no. 122, Division of Research and Statistics, Federal Reserve Board of Governors, April.

Among the determinants of trend productivity growth, R&D has a long history and the role for trade to affect productivity growth a somewhat more recent one. [41] Finding a positive correlation between R&D and productivity growth has been challenging—which has been disappointing for policymakers who want to support R&D as a way to enhance growth. The conclusion of the most recent work that links together trade and R&D is relevant for both the conclusions about policy synergies as well as the recommendations of the KBE report: Innovation policies are not enough to spur productivity growth; innovation must take place in an environment of open trade and investment to reap the reward of productivity growth. [42]

Aggregate and global benefits of the New Economy

There are several ways to approach modeling the potential economic benefits of engaging in policy reforms that yield New Economy performance. This section reviews three different approaches:

Econometric analysis of time-series data that quantifies the macroeconomic benefits achieved from increased economic efficiency associated with the diffusion of network technologies into business;

---

[41] Work by Bartelsman, Eric (1990), op. cit. Griliches, Zvi (1986), "Productivity, R&D, and Basic Research at the Firm Level in the 1970s," American Economic Review, vol.76no.1, March. Griliches, Zvi and Frank Lichtenberg (1984), "R&D and Productivity at the Industrial Level: Is there Still a Relationship?" in Zvi Griliches, ed. R&D, Patents, and Productivity, Chicago: University of Chicago Press, and Perelman, Sergio (1995), "R&D, Technological Progress and Efficiency Change in Industrial Activities," Review of Income and Wealth, series 41, no. 3, September, focus on R&D and productivity.

On the trade side, the tendency has been to consider only the role for imports or the role for exports, depending on the level of detail of the examination. On a sectoral basis, data on imports and exports are generally available—see Mann, Catherine L. (1998), "Globalization and Productivity Growth in the United States and Germany," in Stanley Black, ed. Globalization, Technological Change, and Labor Markets, Boston: Kluwer Academic Publishers, pp 17 – 41 and (1997), "Trade, Technology, and the American Worker," manuscript, Institute for International Economics, December 19, 1997, on how exports and imports affect the growth rate of industry-sector labor productivity using disaggregated data.

At the plant-level, which is becoming de rigor for such analysis, import data are not available. See Jensen, J. Bradford and Nathan Musick (1996), "Trade, Technology, and Plant Performance," ESA/OPD 96-4, U.S. Dept of Commerce, Economics and Statistics Administration, February, Bernard, Andrew B. and J. Bradford Jensen (1997), "Exporters, Skill Upgrading, and the Wage Gap," Journal of International Economics, February, p 3-31, and Baily, Martin Neil and Jans Gersbach (1995), "Efficiency in Manufacturing and the Need for Global Competition," BPEA--Microeconomics.

Other analysis on the trade side include: Bayoumi, Tamim, Coe, David T., and Helpman, Elhanan (1996), *R&D Spillovers and Global Growth*. NBER Working Paper Series 5628. Cambridge, MA: National Bureau of Economic Research, (who use simulations with Multimod), and Helpman, Elhanan. 1997. *R&D and Productivity: The International Connection*. NBER Working Paper Series 6101. Cambridge, MA: National Bureau Economic Research. Nadiri, M. Ishaq, and Kim, Seongjun. *International R&D Spillovers, Trade and Productivity in Major OECD Countries*. NBER Working Paper Series 5801. Cambridge, MA: National Bureau of Economic Research. See also OECD ECO/CPE/WP1(93)6.)

Finally, for the key complementary role of institutions, see George R.G. Clarke, "How the Quality of Institutions Affects Technological Deepening in Developing Countries," Working Paper 2603, Washington: World Bank, April 25, 2001.

[42] The work by the RBA and Australian Treasury, and for the OECD countries overall by Baygan, Gunseli and Catherine L. Mann (2000), "Technological Sophistication and Labor Productivity in the OECD" presented ASSA, manuscript IIE, November suggest that higher labor productivity is associated with greater openness.

Analysis with econometric models that quantifies macroeconomic benefits associated with broad-based trade and investment liberalization, diffusion of networked technologies into business, and domestic policy reforms that ensure that resource reallocations can take place;

Analysis that compares the relative macroeconomic benefits from liberalization of different types of trade—agriculture, manufacturing, and services. The service sector is an area of particular interest because of its key role in access, use, and diffusion of networked information technologies throughout the economy.

Time-series analysis of efficiency gains:

The cost savings associated with the networked information technologies and financial exchange of business-to-business electronic commerce is substantial and pervasive across manufacturing, industrial supplies, and services. Martin Brookes and Zaki Wahhaj of Goldman Sachs estimate cost savings ranging from 10 percent in sectors such as aerospace, paper and steel, and communications bandwidth and media advertising, to more than 20 percent in electronic components and machining, forest products, and freight transport.[43] Cost savings of this magnitude have been confirmed by individual case studies.[44] Because the use of these technologies for business-to-business sales and purchases is so pervasive, cost savings of this magnitude could impact about one-third of US GDP and increase the efficiency of resource utilization. Together these translate into faster productivity growth, which supports a higher sustained rate of GDP growth.

Brookes and Wahhaj apply their evidence on cost reductions in an econometric model ("Multimod" used at the International Monetary Fund). This econometric model of the global economy uses time-series data on many economies in a set of complex models of the individual macro economies as well as their global inter-relationships. The BW simulations suggest that GDP in the specific industrial economies examined (US, France, Germany, UK, Japan) would be almost 5 percent higher after ten years, and the annual growth rate of GDP would be about 0.25 percentage points higher during this period. (A figure that is similar to the increase in productivity growth estimated by Litan and Rivlin.) For example, for the United States, GDP would be higher by about $400 billion at the end of the 10 years on account of the use and diffusion of networked information technologies.

Broad analysis of policy reforms:

The OECD and UNCTAD[45] have investigated the potential benefits for the global economy and for regions of the world from broad-based reforms that incorporated not just trade liberalization but also domestic policy reform and structural adjustment. The approaches are different, but the conclusions are the same: The potential gain to economic well-being is huge

---

[43] Martin Brookes and Zaki Wahhaj, "The Shocking Economic Effect of B2B," Goldman Sachs Economics Paper No. 37, 3 February 2000.
[44] Robert Litan and Alice Rivlin, (July draft 2001) Beyond the Dot-Coms: The Economic Promise of the Internet. Washington: The Brookings Institution.
[45] OECD, World in 2020; UNCTAD, Building Confidence.

from policy reforms that create the facilitating environment in which networked information technologies can take hold.

UNCTAD investigates the same question as BW, but they use a very different methodology. Using the general-equilibrium econometric model (the GTAP model) UNCTAD considers the long-run effect of Internet usage and facilitating policies on GDP in various regions of the world.[46] Adjusting the UNCTAD simulations to be of comparable magnitude to the survey estimates from BW[47], yields the result that GDP in the developed world would be about 4.9 percent greater (about $1 trillion) in the long run—strikingly similar to the figure in the BW study, which uses a very different methodology.

UNCTAD assumes that developing economies do not have the facilitating environment in place. Internet commerce yields only one-third the gains accruing to the industrial world: GDP would be 1.2 percent ($30 billion) higher in Asia and 1.0 percent higher in Latin America ($15 billion). If developing economies did deepen service sector reforms, creating a facilitating environment for information technologies to take hold, and put in place the legal framework to help create an environment of certainty and trust, they could enjoy benefits of more efficient resource utilization much greater than those shown above. Therefore, the UNCTAD study implicitly shows the consequences of incomplete policy reforms: Incomplete reforms cut by more than half the potential gains to be had from the resource efficiencies of networked information technologies.

OECD takes a very broad overview of the potential for gains from external liberalization (e.g. trade and investment liberalization and removal of subsidies) and domestic policy reform (e.g. fiscal prudence and domestic labor market reforms). Together these yield domestic resource reallocations, immigration and capital flows, and a changed structure of production and trade around the world. Or, not—since what the OECD does is compare a "high-performance" (HG) scenario where these reforms and changes take place, and a "business-as-usual" (LG) scenario where polices around the world proceed pretty much on the path that they are now-- some policy improvements, but not very much. (Notice that the scenarios do not consider a back-sliding of policies toward protectionism and large fiscal deficits.)

What are the differences between substantive reforms and continuing on the current policy paths? For the industrial economies of the OECD, GDP growth would be 3.0 percent per year in the HG compared with 2.3 under the LG scenario (compared with 2.5 annual percent growth 1971-1995). For the non-OECD, GDP growth would be 6.9 percent under HG and 4.1 under LG. For China, the difference would be 8.2 GDP growth under the HG scenario and 5.3

---

[46] GTAP was developed at Perdue University in conjunction with a number of international organizations including UNCTAD. See UNCTAD, pages 28-30 for more discussion of the model results.

[47] In one of the simulations performed, UNCTAD examined a 1 percent improvement in resource utilization by industrial economies and a 0.3 percent in improvement by developing economies in conjunction with increased service sector efficiency. They note, "These percentages do not intend to reflect the actual differences in access to the Network...but simply represent a working assumption." Adjusting this parameterization to the same magnitude as the evidence found by Brookes and Wahhaj (op. cit), the UNCTAD "shocks" should be 3.5 times as large.

under LG. For other East Asia (Chinese Taipei, Malaysia, Philippines, Singapore, Thailand) the difference is 7.0 under HG and 4.8 under LG.[48]

All told, these scenarios make clear that the developing world has the most to gain from broad-based liberalization of trade and investment—including the services sectors of finance and banking, telecommunications, and distribution and delivery—operating within a macroeconomic environment of fiscal prudence and where competition policies and appropriate regulation ensures that domestic labor and capital adjustments and reallocations can take place.

Economic gains through trade liberalization, particularly in services:

Trade and investment openness is one of the key policy reforms to create an environment in which Internet usage and the forces of the New Economy can increase efficiency and improve resource utilization. Economic theory and business experience both detail why trade and investment openness increase GDP and economic well-being; this very long history will not be repeated here. As noted, however, effective performance of the services sector is necessary to unleash the power of networked information and communications technologies to restructure and transform the activities of all parts of the economy—including manufacturing, agriculture, the conduct of government, as well as services themselves. Thus, it is reasonable to look at recent analyses of the potential gain to GDP of trade and investment liberalization that focus in particular on the gains to liberalizing the services sector.[49]

Several studies have estimated how much global and individual GDP might increase under different scenarios for a new round of trade negotiations. Table III.1 shows the results for global GDP from CGE analysis by three research groups of liberalization of all sectors, manufacturing sectors, and services sectors. [50] Despite their significant differences (in baseline, in coverage of service sectors and in measurement and scenario for liberalization of service sector protection), two of these studies find dramatic increases to global GDP from service-sector liberalization.

---

[48] OECD, The World in 2020, pp. 92.

[49] For an overview of the approach taken by APEC members with regard to services liberalization, see Sherry Stephenson, "A Comparison of Existing Services Trade Arrangement Within APEC," in Christopher Findlay and Tony Warren, eds. Impediments to Trade In Services, Routledge: London, 2000, pp 287-340. See also Findlay and Warren, "Services Issues in APEC," in the same volume.

[50] Phillipa Dee and Kevin Hanslow (2001), "Multilateral Liberalization of Services Trade," in Robert M. Stern, ed. Services in the International Economy, University of Michigan Press: Ann Arbor, pp118-139 . Thomas Hertel (2000), "Potential Gains from Reducing Trade Barriers in Manufacturing, Services, and Agriculture, " *Federal Reserve Bank of St. Louis Review* , May-June 2000, vol 82, pp. 77-99. Drusilla K. Brown, Alan V. Deardorf, and Robert M. Stern (2001), "Impacts on NAFTA Members of Multilateral and Regional Trading Arrangements and Initiatives and Harmonization of NAFTA's External Tariffs," presented at Industry Canada conference "North American Linkages", June 2001.

Table III.1

	Sectors Liberalized ($ billion gain)	
	All sectors	Services sectors only
World (BDS)	613	390
World (D&H)	267	133
World (Hertel)	350	50

Notes:

BDS: Services coverage includes construction, trade and transport, other private services, government services. Service protection measured by excess operating profits of firms listed on stock markets. Scenario shows liberalization of implied protection of 33 percent. Taken from Table 2, pp. 25.

D&H: Services protection measured by telecom and banking estimates, extended to trade and transport, business and recreational services, and half of public administration, defense, education and health (but not utilities, construction which are assumed to be non-traded). Scenario shows liberalization of protection, including extensive induced of FDI flows and implied change in protection-induced rents. Tertiary = services. Taken from Table 6, p 132.

Hertel: Services coverage includes construction and business and financial services. Service protection measured by deviation from that expected from a gravity model of trade. Scenario shows liberalization of protection.

At first blush, the source of the gains focuses on benefits to industrial economies. Barriers to trade in services (including through barriers to investment) are generally much higher than are barriers to manufactures, so industrial economies generally would export more services if barriers were lower. Global welfare rises through this increased trade in services.

However, a second (and potentially more important) reason for the improvement in global GDP is that developing economies gain resource efficiency through imports and investment in the services sector, which raises their GDP. This is made clear by considering the relative importance of gains to GDP from liberalization of both manufacture and service trade. (Table III.2) It would seem that developing economies would stand to gain much more from liberalization of manufactures both because they export manufactured goods and because their manufactured exports generally face higher barriers than do those of industrial economies.[51] In contrast, it would seem that liberalization of trade in services would not have much of an impact on the developing world because these economies generally do not export services and their domestic service sector is generally quite small.

However, Table III.2 shows that the gains to GDP for developing economies of liberalizing and improving the performance of the services sector are nearly as large as the gains through exports of manufactured goods. Given the generally small size of the domestic service sector in most developing economies, this means that the multiplier effects to raise GDP must be much larger for services liberalization than from increased exports of manufactured goods. In other words, the productivity gains throughout the economy from improved service sector performance are dramatic.

---

[51] See Hertel, Table 2, page 80.

Table III.2

Group	Sectors Liberalized					
	All sectors		Mfg only		Services only	
	%GDP	$Bil	%GDP	$Bil	%GDP	$Bil
World		613		211		390
Canada	1.85	13.5	0.38	2.8	1.46	10.6
Mexico	1.84	6.5	0.32	1.1	1.49	5.2
USA	1.95	177.3	0.34	31.3	1.65	150
Japan	1.9	123.7	0.89	57.8	0.95	61.6
Australia	1.16	5.1	0.56	2.5	0.65	2.8
New Zealand	3.04	2.2	1.88	1.4	1.2	0.8
HK,China	3.36	4.3	1.56	2	1.78	2.3
China	1.50	13.6	0.54	4.9	0.79	7.1
Korea	2.48	14.1	1.4	8	0.91	5.2
Singapore	5.60	4.2	2.85	2.1	2.62	1.9
Chinese Taipei	2.78	9.8	1.58	5.6	0.49	1.7
Indonesia	1.65	4.2	0.06	0.1	0.79	2
Malaysia	2.81	3.4	1.99	2.4	0.54	0.6
Philippines	5.4	4.8	3.52	3.1	1.68	1.5
Thailand	2.62	5.4	1.47	3	1.12	2.3
Chile	2.40	1.9	1.29	1	1.17	0.9

Source: BDS, Table 2

One of the principal channels to get the benefits from services liberalization is through the increase in direct investment that often is the manner in which services trade takes place.[52] Even allowing for some imperfection in capital flows (which is reasonable, because investors do show some degree of risk aversion), Brown and Stern[53] show the benefit to global GDP rises nearly 10 fold (from just $76 billion to $704 billion) as liberalization takes the form of not just allowing trade in cross-border services but also allowing capital to be reallocated to new markets that need more services. What goes unstated in these scenarios, but which is obviously true, is the domestic financial system as well as the competition and regulatory environment play key roles in determining whether capital will be appropriately allocated in this liberalized environment. Thus, these scenarios further bolster the argument concerning synergies among the policy reforms outlined to create an environment conducive to the New Economy.

---

[52] The liberalization of movement of persons is a source of economic gain and fits under the umbrella of services liberalization, but there is no econometric analysis that attempts to quantify the gains of such liberalization for the broad APEC membership.

[53] Drusilla Brown and Robert M. Stern, Measuring and Modeling of the Economic Effects of Trade and Investment Barriers in Services, *Review of International Economics,* Vol 9, no. 2 May 2001. pp 262-286 is both an excellent summary of other's work in this area as well as offering an important contribution by comparing the relative impact of liberalization of trade in services with liberalization of trade and investment in services.

Sub-Regional Trading Arrangements

APEC is a regional grouping. Its hallmark is "open regionalism" embraced in the Bogor Declaration. Open regionalism was designed to allow differential progress toward trade liberalization yet to ensure that trade diversion caused by liberalization among a few would not overwhelm benefits of trade creation among those liberalizing. In the environment of the New Economy where productivity gains are enhanced through liberalization and openness, such open regionalism is paramount, not only for the original reason, but more importantly because those "left-out" of exclusive arrangements are more likely to fall behind. In the contest of the digital, productivity, and income divides in APEC such an outcome would be terrible. Some suggest that the plethora of sub-regional trading arrangements (SRTAs) is an effort to preserve the voluntary non-binding approach, still make progress toward the Bogor goals, and achieve the liberalization contained in the Osaka Action Agenda.

The relationship between regional trade arrangements and multilateral trade agreements (are RTAs stumbling blocks or building blocks) has a long history that need not be reviewed here.[54] Recent analyses of the scope and inclusiveness of the current crop of SRTA in the APEC context add new dimensions to the previous research that are worth mentioning here because of their relationship to the New Economy. On the "building block" side, some of the SRTAs have considered more extensive liberalization of services sectors and have focused on trade facilitation devices including mutual recognition or harmonization of standards, customs procedures, business law, and so on. All of these are of increasing importance in the New Economy. To the extent that SRTAs formulate concensus approaches that are then expanded throughout the APEC region, they act as building blocks. On the "stumbling block" side, however, is the potential for each SRTA to promote "its own" standards, which can raise costs and be just as detrimental to inclusiveness as a differential tariff barrier.

The rise of the SRTA adds a third block-type problem—of the so-called "spaghetti bowl"type.[55] That is, the activities of a single firm are increasingly likely to take place in more than one SRTA member, with trade crossing more than one SRTA boundary. The requirements for being aware of and following more and more rules raises the cost of engaging in trade, even if the rules do not preclude trade. This could impede the productivity gains of the New Economy as well as favor large multinational corporations (who have whole departments to interpret trade rules) and hinder small and medium-size enterprises.

This recent research on the range of proposed sub-regional trading arrangements make it clear that the gains are relatively small (compared with multilateral liberalization). Yet there is the

---

[54] See Jeff Frankel, <u>Regional Trading Bloc in the World Trading System</u>, Institute for International Economics: Washington, October 1997.

[55] The "spaghetti bowl" metaphor was first used by Jagdish Bhagwati, David Greenaway and Arvind Panagariya to describe fragmentation associated with different rules of origin. See reference to the broader issues in Robert Scollay and John P. Gilbert (2001), <u>New Regional Trade Arrangements in the Asia-Pacific?</u>, Institute for International Economics: Washington DC, page 13.

potential for large sectoral shifts in employment, which could be disruptive to those economies[56]

Some of the proposed SRTA among the smaller APEC members might be seen as exemplars of "best practice".[57] Since they would be between small economies the trade gains and any trade diversions would be small. If such "best practice" agreements were exported around the region, particularly under "open regionalism" perhaps there is an argument for further pursuit of this approach.

The detour from open regionalism and pursuit of free trade in the context of multilateral negotiations could be a costly one, for APEC the institution as well as some of its poorest members. Such an outcome is not predetermined, so long as the SRTA works within the framework of WTO rules.

---

[56] Robert Scollay and John P. Gilbert (2001), New Regional Trade Arrangements in the Asia-Pacific?, Institute for International Economics: Washington DC. For analysis of both GDP effects and sectoral employment shifts see: Drusilla K. Brown, Alan V. Deardorf, Robert M. Stern (2001), "CGE Modelling and Analysis of Multilateral and Regional Negotiation Options," manuscript January 23, forthcoming in Robert M. Stern ed. Issues and Options for US-Japan Trade Policies, University of Michigan Press: Ann Arbor.
[57] See comment in Scollay and Gilbert, pp 111.

IV. Case Studies of the New Economy in APEC

The previous section offered reformers in APEC economies a summary of macro-economic evidence that can be used in domestic debates over reforms conducive to New Economy economic performance. This section offers a supplementary toolbox for persuasive reform advocacy: an analysis of case studies of the New Economy collected from government and non-government entities throughout the Asia Pacific region. The raw case studies for this exercise are presented in Appendix 4 to this Report.

By their nature, case studies are anecdotal and offer a partial picture. In total 14 case studies were examined for this Report, including 3 from China. Although we provided a template for these case studies to the drafters, we provided flexibility as well and this resulted in a range of styles and focus. Some concern a single firm, others offer macroeconomic pictures or government strategies. This section is not a comprehensive assessment or roadmap to the New Economy. Rather it is a snap shot of incentives and hurdles, common challenges and concerns, and a demonstration of relationship between policy foundations and productivity outcomes.

Our analysis below focuses on 2 principal themes running through the case studies: that the New Economy is essentially about transformation toward greater productivity, and that reforming structural policy fundamentals is the key to that transformation. Perhaps the most interesting message to be taken from these case studies as a whole is that adopting ICT hardware and software is not the hard part. Nor is training employees to use it. What is most challenging is creating a culture where rational action in response to clear information about maximizing economic opportunities is the principal impulse. This "culture" has both a social basis in tradition and a structural basis in the incentives and disincentives that formal and informal policy conditions provide. This is to say that both government on the one hand and firms and individuals on the other play a role in creating an environment of productivity. This cultural dimension is exceedingly difficult to derive from empirical approaches to the New Economy based on econometrics, such as provided in the previous section. It is in this regard that case studies such as these, which chronicle the stories behind economic transformation, can be most valuable.

Restructuring and Transformation

Case study respondents were not asked to enter the competition for an end-all definition of the "New Economy" as a prelude to their contributions. Explicitly or implicitly all of them have a view on this subject however. All referenced information technology, and most commented directly on at least some aspects of policy that shape the use of ICTs. But what is most germane in the narratives they present is the process of restructuring and transformation taking place at the governmental, corporate and individual levels across the Asia Pacific.

The adoption of ICT by the Hong Kong Trade Development Council (HKTDC) over the past 2 years is described in the Hong Kong case study[58] as transformative. The TDC exists to promote international trade for HK, China companies – especially small and medium export-oriented firms. The use of ICTs has permitted the organization to increase the volume of information it swaps with its members. The volume of inquiries from parties interested in Hong Kong, China suppliers processed has also been increased dramatically. The mix of services has also evolved: now real time information can be exchanged through the Council's website, and hence the organization is being pulled toward opportunities to help provide attendant business services such as one-click insurance, financing and the like. A conversion is taking place from an old, low-tech attitude about bringing Hong Kong, China businesses and customers face-to-face mainly through trade shows, to a new attitude that is very tech-centric. HKTDC has become an active proponent of ICT uptake with its members because it now knows the benefits first hand, needs to have them become tech savvy to maximize its own new offerings, and in order to fulfill its statutory mission of helping HK, China firms maintain competitiveness in the international economy.

This is not an easy task. Table IV.1 reproduces results from Hong Kong cited in the case study showing that small and medium sized firms, as compared with larger firms, may be slower in taking up e-business, in particular at the initial stage. Over 80% of the survey sample was small firms with less than 10 employees. A substantial number of them belonged to the retail sector and personal service sector. These firms were relatively slower in their IT uptake for reasons ranging from reluctance to spend the money required to limited numbers of IT professionals (though that doesn't seem to be stopping neighboring Shenzhen from undergoing a high-tech boom[59]) to wariness about on-line banking and services (which could relate to concerns about either tax data or information leakage).[60] (These figures are further elaborated in supplemental case studies HK2 and HK3, which were not analyzed for this section but are included because they contain valuable data.) By contrast for larger firms having 50 or more employees, over 90% of them had reached the "basic adoption" level or above, i.e. they had e-mails and webpages and some may also have their business fully integrated with IT. Hong Kong, China's greatest challenge appears to lie with adoption of IT by smaller firms. Were those smaller firms to be value chain partners to Hong Kong's larger firms, the challenge would be somewhat compounded.

On the other hand, the supply side has been very active in Hong Kong, China, and once firms are ready to fully plug into the network, they will find one largely built. How the builders will

---

[58] Prepared by Christine Loh of the Hong Kong non-profit Civic Exchange.

[59] On June 26, 2001 the *South China Morning Post* online addition reported that "The Hong Kong Retail Management Association (HKRMA) estimates shoppers from Hong Kong spend HK$100 million a day in Shenzhen."

[60] Information leakage involves the unintended disclosure of confidential or proprietary information, which in turn can aeffect markets or market expectations in a manner counter to the economic interests of the owner of the information. The need to use human brokers to divide and transact very large securities market trades, often over several days, commonly leads to information leakage which moves the price against the transactor before he has finished executing his position. But the Internet can help fix the problem – it is not inherently the source of the issue: losses for transactors from information leakage have motivated the formation of internet-based private securities- trading systems like *Liquidnet*.

recover their costs without subsidy should demand sit idle for a prolonged period (say, half the length of a business cycle) is a separate question. The trend is toward broader uptake in Hong Kong, China and certainly compared to many economies this one is in pretty good shape on the supply side.

Table IV.1 e-business Adoption Index (Hong Kong, China)

Levels 0-5	Identifiable features	% in Sept. 1999	% in Sept. 2000	% in May 2001
0: No intention	No e-mail address and no intention in next 6 months	60%	54.4%	51.4%
1: Show intention	Plan to set up an e-mail account and/or a website within next 6 months	40%	45.5%	48.6%
2: Basic adoption	E-mail usage only	34.5%	42.4%	45.8%
3: Prospecting	Well-established web page and e-mail communication	10.2%	15.3%	12.4%
4: Business integration	Web application for online transaction or basic integration with internal operational systems or with external business partners	3.7%	3.8%	3.8%
5: Business transformation	On-line transaction, on-line payment, internal and external integration, web page, email	0.2%	0.3%	0.3%

Nonetheless, HKTDC's transformation will only be meaningful if the firms it exists to serve can transform too: smaller traders need to be encouraged to have email and web browsers so as to see the Trade Council's spiffy new site or email addresses to get business opportunity flashes electronically. And as the Council has learned by taking the plunge, adoption of transformative business practices in the New Economy is not something that can be achieved by official decree or even promotion (though such programs help). A culture shift is required here. This may depend on 'big' players taking the lead in developing applications and driving the market in the Hong Kong case (though it may be argued that in the United States the initiative of smaller, start-up firms using technology to obviate the barriers to entry traditionally held by established players were the primary source of productivity impetus). With the increasing number of applications in various sectors, e.g. Internet stock trading, e-supply chain, e-logistics, EDI services for the trading sector, there has been increased adoption by small and medium sized firms. This is reflected by the significant increase in their adoption over the 18-month period from September 1999 to May 2001.

While Hong Kong, China ranks as one of the most open economies in the world, it is important for it to continue to introduce competition into "non-tradables" – which are *increasingly tradable*, thanks to ICTs and the global business impulse of the New Economy – to ensure it can keep pace with rapidly adjusting neighbors less vested in the prosperous guilds of key professionals.[61] This is highly consistent with the empirical findings about the importance of transformation entering an economy through the import trade channel as noted below.

The case study of New Economy developments in Japan also captures the flavor of transformation and deep restructuring. The case study, drafted by analysts in the Japanese Cabinet Office[62], provides an overview of the New Economy changes taking place in Japan as a result of ICTs and evolving underlying policy conditions, rather than a specific firm. But the signs of corporate transformation are abundant. For example the study presents data showing a shift in corporate IT spending from areas related to marginal cost savings and efficiency, such as personnel/human resources and accounting[63], to core components of how firms compete, including management planning and procurement. As the study states:

> There have also been changes in the objectives of IT investment. While "speed up of operations" is becoming less important, other objectives are getting more important, such as "Strengthening business and sales force," "Organizational reformation," and "Reduction in procurement cost." From this it can be seen that IT investment is being undertaken as an active corporate management strategy.

The Japan case study is also very explicit in observing that only in cases where "corporate flattening" – a Japanese way of saying restructuring – took place along with the move to ICT did total factor productivity tend to increase. (Human capital was also identified as a necessary co-factor.) Attempting to install the ICTs without permitting the change in corporate culture and behavior that comes along with greater information and fewer constraints (policy and market structure) to use that information (i.e., a more contestable marketplace) does not lead to the gains of the New Economy. In fact *it is actually value-subtracting*, because it requires capital expenditure but does not produce a return on the investment. The case study offers us an example of what a shift in attitude would mean in Japan:

> Employment relations from now on are expected to develop more along the lines of "Treatment based on merit and ability," "Securing human resources with priority on competitiveness and expertise." These responses seem to foresee that enterprises will try to link IT to their competitiveness more strategically by advancing restructuring of the human resources within their organizations.

That such a shift is still required in the world's second largest economy toward using *expertise* as the decisive factor in making hiring decisions says much about the "structural" aspect of Japan's economic reform challenge.

---

[61] See Michael Enright et al's study of HK noting that until recently "the non-competitive delivery of non-traded services was not a matter likely to jeopardize the territory's competitiveness;"[61] but that today it matters tremendously.

[62] Prepared by International Economic Affairs Division, Cabinet Office -- Japanese Government.

[63] This is not to say that incremental changes in the conduct of business functions such as HR and accounting are not important New Economy events, or do not add up – when they take place across the whole economy – to potent economic gains and transformation.

As suggested above, the incentives present in a more competition-driven economic environment are the key to altering the culture to better emphasize efficiency, talent, merit and ability in human resource, and in the board rooms and corporate strategy sessions too. In Japan's case, the dampers to domestic competition are fairly well known. But they are not the subject of this case study, nor is it the objective of this Report to catalogue them or tell Japanese officials what they need to do. Rather, the goal here is only to clarify the connection between structural policy factors and the benefits of the New Economy phenomenon too often associated merely with having a lot of information technology around the office. For the purpose of this Report, it is enough to note that work remains in this case in each of the 4 domains of policy that Chapter 1 identified: fiscal, financial, trade and investment, and competition and legal policy.

Korea is coming to grips with the centrality of firm and market transformation in the New Economy story as well, as the case study on the merger of Samsung Corporation and Tesco of the UK attests.[64] Unlike the Japanese case, the Korean case describes a specific firm, and the imperative for transformation in the narrative is unambiguous: the alternative was bankruptcy. The case study shows that adjusting to the notion of a foreign firm as part of the solution for Samsung was just the beginning. The real work of transformation entailed changing the culture at the human level within the firm. Thanks to considerable openness in Samsung-Tesco's sector (retailing) the domestic competition needed to motivate transformation was clear, what was more difficult was training the firm to act differently, unlike in Japan where key sectors still have limited contestability. But like Japan, a shift toward "rationality" in personnel and strategic management was identified as key. As the case study puts it:

> It is relatively easy to adopt just the new hardware and train employees the new skills that are required by new technology. The harder part is the balancing of different culture (in this case, British and Korean).... As New Economy thrives on the network and the network connects different regions and cultures, the balanced (globalized but also localized) mindset of the workers plays critical role in utilizing the benefits of a global network.

And,

> The morale of the employees was quite low due to cultural difference caused by merger, language barriers, and communication difficulties. The major conflict was that employees perceived the new management process of Samsung-Tesco to be too rational and lacking humanity.

Once again having ICTs in the office, or even exporting a lot of high tech manufactures, is not what generates the New Economy benefit: using the information generated by using the ICTs to make more rational choices – which is what information is for after all – is the source of the gain. And often, using information rationally requires transformation of a company, its culture, and the structural policy context in which it operates.

---

[64] Prepared by Youngmin Jang of the Korea Institute for International Economic Policy (KIEP).

The other wealthy economies of APEC for which case studies were submitted also focused on the transformation entailed in the New Economy. The Singapore case study, focusing on electronic government, is conspicuously about transformation.[65] It stipulates a necessity that "Government…fundamentally re-think all aspects of governance to see how we can leverage on technology and new business models to improve efficiency of internal processes as well as change the nature and quality of government interactions with both individuals and businesses." It pointedly notes that, "Strategies that have worked well in the past may no longer be as relevant for this New Economy paradigm," and that "Public officers must therefore be prepared to change their tried and tested ways in transforming government."

For Australia, in regard to the banking sector, the case study analyzes the wholesale transformation of the market structure and incentive of firms within it to use ICT to change what they do and how they do it.[66] The decisive factor in commencing these changes within Australian banking is identified as the opening of the sector to competition. As the case study puts it:

> The main driver of [IT uptake] all of which involved substantial up-front costs, was competitive pressure from other banks and financial institutions. These forced ANZ [Australia-New Zealand Bank] and the other major banks to seek efficiencies and productivity gains wherever they could. ANZ sought "to optimise use of our electronic as well as our traditional branch delivery channels, to serve customers better and to provide ANZ with a permanently lower cost base". Plus it could not afford to look old-fashioned compared to its competitors, as information technology rapidly evolved.

The study cites the CEO of ANZ bank as arguing "[T]he advantages of incumbency are being rapidly eroded by the technological and business developments of the 'New Economy '". But while opening to competition sounded the starting gun for bank sector transformation, it did not proceed in a vacuum: a much broader context of change made such profound restructuring necessary and viable. The Australian study indicated that a government willing to encourage "competition in telecommunications (and thus innovation and lower costs) and a strong education and training system to give the necessary technical and commercial skills base" was key. Telecom competition has a major role in fostering an environment of transformation, but a policy of engendering dynamism and productivity enhancing restructuring in a given enabling sector – telecom or finance/banking, e.g. – would be meaningless without a broader context of reform.

The Canadian case study of general merchandising retail, prepared by staff at Industry Canada[67], echoes the study of the same sector in Korea. Information technology and a policy

---

[65] Prepared by the e-Government Planning and Management Division, Government Chief Information Office, Infocomm Development Authority of Singapore.

[66] Submitted by Tony Weir of the New Economy Branch of Australia's Department of Industry, Science and Resources, but the paper is a personal view only not necessarily representing an official view.

[67] Prepared jointly by Philippe Richer, Service Industries Branch (Industry Sector) and Raymond Lepage, Electronic Commerce Branch (SITT Sector), although again the paper does not necessarily reflect the views of Industry Canada.

environment conducive to its use (i.e., one that *doesn't* preempt rapid, transformative shifts in market structure and *does* support the profit incentive to undertake the risks entailed in such shifts) are transforming Canadian retailing: the nature of the business is changing. The core competency in the industry has become one of value chain management as much as stocking shelves. As the study says, "The objective essentially consists in accelerating processes through better planning and execution among partners." Adding to the transformed nature of achieving that objective in the New Economy is the disintegration of traditional positions in the market:

> Not only is competition fierce, but firms are also becoming more uncertain of their competitors' identity. In the retail sector, the traditional value chain of supplier, distributor, retail and customer is changing rapidly. The Internet adds to this insecurity, as prominent manufacturers now sell their products directly over the web - bypassing whole sellers, distributors and retailers. As a result, retail organizations are often faced with the difficult situation of competing among both other retailers and their own suppliers in certain cases.

If the leading firms in an industry are having to relearn who their competitors and who their partners are, constantly re-calibrating the two groups, then how much less able government is in trying to shape market structure in an industry. But that does not mean the virtuous process of transformation happens without a seminal government role. The Canadian study was one of the most explicit in drawing a connection between industry restructuring and the role of government in assuring a desired outcome, noting: "[I]t is important that the government provide a sound fiscal framework, low inflation regarding stable price as well as stable interest rates. It is especially true for retail sector as the large merchandising firms must be convinced that the economic environment is conducive to sustaining economic growth before they make large capital investments."

The case studies from middle and lower income APEC economies – Chinese Taipei, Malaysia, Peru, Viet Nam, and China – have just as much to say on the subject of transformation and restructuring. These case studies remind us that aggressive transformation is not taking place everywhere equally, and, too, that it is relatively more jarring the fewer resources are available to absorb losses in the process. But the message comes through just as clearly that in talking about the New Economy we are talking about wholesale transformation of organizational behavior on the micro and macro level, but the bumps in the road are more apparent is the less wealthy cohort.

In the case of Chinese Taipei, we must read what the case study tells us about the evolution of Taiwan Semiconductor Manufacturing Corporation (TSMC), but then must read outside the text (or between the lines) in order to understand this evolution in context[68].

---

[68] Dr. Chen Shin-Horng, Research Fellow and Deputy Director of the International Economics Department of Chung-Hua Institution for Economic Research.

The case study describes with admirable clarity how institutionalized the habit of flexibility and transformation has become at TSMC. The firm constantly reassesses its place in the value chain of semiconductor design, manufacture and use. For TSMC the product is the process:

> In TSMC's B2B e-commerce model, goods and cash flows are secondary to information flows. As a pure-play foundry, its inventory costs for finished products are not an important issue, whereas in contrast, customer relationship management is regarded as central to TSMC's operations as a means of securing its rates of capacity utilization and profitability. In addition, from their own view, B2B e-commerce is necessary for foundries to come to terms with the trend towards SOC. Therefore, TSMC's e-commerce initiatives aim to meet the across-the-broad needs of its customers, in order to enhance customer loyalty.

As a leading firm in a global ICT sector, TSMC has its finger on the pulse of the New Economy. But what makes it a New Economy company is not so much the fact that it manufactures computer chips, but that it uses ICT comprehensively to run its process and interaction with customers and suppliers in a flexible, adaptive manner. It would be a mistake to think that TSMC's greatest accomplishment is its prowess as an exporter. Its system to manage information flows among the many parties in the IC value chain is its crown jewel. Moreover, it is not just mobilizing information, but a culture of liberty to *act* on this information in pursuit of profit that is key.

The cyclical downturn in technology, and the mix of value chain modification and special circumstances that exist with neighboring economies, will put TSMC's flexibility to the test in the years to come. It will be a test of the ability of Chinese Taipei policymakers to ensure the fundamental policy conditions for New Economy transformative behavior as well.

The lack of constraint on trade and investment flows in Chinese Taipei has contributed to TSMC's adaptive ability to move quickly up and down the value chains of its customers in order to build partnerships that preclude "commodity" status for the firm in an increasingly crowded market. A transformation-ready firm needs a transformation-willing policy environment as well. To a considerable degree TSMC is as valuable to Chinese Taipei offshore as it is for other economies from a Chinese Taipei base today: its value lies in the power of its semiconductors to harness information that can make Chinese Taipei more productive across the boards, not just in tech sectors.

The Malaysian case study also examines a single firm and its experience of the New Economy, but differs from Chinese Taipei in that it is a small family firm instead of a global powerhouse ($12.5 million annual turnover, versus a market capitalization for TSMC of over $50 billion as of May 2001)[69]. The firm is described as "privately owned trading and distribution company involved in the import and export of industrial products." Though smaller, the firm's business is inherently international, they maintain offices in Hong Kong, China and Singapore in addition to Malaysia, and they are in a sector where comparative

---

[69] Contributed by Karim Raslan, a Kuala Lumpur-based lawyer and regionally syndicated columnist.

advantage has the potential to shift significantly given the investment in ICT by firms elsewhere.

For this particular small family firm, the use of ICT may not be transformative, mainly because of the firm's reliance on face-to-face and personal interaction, and a reluctance to do business or negotiate on-line. Factors including volatile technology prices and concern over on-line security contributed to this Malaysian firm's concerns. But the overarching view was that low tech approaches were just better suited for their business.

A few quotes sum up their perspective:

> There is no doubt that the reduced costs have been a direct benefit to the bottom line. Furthermore the accelerated operation times has reduced inventory costs. However the Internet has not resulted in an expansion of either the customer or supplier base. The clients stressed that in the industrial supply business the element of personal relationship remains crucial.... Clients were adamant that a good track record of service, reliability and a strong market reputation helped them maintain their competitive edge. [T]here were, at least in late 1999 and early 2000, very high expectations about the Internet and its ability to cut business costs. However, they have not yet found that many apparent advantages have been applicable in their particular business.

As discussed earlier, this preference for the personal is prevalent in wealthy Hong Kong, China as well, where over 50% of SMEs appear uninterested in transforming even so much as to use e-mail. The commonality here may be smallness. It is unclear why a firm cannot maintain personal contacts and employ information technology at the same.

The Peruvian and Vietnamese cases implicitly demonstrate the need for transformation. The Vietnamese case describes an on-line medical clinic service claiming to have 6000 unique visitors a month in an Economy with only 130,000 dial-up internet users[70]. In Peru meanwhile, 83% of an estimated 1 million internet users are said to want pre-paid internet debit cards to do transactions on-line[71]. Numbers like this reflect an extraordinary latent demand for alternative consumption channels. Though neither case study addressed the question of the New Economy making marginal changes to economic behavior or, rather, transformative changes, it is clear that this level of on-line demand in relatively poor economies reveals a big up-side potential from transformation. It is little surprise then that Viet Nam has signed a comprehensive bilateral trade and investment treaty with the United States that will serve as a template for wholesale restructuring of both externally and internally oriented commercial regulations and barriers. Or that Peru is the second most improved economy in 2001 over 1994 in FTAA negotiation readiness indicators soon to be published by the Institute for International Economics.

---

[70] Contributed by Dr. Mai Anh of Vietnam's Ministry of Science, Technology and Economy (MOSTE).
[71] Christian Rodríguez Ramos of the non-governmental Peruvian Institute for Electronic Commerce (IPCE) prepared this case study.

Finally, this Report includes fully 3 case studies concerning China. We decided to solicit multiple cases concerning China for three reasons. First, China is APEC Chair this year, and we believe the opportunity for many ministers and leaders to visit various parts of China for APEC meetings can be heightened with additional case study materials to provide context on the setting. Second, China is exceptionally diverse in terms of levels and conditions of development and large in terms of market size, arguing for a broad set of views. Finally, and most importantly, the combination of rapid ICT uptake and rapid structural policy adjustment already taking place in China is in and of itself a principle driver of the New Economy imperative for all other economies in the APEC region. Does this mean China has achieved New Economy status? In some ways yes, in some ways no: the story is a complicated one, hence the multitude of China case studies. Our goal here is not to decide that question, but to learn what we can about the New Economy from experiences in China.[72]

The three China cases include an assessment of the environment for e-commerce in international trade with China, done by a MOFTEC subsidiary unit charged with its promotion (CIECC)[73]; an assessment of the quasi-statal conglomerate TCL Holdings and its transformation to take advantage of new demand for ICT[74]; and a study of difficulties promoting retail business automation software systems due to market distortions, contributed by an expatriate business professional with long experience in China.

Each China case reflects the profound changes that have taken place in China, but also illustrates the benefits still unrealized due to residual restraints on transformation, and the challenges of overcoming them. Take the CIECC study. It describes an elaborate electronic trade network that has been built to facilitate and streamline international trade, especially exports. The trade network, called CIETNet, is said by the MOFTEC unit to have 97 nodes covering China with an integrated network for data exchange and trade processing, with links to international networks. The case says that last year (2000), "...about 40 billion U.S. dollars export transactions used CIETNet to transmit export documents." This achievement testifies to the transformation that has taken place using ICTs.

But we also know from copious research and from senior Chinese officials themselves that serious local distortions, including intra-provincial trade barriers, prevent full rationalization of commerce. The ICTs cannot transform the market structure alone, rather central policy reform must occur in order for the network to realize its full potential. Otherwise, regions utilizing the efficiency benefits of the network (e.g., permitting online financial services) will pull ahead while regions resisting network-borne competition in order to promote local infant firms will fall behind. The resistors will hobble the non-high tech, old economy by denying it the benefit of competitive value chain partnerships. The CIECC study correctly reveals the likely transformation of government, too, that will occur as the network is allowed to function fully: "It [the network] also makes the governmental administration on trade more efficient and more transparent, eradicates low efficiency, arbitrary, and bureaucracy and helps to build

---

[72] The purpose of this Report is not to arbitrate who is and who is not a New Economy. Rather, it is to provide evidence on the nature and benefits of the New Economy phenomenon that policy professionals in APEC can use in advocating reform.

[73] **China International Electronic Commerce Center of the Ministry of Foreign Trade and Economic Cooperation.**

[74] Prepared, like the Hong Kong study, by Christine Loh of the non-profit Civic Exchange.

an administration-service system of standard, efficiency, justice and transparency." What that means is that the *status quo* in governance and regulatory behavior in most of China as it pertains to commercial activity is about to change – radically.

This forecast is substantiated by the other two China case studies focused on the fortunes of particular businesses in China. From the retail automation systems study we see first hand what the countervailing local forces are that must be transformed if CIECC's network is to realize its value, and in the TCL case we can extrapolate what sorts of top level structural policy reforms will be needed to permit a Chinese success story in the journey from state owned-follower of policy to dynamic mid-sized-competitor for national market share to make the next step: to world class, world scale competitor.

The case study by a small private retail automation systems company is valuable, as it is from the perspective of a firm that offers the nuts and bolts of information processing technology for the New Economy. From the case study:

> [The] product is a Consumer Relationship Management software suite, which gather information about consumers and analyze demographic and purchasing characteristics in order to enable companies to improve operating margins. Profitability is increased through better targeting of marketing campaigns, early identification of attrition risks, improved management of customer service, and other technology-aided marketing and sales activities.

This is precisely the kind of product that permits managers of a business to quantify the advantages and disadvantages of how they are currently using scarce capital and labor for commercial ends. Once again, the rational reaction to that data is – so long as the market incentive exists – to transform a business using new information, because it is no longer ambiguous what is fruitful and what is wasteful in the present activities of the firm. The case study describes, however, how the normal market incentives that would bring about that transformation, and with it – quite possibly – increased profits, jobs and efficiency in resource use, are stymied by policy inadequacies. The next section explores the policy specifics; our point here is that transformation is the mother of productivity, and transformation is impeded by distortions in the policy environment.

TCL electronics is another proof of the transformation that is taking place in China. Its ownership structure is partly state, partly market (with HK and BVI listing vehicles), and the firm was one of the first to list in the Shenzhen stock exchange in 1993. Concurrently, the firm made a conscious shift up-market toward higher value added, more technology-intensive products, starting with simple consumer electronics and moving toward computer related goods. It has shifted from a local orientation to an international mindset, forming joint ventures and alliances with Chinese Taipei and American high-tech firms. Starting in 1996 TCL established a research and development function in the United States to acquire expertise in high definition television technology. Firms like TCL are transforming expectations about China: this is no longer an economy foreign firms come to on a one way street to find cheap labor alone; Chinese firms are reaching out just as aggressively, positioning themselves for a future that is thoroughly global.

Two dynamics are most worth noting here. First, the principle transformation at TCL was the mindset that senior managers had toward the firm and its purpose. Second, the vision of those managers required more than tech-sector opportunities or internal installation of ICTs to be achieved: it required critical shifts in the policy environment. Without steps toward financial liberalization it could not have financed its up-market transition, without trade and investment liberalization it could not have maximized earlier opportunities in contract manufacturing. As a firm growing based on domestic demand, especially in telecommunications and media, TCL has been most aided by the introduction of competition into these niches domestically, which is spurring consumption and network build-out. Its further success will be predicated even more directly on a pro-competitive stance by central authorities, as its increasing market share may well come at the expense of less competitive domestic and foreign firms which will argue against competition unless the interest of consumers and macroeconomic growth are defended by the center.

Conclusions About Transformation

This section has drawn from APEC case studies to demonstrate that the New Economy paradigm, characterized by new firms and new use of technology by existing firms to lift productivity – with positive consequences for the macroeconomy – is found in the transformation and restructuring of how economic agents behave in the market, not just in the manufacture or adoption of computers and phones. The next section will draw on these case studies again to clarify the connection between that transformation and the specific policy domains that are identified as critical to the New Economy at the beginning of this Report.

Transformation and Policy

Policymakers have over-emphasized the power of manufacturing and selling ICTs alone in generating productivity gains and attendant macroeconomic benefits associated with the New Economy. By contrast, we have stressed that those gains result from more profound transformations in economic behavior that occur when key policy reforms empower firms and individuals to maximize the use of ICTs and information resources they make available. The previous section drew on case studies to illustrate the character of the process of transformation; this section illustrates the connection between that transformation and policy. Both sections are meant for the use of policymakers in the Asia Pacific to draw upon in demonstrating to fellow decision-makers domestically the imperative of policy reform in maintaining pace with other New Economy economies.

Six factors will be examined in this section: the 4 structural policy domains that are the foundation of clear market incentives (fiscal, financial, trade and investment, and competition and legal), and 2 policy concerns that deal in culture as much as the realm of economics, namely human resource policy and national e-commerce promotion strategies.

Fiscal Policy

The case studies show the relationship between fiscal policy reform and New Economy style transformation, both affirmatively and negatively.

Recall from Chapter 1 the constitution of the fiscal policy domain. An illustrative list of fiscal policy tasks any government needs to address would include the factors in this restatement of the fiscal domain:

Fiscal policy: Government has a large labor force, is a big spender, and interacts in many ways with citizens, business, and economy. Ensuring low administrative costs, efficient procurement, and transparent communication are important, particularly as information and networked relationships have greater value. Poorly allocated or politically driven fiscal spending and inefficient tax policies bloat the government and damage both the macroeconomic environment and microeconomic incentives. ICTs both increase the premium on efficient government and help enable it. Private sector participation and public-private partnerships in the delivery of government services can increase efficiency. Moreover, information technologies can enhance the transparency of procurement and regulations that allow the private sector to focus on productive economic activity as well as enhances the role for civil society.

A key point here is that governments evince sufficient fiscal discipline on the spending side – for several reasons. Traditionally, this concern was so not to tempt recourse to "inflation taxing" in order to reduce the burden of debt. Several more dynamic points come into play in the discussion of APEC economies. First, fiscal spending plays a role in supporting consumption, thereby moderating business cycle fluctuation; but it can have the unintended consequence of *deferring transformation and restructuring* if it simply makes up for poor economic performance that is structural in nature, not cyclical.

Second, public expenditure priorities can prevent adjustment quite apart from aggregate demand management efforts (though the latter is often used as a cover) when a large share of public spending goes to support *specific* firms for the sake of industrial policy. Not only can such efforts crowd out competitive new firms – both foreign and domestic – from acquiring the market share that is the life blood incentive for investment, but these goals crowd out more productive avenues for expenditure such as primary health and education, or environmental reclamation that national resources might otherwise be directed toward. Finally, the tax side is fiscal spending's twin, and it is imperative that fiscal outlays be tamed so that tax rates can be held lower enough to attract investment and innovation while still providing for basic high-return government tasks.

This quote from the Korea Samsung-Tesco case study is both instructive and fascinating:

> Had the macroeconomic conditions been favorable, Samsung Corporation would
> never have considered a merger with Tesco PLC and the result would not have been as

good as now. Strategy and Planning department of Samsung-Tesco pointed out that while favorable macroeconomic condition is important and much more preferred, it is also the case that the unfavorable macroeconomic condition sometimes boosts restructuring and creates an environment for what Samsung-Tesco calls a 'step change'.... When the organization does not have capability of conducting 'creative destruction', unfavorable macroeconomic conditions could stimulate the innovation process, but it should not be (and cannot be) deliberately created for its risk is too big.

The message here is extremely clear: the until recently-prevailing strategy in Korea of using fiscal subsidies directly or indirectly to offset the commercial shortcomings of firms in a changing, increasingly global economy stymied transformation which – though unpleasant to go through – is the source of subsequent corporate strength. In the end, as difficult as transition was for Samsung, it probably can be thanked for the continuing viability of countless jobs.

Very little is said *directly* in the case studies about fiscal policy issues, aside from a pointed comment in the Canadian retail sector case study:

> [I]t is important that the government provide a sound fiscal framework, low inflation regarding stable price as well as stable interest rates. It is especially true for [the] retail sector as the large merchandising firms must be convinced that the economic environment is conducive to sustaining economic growth before they make large capital investments.

As this quote notes fiscal policy has an important role to play in minimizing the disruptive effects of business cycles and thus in girding investment, and that is something that many of the case studies emphasize. Malaysia; Hong Kong, China; Peru; Japan and Korea, for example, in addition to Canada, suggested that ICT investments had been reduced by lean economic conditions (though often these were considered exogenous and hence less amenable to proper domestic fiscal action).

> A thesis consistent with many of the case studies but not directly stated is that the tax regimes in some APEC economies are an impediment to the adoption of ICTs and thus to productivity transformation.

The reason behind this may be as simple as a highly atomistic market structures marked by a predominance of SMEs. Or, it may mean a tendency to tax avoidance among many firms that would work against the uptake of online modes of commerce which leave a tax trail of information for authorities to follow. That tax avoidance is an impediment to moving on line in most of the APEC economies is clear; for research purposes here, names need not be named, but the problem needs to be recognized. One could posit that movement to online modes of business is in fact inevitable, and therefore that Asian governments most afflicted by tax evasion today *are on the cusp of a major windfall in revenues*, which will permit them to better invest in social safety nets and services while simultaneously reducing marginal rates for the few firms that are regular payers. However, *they must ensure that the reasons for evasion are not so structural that firms would rather move operations offshore or fold up shop rather than face the statutory tax burden.*

Financial Deepening

The case studies offer many examples of the importance of financial deepening to fully propagate a New Economy outcome. Recall that by financial deepening we are concerned with an outcome: the most efficient allocation of financial resources toward investments with the highest returns on a long-term basis. The ingredients for such an outcome include enough bank and non-bank financial institutions is engender competition and competitive offerings that are a central input for every other sector in the economy. Deep financial markets operating within an environment of appropriate prudential management yield market-determined interest rates. Part of the New Economy mindset is institutional flexibility to adjust to the most promising opportunities available; access to efficient financial services is like the grease in a motor that permits that flexibility. Adequate prudential regulation is an essential part of making that possible.

Financial institutions were early adopters of information technology, using it to cut operating costs by processing transactions more efficiently as seen in the Australian banking case study. They did old tasks, but more efficiently. But ICTs meant offering whole new services as well, like remote banking and 24 hour services. Spreadsheet software, an early but revolutionary ICT offering, has directly influenced the trend in mergers and acquisitions, and financial decisionmaking by everyone from the largest conglomerates to individuals, thus changing the demand for financial services dramatically. The case study reflects the globalization of finance: an individual can now manage a Citibank account in New York from literally any place on earth, and indeed, many do.

In Canada "Company A continues to leverage traditional EDI technology to process transactions with suppliers. Company B receives more than one thousand orders on its web site per day. In 1999, Internet sales exceeded $ 22 million. Company C uses its network to place orders, submit invoice, track shipments of goods and pay its suppliers." All these uses of the Internet increase efficiency and competitiveness, and all require both policy willingness to permit financial service innovation and provision in a new way, and a competitive finance industry where firms foreign or domestic strive to expand the utility of their services for consumers and businesses.

The Canadian retail case study shows how retailers are integrating all financial tasks into their B2B networking practices. By contrast, the China case study documents that similar types "of simple financial service [are] off limits to the private sector in China, not obtainable from any of the state-owned banks, and therefore not, currently, an option." The biggest problem identified by Samsung-Tesco in Korea was also a government prohibition against private businesses offering new financial services to customers who wanted them. In Peru, "Many projects to build Internet focused SMEs have been halted because of the high interest rates in the Peruvian financial system."

The global provision of financial services we see in the Australian study makes it increasingly fruitless to maintain restrictions on innovation in finance domestically. At the very least, domestic citizens will be highly aware of the superior value and quality of financial services offshore, and therefore be discontent with their local providers. Moreover informal arbitraging to take advantage of the value elsewhere will emerge and entrepreneurs will go abroad to access efficient finance.

It is also clear how important the prudential function is for financial deepening to lead to long-term benefits. In Malaysia, the studied firm worried that online finance: "...depended on the quality of management and supervision. 'We are concerned about the calibre of the people inputting data and supervising the process.'" In Viet Nam, the lack of regulations covering financial transactions on the internet leads the entrepreneur in the case to be cautious about on-line payments. Even the case study from advanced Japan fretted that "we cannot deny that IT has served to destabilize financial and capital markets." These concerns are totally justified, they range from the microeconomic needs such as consumer protection to macro concerns like interest rates, and they require a trusted and competent organization of financial regulators and policy reformers to remedy.

Economic transformation yields benefits, in terms of profitability, jobs created, quality of life and environment and prevented adjustment shocks in the future. But it requires inputs and finance is perhaps the most important one. The financial sector must send some of the most sensitive, critical and powerful signals through the whole economy in the form of the prices it sets for finance, therefore it is critically important that it performs efficiently. The financial sector itself must be permitted to transform to be viable in the New Economy, but then it must be empowered by its independence to help all other sectors transform as well. Ultimately, given the size of the rest of the economy compared to the finance sector, it is most important that this input to transformation is provided efficiently, and of very little importance whether it is provided by a domestic firm.

Trade and Investment Policy

The case studies offer plenty of examples of and support for the broadly understood notion that liberalization of trade and investment policies is key to stoking domestic productivity growth. The inflow of foreign know-how, technology, competition, culture, products, and finance, as well as the "inflow" of foreign demand, can each bring about transformation and restructuring in domestic firms. Failure of policy to encourage openness to trade and investment conversely defers that restructuring, and during that deferral – especially during moments of profound technological change in the external economy such as is taking place today – domestic commercial prowess will generally erode.

The case studies mostly reflect the upside of the New Economy for trade and investment openness. In Hong Kong, China, the Trade Development Council may now process over 1 million inquiries about local businesses a year. The CIETNet e-commerce network in China is expected to help precipitate a fully paperless trading environment there by 2010, which is expected to also help eliminate false trading license problems between China and the US and other economies. (Indeed, the CIETNet case study notes the importance of APEC in helping coordinate progress toward that paperless environment.) Peruvians send large amounts of goods home through internet commerce, along with $800 million a year, and the customs authorities hope to be paperless in the medium term. Competition successfully impelled the Australian banking industry to dramatically improve competitiveness.

But for each of these successes and hopes, there is a dark side: the prospect that for whatever reasons, the domestic policy changes needed to implement these improvements to the trade environment will not happen everywhere at once, resulting in at least temporary new comparative advantages for early movers and corresponding disadvantages for laggards. The implications of this are dealt with at length below, in the section on *Digital Divide*.

Competition and Legal

At the macro level, competition policy must support an efficient market structure outcome. Consider the following quote from the Canadian case on the subject of market structure. "Not only is competition fierce, but firms are also becoming more uncertain of their competitors' identity. In the retail sector, the traditional value chain of supplier, distributor, retail and customer is changing rapidly. The Internet adds to this insecurity, as prominent manufacturers now sell their products directly over the web - bypassing whole sellers, distributors and retailers. As a result, retail organizations are often faced with the difficult situation of competing among both other retailers and their own suppliers in certain cases." This concern from the business perspective has an analogue for policymakers: it is increasingly challenging, yet increasingly important, to estimate the market contestability results (and hence consumer welfare implications) of new horizontal and vertical arrangements among firms. Policymakers must take heed of the confusion even among firms about market power to redouble domestic efforts to provide fair trade governance, taking care not to stifle innovation in the process, so that the New Economy is characterized for easier entry and exit from market.

At the micro level, the competition regime must permit productive firms to use ICTs to create efficient business models and take commercial risks without arbitrary restrictions on scope and scale of business. One case study of China described the effects of market licensing and structure authorities that are still more concerned with the welfare of a handful of threatened producers than the welfare of the myriad of consumers.

> "[R]egulatory restrictions on operating retail establishments across provincial lines make it difficult for the company to grow enough to increase efficiency by lowering overhead costs. [L]icense-scope restrictions make it hard to come up with internal financing arrangements to facilitate coordinated, group activity. [G]eneral retailing licenses, permitting sales of different product lines, cannot be obtained by small or private companies. Instead, to conduct its business, the company must use surrogates to act as the seller-of-record for the various product lines."

Not only does such a situation harm consumers, but it hobbles what ought to be a new generation of competitive firms from taking off because they cannot access such services, while new foreign competitors post-WTO most certainly will be able to even if they consume them offshore for onshore use.

In instances, the pro-competition function of government must be to actively look for potential sources of competition to incumbent domestic firms. This is why in Australia the "roles of government that have facilitated e-commerce include encouraging competition in telecommunications (and thus innovation and lower costs)".

There are also indications in the case studies of how important reforms to the basic legal environment are, including of course sound regulatory stances in areas discussed above (fiscal policy, financial, trade, etc.), and just as importantly deregulatory moves where needed. There wariness of businesspeople to use online modalities for commerce expressed in many case studies (e.g., Malaysia) reflects the fact the in many Asian economies informal means to approximate a predictable legal environment have been fashioned over time through personal relationships and individual, local political leadership – such as a mayor in a port town ensuring foreign investors are not cheated even though national legal mechanisms are not fully in place to guarantee that. The promise of the networked economy must inherently go beyond such a bundle of local "islands" of legality to take advantage of broad economies of scope and scale unbounded by geography. If the power of information cannot be used because only a fraction of jurisdictions have a sufficient legal environment to support its use, then the losses to an economy are exponential. This is why the low legal risk opportunities such as transmitting export documents have already gone on line in a case study such as the China CIETNet, while the higher risk but higher value added opportunities such as managing intra-firm payments online have not.

Although it does not arise in the case studies, nor does it come up in conversation too much in Asia, a taxonomy of legal and regulatory reforms conducive to a maximum growth outcome in the New Economy would not be complete without mention of property rights – including the disposition ownership of state owned enterprise assets. The Report does not propose a blanket prescription of privatization and titling. However it does propose that the burden of proof lay with government as to why assets should be held by the state and not the people. The case studies show many instances where New Economy firms are blocked from transforming toward productivity by the crowding out effect of state subsidized firms. Entrepreneurs are hungry for financial leverage that could be afforded by a proper assignment of rights to property or national wealth tied up in state enterprises. State enterprises are eager to reform, but partly constrained by the ambiguity of the ownership of the fruits of their labors. But neither does the Report pretend that the resolution of these ownership issues will be simple. Some Eastern European nations did indeed have unfortunate experiences with the process. Nonetheless, for those APEC economies facing this dilemma the alternative to pressing forward is even less desirable, as it means eroding performance vis-à-vis economies better able to mobilize assets through assignment of property rights. What's more, the experiences of others are now available to help.

The Place of Human Resource Policy

In this Report we have steered away from a direct treatment of appropriate human resource policies, because the subject can be addressed in the detail it deserves only in lengthier reports elsewhere, and because the primary concern in the Report is with those structural economic policies which have been more neglected in New Economy analyses. However the number of comments concerning human resources in the case studies necessitates that several principal topics are noted.

Three broad topics that arose were overall national human resources policy, human resource availability, and human resource training in the firm. First off, in terms of overall policy, many case studies emphasized the importance of incorporating technology awareness into basic education nationwide. Firms appreciated the value of new employees possessing a level of ICT awareness that prepared them for new skill requirements in the marketplace. This is related to another overarching role for government in human resources: to promote broader awareness of ICT and the new competitive environment created by policy reform so that those still in the basic education system and those already in the marketplace alike will have the contextual awareness to understand the profound importance of using technology to participate in society more productively. As the case studies show, in some APEC economies ranging from the less developed to the most developed a surprising number of businesses still think ICTs are just an incremental, not a revolutionary, addition to the marketplace. Such an attitude is not conducive to transformation.

Second, a number of cases reflected a concern about human resource availability. The need for skills-oriented special visa programs was mentioned. The under-use of software tools due to scarcity of relevant skills was noted. Some cases recognized that the urgency for human resources in technology was transforming the structure of labor markets, with high-skill scarce professionals working on a temporary basis without needing to form longer term bonds with big firms, while women with skills especially have new opportunities to telecommute via ICTs to fill the personnel gap. New firms and strategic alliances are being formed, often cross-border, to provide critical skills.

A related concern is that the best and most talented workers are snapped up by multinational firms. There are some structural reasons for this. MNCs are fully cognizant of the value of these workers and compensate them accordingly. They have heavily invested in ICTs and give tech workers a large and growing role in building the foundations of the business. And in come cases the more flexible culture of these foreign firms presents a more attractive environment to workers trained to think flexibly and creatively. This tendency, if in fact it is broad-based, can of course be reversed. Many talented Chinese workers, for instance, are increasingly leaving foreign invested enterprises to join Chinese firms or start their own now that they have acquired experience and training with them. But that reversal is contingent on local firms matching the zeal for transformation that make some foreign firms a dynamic and rewarding place to work, and upon adequate finance available for local start-ups to get going and invest adequately to be competitive.

Finally, the subject of training within the firm arose in case studies, again ranging from poorer to wealthier economies. The message here was that pre-employment, basis education was important for producing a pool of New Economy workers, but that the most important skills had to be taught, and maintained, once inside the firm. One of the characteristics of modern ICTs is that they don't have to be one size fits all – they are adaptable and are tailored for each business in which they reside. This is a source of proprietary, competitive advantage for many New Economy leaders, including the old economy firms that employ them. It follows therefore that the basis education platform cannot prepare workers for the specific technology that they may use in their jobs, that firms must be prepared to do that thoroughly themselves, and that policymakers should not delude themselves into assuming that basic education is a panacea. The return to firms from investment in HRD must be the engine for a skilled populous.

National E-Commerce Promotion Strategies[75]

Almost every case study made mention of the need for a national or economy-wide policy function to promote the New Economy or e-commerce. The reasons are various and include concerns that the policy problems noted above will not be remedied quickly enough without a coordinated government perspective. Some see national policy as the key to providing new services and regulations needed to nurture the net, such as e-commerce laws, cyberspace consumer protection, or other "soft-infrastructure" needed to support transformation. Others focused on the negative side of the story: that existing government policies designed for an old paradigm in which competition and transformation were not unambiguously good were themselves the problem, and had to be scrapped in order to facilitate progress. Several studies honed in on the government's role in assuring domestic firms unfettered access to the emerging global online trading environment, whether that meant negotiating to make sure they weren't shut out by collusive competitors or that the necessary domestic ICT infrastructure (telecom, legal) was in place to ensure the global network had a local socket to "plug into". Others, meanwhile, showed an awareness that such efforts to guarantee open competition internationally were no more important than efforts to secure open competition domestically.

We add a final point from the case studies that is as much a reminder to policymakers in developed economies as for the developing. More than half the studies underscored concerns about network security or robustness. Businesses in the United States worry about system failure as well, no question about it, and expend serious resources to protect themselves. But in many APEC economies the network is still far less secure. Telecom problems regularly interrupt email communication. Maintenance and support services can be hard to come by and insufficient. Some would say the answer to such problems is greater foreign competition to permit more competitive products to be offered, and indeed in markets with more open telecom sectors price does decline while quality goes up more rapidly than in closed economies. But these things take time, and in the meantime APEC firms that want to climb the learning curve along with their global competitors must work twice as hard, backing up

---

[75] See also the discussion of e-commerce promotion (with assessment of specific cases) in Chapter 10, Government and Development: Closing the Digital Divides, in <u>Global Electronic Commerce: A Policy Primer</u>, op. cit.

business processes with fax and hardcopy and whatever else is needed to prevent over-dependence on the new networks. It behooves policymakers everywhere to respect the urgency of these challenges for (especially small and medium) businesses going forward, understanding the role of structural policy reform in making that network more dependable but also the natural speed limit toward that goal for many economies.

V. Implications of New Economy Divergence: Digital Divide

Introduction

As with the Gutenberg printing press information revolution in the 15th Century, the industrial revolution of the 19th Century and the micro-processing revolution of the mid-20th Century, the networked information technology revolution characterizing the New Economy today has the potential to invigorate economic productivity greatly where it unfolds. Thus have Chinese leaders, for example, noted that they "missed the industrial revolution, and must not miss the IT revolution".[76]

The preceding section developed evidence and examples for policymakers seeking to secure these gains for their economies. But for a variety of reasons, policy reforms will not occur evenly around the world. Old inequalities could be exacerbated and new tensions introduced as relative economic competitiveness shifts among nations. (Although, we hope that this Report will help point the way toward ameliorating some of those inequalities.)

The rate of absorption differs, so a productivity and development divide within and between economies is inevitable, at least for a period. At issue for this Report is to consider the consequences of divergence in economic performance between "adjusters" that undergo the full panoply of economic and social transformations from embracing the New Economy paradigm, and "laggards," which will not. No one *wants* to be in the lagging column, but some will end up there.

In the parlance of the New Economy, these differences in initial conditions and in subsequent growth and development have taken on their own new definition—the digital divide. Just as it is both wrong and (from a policymaking perspective) dangerous to conceive of the New Economy narrowly in terms of ICTs alone, it is both wrong and dangerous to think that the growth divide among economies has come from and will worsen simply on account of differences in measures of access to ICTs and the global network. As we have seen in the discussion of US and Australian productivity experience, the presence or absence of ICTs is a first step, but the diffusion and use of the ICTs, which depends on the policy environment, is the more important step towards higher sustained growth. Consequently, whereas we will often use the colloquialism "digital divide", what we are concerned with is the broader concept of the productivity and growth gap among APEC members. The Report speaks to that divide.

This section will examine the productivity divide from three perspectives:

- Initial conditions, with respect to growth, development, and digital indicators.

---

[76] Ironically of course it was in China that movable type was first developed, yet was never employed in a manner that contributed mightily to national productivity. This is not the case with the information revolution, wherein already IT and the internet are enhancing the productive activities of Chinese firms and entrepreneurs.

- Possible consequences for trade competitiveness of different policy conditions.

- Implications for international economic institutions.

Initial conditions and Predisposition to Policy Reform

Before addressing how the forces of the New Economy might transform economic activities to change productivity growth and the capability of an economy to grow rapidly without inflation, we should establish where the various APEC economies are starting. Initial conditions likely will affect the extent to which an economy can embrace the potential of the New Economy.

Clearly the relationship between development, technology, and policy is complex. It is impossible in this Report to give a substantive and complete analysis of the relationship—nor indeed are we, as advisors to policymakers, likely to ever have enough evidence to complete a road map to prosperity that highlights route, speed, and good places to stop and rest along the way. The purpose of this section is simply to show some indicators and some relationships that are particularly germane to this study.

Chart V.1. Initial Conditions in APEC:
Real GDP per capita and Productivity Growth

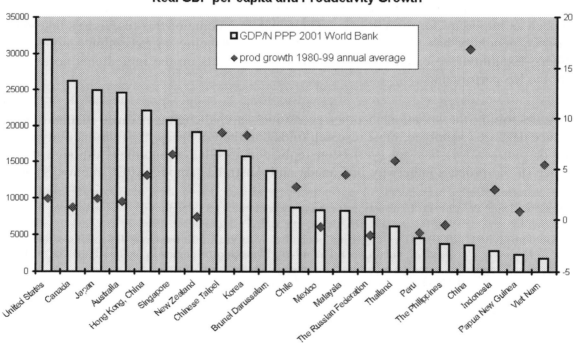

Productivity and Growth

Chart V.1 shows GDP per capita and the average annual rates for productivity growth for individual APEC members (1980-1999). From this presentation of the data, there is some suggestion of "convergence" within APEC—that is, the economies with the higher per capita

GDP have lower rates of productivity growth, and the economies with the lower per capita GDP have higher rates of productivity growth (see Chart V.2). But the evidence for convergence is weak and more apparent is the wide range of experience.

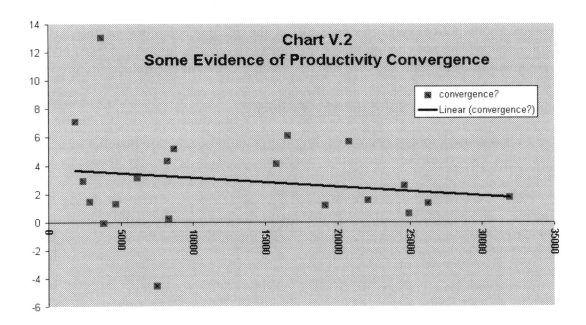

Moreover, Chart V.3 shows that for many members, productivity growth in the last half of the 1990s (right bars) fell short of the average productivity growth of the 1990s (middle bars). While some might argue this is on account of the financial crises, the 1990s

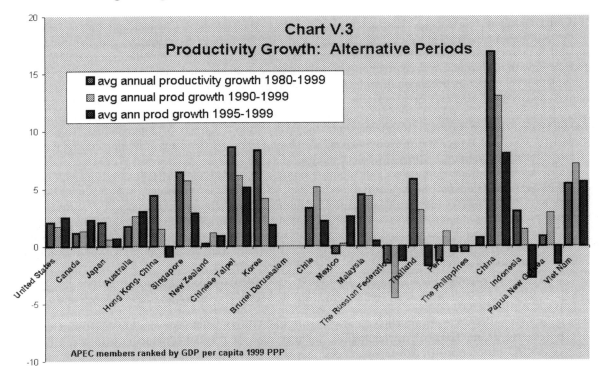

productivity performance is often lower than that of the averaged for the whole of the 1980s through 1990s (left bars). Only for some members—US, Canada, Australia, and Mexico—has recent productivity performance exceeded that of the 1980s-1990s. These charts imply that the productivity divide, and therefore the growth divide, are widening in APEC.

Some might argue that GDP per capita is too narrow a measure of well-being so that focusing on productivity growth to raise GDP per capita is too narrow. Chart V.4 shows a scatter plot and polynomial trend line relating GDP per capita and the UN's Human Development Index, which includes education, health, and environmental measures. There is a close relationship between these two measures for the APEC members, particularly at lower levels of GDP per capita. This suggests that raising GDP growth via increased productivity will raise the broader measure of well-being of the Human Development Index as well. So, the Report's focus on productivity growth and the New Economy is not misplaced.

Chart V.4
Relationship Between Per Capital GDP and the UN Human Development Index

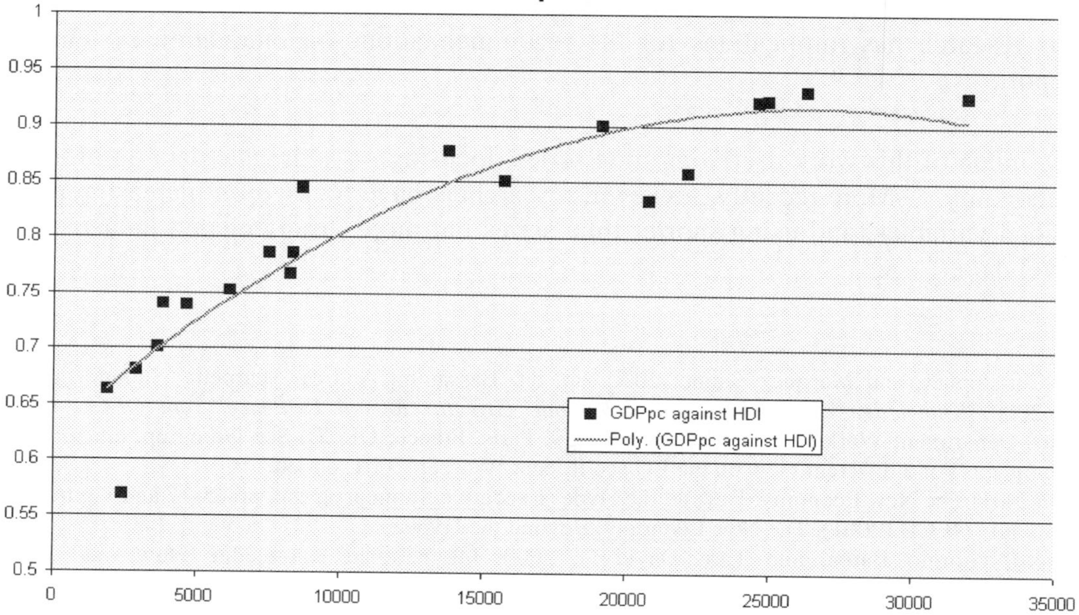

Digital Measures

Even before going "digital" it is clear that there is a "divide" in APEC. And, indicators of productivity growth do not suggest any rapid closure of that divide soon.

But, what about the digital divide? First, it is important to establish that there are two divides—*between economies* which is associated with different levels of income as well as infrastructure—and *within economies,* which is associated with a number of factors, including income, education, culture, and geography, among others. The "between-economy" divide is well known, but the "within-economy" divide may be more difficult to remedy, and, is in evidence in many economies even those with a high average level of income of the economy.[77]

What evidence shows a digital divide within APEC? Chart V.5 shows the relationship between income, two key aspects of infrastructure—teledensity (which is necessary for networking ICTs) and PCs (which are key delivery devices)—and users as a share of the population. The relationship between income, infrastructure, and usage is clear, and the digital divide in APEC is striking.

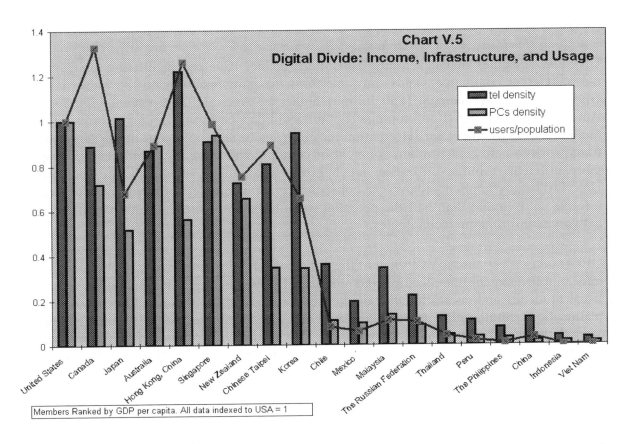

Would closing one aspect of the digital divide—say, by producing and exporting high-tech products (which includes telephone gear, PC pieces, as well as a variety of other products) be a way to jump-start economies that are at risk of falling further behind? The discussion of the US and Australian experience of the 1990s concluded that an environment that facilitated the *diffusion* of ICTs throughout the economy was critical to raising productivity growth. But, perhaps economies with large high-tech export sectors could use this as a spring-board for domestic use and diffusion throughout the economy, to yield overall greater benefits. Unfortunately, there is no such simple path. Chart V.6 shows no strong relationship between the share of hi-tech exports in manufacturing exports (World Bank data) and the average productivity growth experience of APEC members over the 1990s.

---

[77] See the discussion in <u>Global Electronic Commerce: A Policy Primer</u>, (2000) Catherine L. Mann, Sue E. Eckert, and Sarah Cleeland Knight, Institute for International Economics: Washington, pp 173-188, Chapter 9: Government and Development: Closing the Digital Divides.

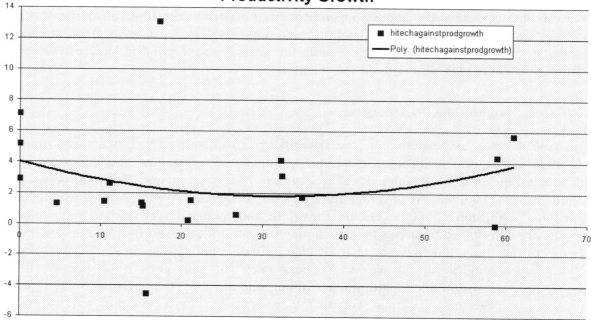

Chart V.6
HiTech Exports Have No Strong Association With 1990s Productivity Growth

Finally, returning to Chart V.4 we note that the relationship is not linear, indicating that even members at higher level of GDP can do more to improve the human development of their citizenry. Members with higher per capita income and high human development index should have a greater capacity for transformation. But wealth and health are no guarantee that reform will proceed, and indeed wealthy and healthy economies can be more satisfied with their situation, more risk averse, and thus less prone to accept reform.

KBE Status Indicators

The KBE Report from 2000 recommended that "KBE Status Indicators (KSIs)" be included in the annual APEC Economic Outlook publication. The lead economies (Australia, Canada, Korea) have submitted a proposal and implementation plan to the Economic Committee of APEC to further this objective.

Chart V.7 presents recently updated data on the indicators for Australia, as an example. The complementarity between this Report and the follow-on from the KBE Report of 2000 is clear. In fact, many of the indicators that are shown here are used in the aggregate measures of policy environment presented later.

Indeed, the KSIs in conjunction with the digital measures (previous) and the overall measures of policy conditions (discussed extensively below) should help policymakers target their efforts to those areas where they might reap the greatest gain. That said, we must remember

Chart V.7. Australia KBE Status Indicators

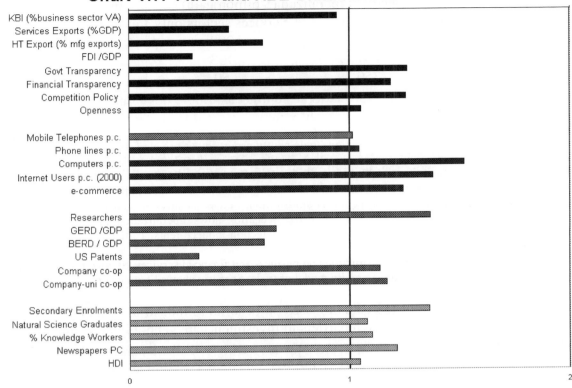

that achieving an environment to promote uptake of networked ICTs and facilitate transformation of activities is more than simply "checking the boxes" one after another.

Challenges to and Predisposition to Reform

In sum, by a variety of indicators and regardless of income levels, APEC members must renew their commitment to broad-based reforms so as to raise potential growth and human development of their economies. This is why in this Report the focus is so exclusively on the policy environment.

What determines the predisposition to policy reform, how is this endogenous to the process itself, and how can the forces of the New Economy help the process? First at issue are adjustment pains—ranging from reduced corruption income, to loss of power and profit of vested interests, to sectoral and demographic dislocations, to individual job losses. Some of these adjustment pains are worthy of a response to ameliorate them, some of them may require a response so as to mute the resistance, and others will simply take care of themselves. However, the longer an economy defers structural adjustment, the more challenging in terms of bankruptcies, transitional unemployment, skills mismatch and fiscal expenditure the process will be. Both high income and lower income economies in the APEC region have had to face this truth over the past decade. The adjustment pains at home also are a function of reforms abroad. To the extent that New Economy policy reforms pervade neighboring economies, the greater the need for policy reforms at home, but the more wrenching the change needs to be. In this regard, being a first-mover may reduce the depth of economic restructuring. But, by the same token, the forces of the New Economy once released may help policymakers undertake reforms. For example, introducing new technology can erode the power of vested interests, as for example in telecommunications, and release more resources to the private sector activities. A commitment and vision by policymakers to the overall reform process will speed up the process.

Past successes can blind policymakers to current needs. Some policymakers still believe that there is a short cut to high growth without structural adjustment. Some would argue that the focus of "export-oriented" growth with governments picking industry sectors based on a view to the international leaders still has currency in the New Economy. Today, most of these economies are at or near the technological frontier, and the adjustments needed to their "export-oriented" industries and to their domestic economies are greater for not having at home a vibrant marketplace designed to find through the trial and failure the new "winners".

Institutional and social assets in an economy are essential supports to reform. The United States, for example, entered the information age with a well-developed legal system capable of instilling confidence among investors so that they would put at risk literally billions of dollars toward research and development in innovation and implementation of technology. For another example, China and Viet Nam – by virtue of past investment – enjoy literacy rates of over 80 and 90% respectively as they go forward, a key asset for a knowledge based economy, whereas India, by contrast, has a rate of only somewhat over 50%. These institutional factors facilitate fundamental policy steps, such as a mature legal system does in advance of broad financial liberalization, or can determine the pace of movement toward the KBE-type mega-phenomena, such as literacy is for human resource development to be pervasive.

Just because an economy is not making the *comprehensive* policy reforms described above necessary to produce a New Economy outcome does not mean it is making no reforms, of course, or that its policy regime and economy are not becoming more efficient and productive. Thanks to piecemeal reforms a particular economy may not decline in *absolute* terms, but the differential pace of overall reforms will increasingly be observed in different outcomes in terms of growth performance.

Policy Conditions, Sectoral Transformation and Trade Competitiveness in the New Economy

Trade has always been an important channel for changes in global demand and production technology to affect productivity and growth. The forces of the New Economy operating in the global marketplace are transforming production methods and production patterns. How does an economy's *policy environment* combine with its *trade patterns* to create new opportunities for businesses in economies; and how might the failure to have a facilitating policy environment lead to a loss of competitiveness in the international trade arena?

Even small changes in the pattern of trade will be important. In 1999 industrial economies purchased $1.2 trillion worth of merchandise from developing economies, compared to development assistance to them totaling only $52 billion net, after repayments. Even after taking into account exports to developing economies from industrial economies of $985 billion, the net payment for traded goods to the developing world was $224 billion, more than four times the value of aid (hence the slogan: "trade not aid"). For developing economies, this market share in the industrial world is critical. Relatively subtle changes in the competitive landscape among developing economies are certain to have major effects on trade flows and thereby on income and productivity growth. Since the latter are the macro-level manifestations of the APEC "divide", examining the nexus of policy conditions, sectoral transformation, and trade patterns makes sense.

The methodology presented in this section should be thought of as a tool for analysis and consideration by individual APEC members. Rather than reach definitive conclusions, APEC members will have the opportunity to compare themselves against others in the group according to a common set of indicators and focusing on an arena in which they do compete—international trade. While these common sets of indicators necessarily cannot capture the nuances of individuality of each economy (for which the KSIs do better), they do yield powerful inferences. Moreover, it is important to remember that third parties (such as investors) make these comparisons using common measures, appropriately or not.

Measuring Overall Policy Conditions in APEC Economies

Evaluating and measuring an economy's policy conditions and preparedness for engaging in and enjoying the benefits of the New Economy is somewhat of a cottage industry. Some measures focus on specific indicators that are important for specific aspects of the New Economy (e.g. telecom density or number of knowledge jobs). Other measures add in broad issues that are increasingly relevant given the transparency inherent in the information flow of the New Economy (e.g. corruption, arbitrariness of regulations, or opacity of corporate governance). Still others include indicators that are important for all kinds of commerce (e.g. macroeconomic stability, global openness, or performance of financial institutions). And, all indexes are a combination of the policy inputs and the environment that results. As discussed early, APEC is preparing data to measure progress along the dimensions of the four KBE phenomena.[78]

Clearly, there is no one right measure. Moreover, evaluations can be undertaken for a range of purposes, from promoting introspection and internal policy debate within an economy to an international firm deciding which economy to consider for a new investment. The purpose of this section is simply to show some indicators of overall policy conditions that include the dimensions deemed important for creating a facilitating environment.

Several Charts and Tables show both general and more specific measures of policy conditions and preparedness for the New Economy. Chart V.8 shows several widely available summary measures of policy conditions for most APEC members: Economic Intelligence Unit/Pyramid Research E-readiness ranking; World Economic Forum Current Competitiveness Index; the

---

[78] APEC (2000), Towards the Knowledge-Based Economy Report, Appendices and submission by lead-economy Australia to the Economic Committee II in Dalian, China August 2001.

Global New Economy Index from MetricNet; the World Competitiveness Score from IMD in Lausanne Switzerland; and, with more limited coverage, PriceWaterhouseCoopers Opacity Index. APEC members are shown in descending order of per capita GDP. If all measures ranked the APEC members identically, all bars would be the same length.

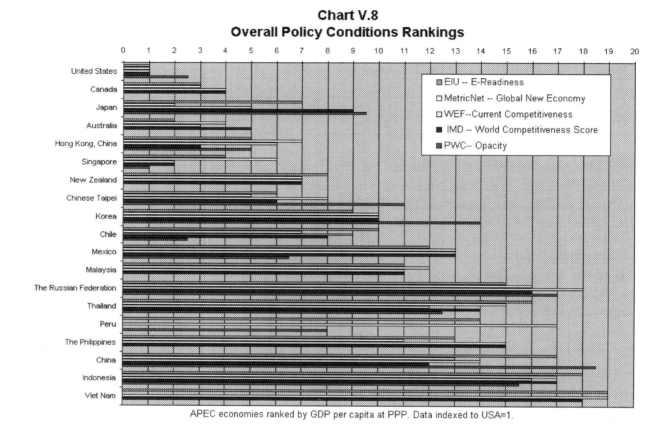

Chart V.8
Overall Policy Conditions Rankings

APEC economies ranked by GDP per capita at PPP. Data indexed to USA=1.

The data and surveys underlying these broad-based indicators are, in many cases, exactly the same as the disaggregated indicators shown in the 2000 <u>KBE Report</u>. The advantage of examining broad-based indicators is that they summarize the overall policy environment. We believe that synergies among policies in the four domains are key to creating the New Economy environment in which transformation of economic activities can take place in response to technologies and information. Moreover, it is clear that firms experience the whole picture for an economy. Disaggregated indexes are useful too, because they provide insights for policymakers to discern which policy area needs the most reform. On balance, for the purposes of this analysis, purposes, aggregate measures are superior.

What underlies the different indexes presented here? The concept of *e-readiness* by the Economist Intelligence Unit/ Pyramid Research[79] is shorthand for the extent to which an economy's business environment is conducive to Internet-based commercial opportunities.

---

[79] The Economist Intelligence Unit (2001) *The Economist Intelligence Unit/ Pyramid Research e-readiness rankings.* http://www.ebusinessforum.com/index.asp?layout=rich_story&doc_id=367

The model tallies scores across six categories – including the EIU's business environment rankings – and 19 additional indicators. The six categories comprising the ranking are, with decreasing weight: 1. Connectivity; 2. business environment; 3. e-commerce consumer and business adoption; 4. legal and regulatory environment; 5. supporting e-services; and 6. social and cultural infrastructure. Where possible, the variables – connectivity in particular – rest on quantitative, statistical data; others reflect qualitative assessments by EIU economy analysts.

The *Current Competitiveness Index* by the World Economic Forum purports to measure the conditions that determine an economy's sustainable level of productivity. [80] Factors underpinning current competitiveness are divided into two major categories: The sophistication with which an economy's firms compete and the quality of the economy's business environment. A variety of measures (some 65 of them, all statistically related to GDP per capita), are combined into the indexes. The content of the overall index includes indicators on infrastructures (air, sea, land, communications, administration) capital availability, human resources, science and technology, and business and regulatory environment (transparency, entry and exit, and trade openness).

MetricNet's *Global New E-Economy Index* represents a measure of the economic dynamism and strength, as well as the technological capabilities and potential of an economy. The categories of the indicators in the Global New E-Economy Index are: 1. knowledge jobs; 2. Globalization; 3. economic dynamism and competition; 4. transformation to a digital economy; and 5. technological innovation capacity. The GNEI uses data for the categories and factors specified above from the following sources: *The World Competitiveness Yearbook, 2000; The Computer Industry Almanac and The Internet Software Consortium.*[81]

The *World Competitiveness Score* from IMD, International measures and compares the extent to which an economy provides an environment that supports globally competitive companies. It is sold to businesses so that they can monitor markets and investigate new sites for investment and to governments to judge their own policies in practice. The components of the Score include: Economic performance (domestic, international, employment, prices, and forecasts), government efficiency (public finance, fiscal policy, institutional framework, business legislation, education), management efficiency (productivity, labor markets, finance), and infrastructure (basic, technological, scientific, quality of life and value systems). Some 139 criteria are involved in generating the Score.

The *Opacity Index* by Price Waterhouse Coopers is a more narrow measure, but one of particular importance for the information flows and investment climate of the New Economy. This index estimates the adverse effects of opacity on the cost and availability of capital in 35 economies. The composite score for each economy is based on opacity data in five different areas that affect capital markets: 1. Corruption; 2. legal system; 3. government macro-economic and fiscal policies; 4. accounting standards and practices (including corporate

---

[80] Porter, Michael E.; Sachs Jeffrey D.; Warner Andrew M; Cornelius Peter K.; Levinson, Macha and Schwab; Klaus (2000) *The Global Competitiveness Report 2000.* The World Economic Forum. New York: Oxford University Press. See in particular pp 16 and pp 44-47.
[81] Metricnet.com (2000) The Global New E-Economy Index: A Cyber Atlas.

governance and information release); and 5. regulatory regime. The data is based on average survey responses for the five types of opacity. [82] Since the coverage of the O-factor is more limited than for the other indexes, the scale of an economy and its position in rank has been adjusted to be comparable to the other measures.

Considering the range of indexes, the similarity in ranking of the member economies is striking. For a few of the economies, the different rankings vary by more than two or three places: Japan, Singapore, and China for example. A closer examination of the underpinnings of the indexes would reveal the specific differences among the overall, and policymakers in these individual economies no doubt should wish to make this examination. [83]

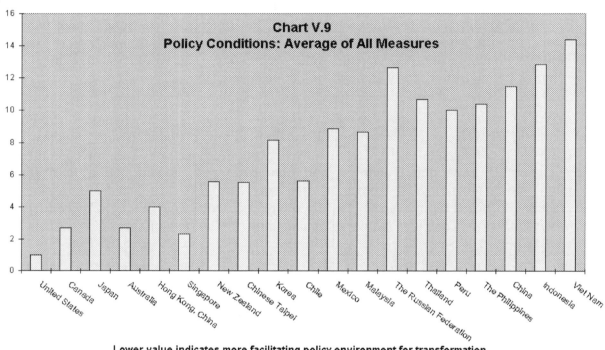

Lower value indicates more facilitating policy environment for transformation.
APEC economies ranked by GDP per capita at PPP. Indexed to USA=1

However, for the analysis focusing on trade competitiveness for the full APEC membership, the policy conditions rankings must be distilled and simplified. Chart V.9 averages the five indicators of policy conditions with the most complete coverage of economies and orders this average by GDP per capita of the APEC economies. Economies with shorter bars have policy conditions that are more facilitative to the environment and transformations of the New Economy.

---

[82] PriceWaterhouseCoopers (2001) The Opacity Index. Launching a new measure of the effects of opacity on the cost and availability of capital in economies world-wide. www.opacityindex.com

[83] The original sources present the inputs to these measures and methodology of aggregation to the composite measures shown in the Report.

Measuring Sectoral Transformation In the New Economy

The nature of the production process (comprising both manufacturing and services) is becoming increasingly fragmented and globalized. Multinational firms and strategic business alliances communicate, get price quotes, submit bids, transfer data, offer customer service, produce product designs, code software, and basically *do business* using networked information and communications technologies in the international arena.[84] Economies that do not have a facilitating environment to allow the forces of the New Economy to transform business activities will be marginalized from the global production process and global economy, at increasingly great cost to their citizens.

But, the uptake of network and information technologies differs across sectors and can be measured several ways: By cost savings when used, by how these capabilities are being used (static Web-site, interactive Web-site, financial exchange over the Web, supplier information exchange, fully integrated operations). For this Report, several different analyses of how network and information technologies have affected the operations of US and European industries are considered to derive a summary indicator for each sector of the intensity of transformation due to use of networked ICTs: we call this the Technology Transformation Intensity (TTI).

For most APEC economies, we would not expect their industry sectors to use the network and information technologies as intensively as the US or European counterparts. But, the TTI measure should indicate which sectors are likely to feel pressure to use these technologies first. For example, if a firm in an APEC economy is currently part of a multinational value-chain, and its partner and parent firms use ICTs, it will be expected to use them as well. [85] Thus, using the US and European analyses as a benchmark makes sense.

Measures of 'Technology Transformation Intensity' by sector summarizes various approaches to estimating how intensively industrial sectors are using networked ICTs to transform their operations. This research is distilled into the Table below which ranks industry sectors by the extent to which they are being transformed by the use of networked information technologies. A lower value of TTI means less transformation is being undertaken by this sector in response to New Economy opportunities.

---

[84] The measures of business to business (B2B) transactions overwhelmingly dominates Internet commerce and many B2B sales take place across the border and between multinational and local firms. Forrester estimates $2.7 billion on B2B exchanges by 2004 http://ebizchronicle.com/slp_reports/march/erp04_oracle.htm). Jupiter estimates increase from $336 this year to $6.3 T in 2005 accounting for 80% of B2B transactions (http://ebizchronicle.com/editorials/editorial_09_ebizover.htm). Boston Consulting Group estimates rise from $1.2T (13 percent of inter-company gross purchases) to $4.8 T in 2004 (40 percent of inter-company gross purchases; include EDI. (http://ebizchronicle.com/backgrounders/dec00/b2snapshot.htm).

[85] Indeed, several firms in several economies have made this point in the course of field research. The firms worry that if they do not have a facilitating environment at home that they will be dropped from the supply chain. They also worry about the cost of capital and human resource issues. These points were made as well in the case studies.

Table: Technology Transformation Intensity: Benchmark	
Foods	4
Consumer goods and textiles	3
Energy, chemicals, natural resources	1
Pharmaceuticals	4
Forest/paper products	4
Steel/metals and metal products	1
Industrial equipment & Supplies	3
Electronic Components	5
Autos	3

It is worthwhile discussing the research underlying the Table (which is presented in detailed form in Appendix 1). Survey research of US industry in 2000 (Brookes and Wahhaj) suggests cost savings ranging from 10 percent in sectors such as aerospace, paper and steel, and communications bandwidth and media advertising, to more than 20 percent in electronic components and machining, forest products, and freight transport. New research, edited by Litan and Rivlin of Brookings, takes a more comprehensive look at the impact of information technologies on productivity growth in different sectors in the US and sums up the impact on US productivity growth at between 0.25 to 0.5 percentage points.[86]

Forrester Research[87] considers two inputs: "industry readiness" and "product fit" to yield a measure of "ultimate marketplace saturation" for how much different industry sectors might use networked ICTs. Computing and electronics for example has a measure of greater than 70 percent "ultimate marketplace saturation" because the industry is "ready" and the "product fit" is high. For industrial equipment and supplies, the industry is "ready" but the "product fit" is not as good (since a great degree of customization is common); thus a measure of only 60-70 percent "ultimate marketplace saturation". And so on. These measures of both "industry readiness" and "product fit" help to characterize which sectors are or will be transformed the most by the use of ICTs, and therefore, which sectors may demand a heavier use of networked information technologies by their supply chain partners in the APEC economies.

EITO from Europe[88] presents another analysis of how e-commerce is affecting industry sectors there. This study rates European industries and partners by internal use of the networked ICTs (e.g. whether firms in the sector are reorienting their internal organization and operations toward using the Internet) and external use of networked ICTs (e.g. whether external relationships and marketing are being done via the Internet). The two scores weighted-up yield the overall score for the sector. By and large, the analysis suggests that US

---

[86] Robert E. Litan and Alice M. Rivlin (2001), Beyond the Dot.Coms: The Economic Promise of the Internet, Brookings Institutions, July 2001 draft.

[87] (http://ebizchronicle.com/backgrounders/march/forrest_b2opportunity_onlinetrade.htm) last visited June 26, 2001.

[88] EITO (2001), European Information Technology Observatory 2000 Millennium Edition Part Two, The Impact of E-Commerce on Five Vertical Sectors (prepared by GartnerConsulting in close collaboration with EITO Task Force and Enterprise DG of the European Commission).

and European firms and supply chains are responding similarly to the opportunities offered by networked information technologies.[89]

The National Association of Manufacturers and Ernst&Young[90] classify stages of Internet usage and adoption by different industry sectors. Stage 1, e-Information is where firms use the Internet for information. Stage 2, e-Interaction is where firms use e-mail actively. Stage 3, e-Commerce is where firms buy and sell using Web-sites. Stage 4, e-Company is where firms link together their supply-chain partners. Stage 5, e-Economy is where a whole economy is populated by firms that actively use information technologies throughout their operations. NAM/E&Y evaluate what share of US firms in a particular sector have reached a Stage. For this Report, the industry sectors that have moved furthest through the stages of application of e-commerce are given higher values for technology transformation intensity. So, for example, chemicals and natural resources have lower TTI values because this sector has moved less far along the stages of application. The consumer goods sector has moved farther, so is more Internet intensive.

This latter research maps well into the policy dimensions that are the focus of this Report: An economy needs to have adequate network access to achieve Stage one (e-information, which, for example, is having a "brochure-ware" style Web-site with company information). An economy needs to have reasonable network pricing, and use information technology at the desk to reach Stage 2 (E-Interaction, allow businesses to send and receive e-mail from a Web-site. Such capabilities are important for setting-up business appointments.) An economy needs to have a good banking and finance infrastructure to move into Stage 3 (E-commerce, which for example, allows the buying and selling of products from a Website). An economy needs to have adequate network security and safeguards as well as rapid distribution capabilities to move to Stage 4 (E-Company, which, for example might mean a company intra-net to keep track of inventory and do just-in-time supply). An economy needs to have all these infrastructures, a facilitative business climate, and a population of e-businesses to move to Stage 5 (E-Economy).

Putting These Together with Trade Patterns: Competitive Pressures and Opportunities

Suppose an economy currently has a high share of trade in electronics products, which has a high technology transformation intensity (TTI), but the economy has a poor ranking when it comes to policy conditions. This economy could lose competitiveness, production, and employment in the industry to an economy with similar trade characteristics but better policy conditions. This observation may induce policy reform in the target economy, it certainly will impact economic activity and, through the trade channel, productivity as well. (Recall the discussion of the evidence for the US and Australia, among others, on the role for trade to affect productivity growth.)

---

[89] The textile sector is somewhat different, with the US sector using the Internet more intensively than its European counterparts. Since the textile and apparel sector has had extensive protection via the MultiFiber Arrangement, this could account for different uptake. Indeed, see the discussion in EITO.
[90] The National Association of Manufacturers and Ernst&Young (2001); E-Commerce Trends Index

On the other hand, suppose an economy has a high share of trade in a product that has a low TTI and the economy also has a rather poor showing on policy conditions. Such an economy is insulated from the forces of the New Economy coming through the trade channel. Whereas such an economy would be better off in a macro sense from improving its policy conditions, the trade channel is not likely to be the factor forcing domestic policy change.

There are several ways to show the relationships between policy conditions, trade patterns, and sectoral technology transformation intensity. The first approach is to examine each economy separately and consider how the New Economy forces are working through the trade channel of different *industry sectors within the individual economy*. The second approach is to examine each industry sector separately and consider how the New Economy is working through the trade channels to differentially affect the competitiveness of economies, *comparing economies within an industry sector of trade*. [91]

Consider this second perspective first. Appendix 2 presents a series of charts which incorporate data on the composition of trade (exports and imports) by major industry sector and also incorporate the benchmark TTI for each of the industry sectors. [92] Chart V.10 is a prototype of those charts. The vertical axis measures share of exports and of imports of different industry sectors in trade of the economy, which are arranged along the horizontal axis by SITC classification, starting with foods and ending with autos. (To avoid too much clutter, bubbles for trade shares of a sector less than 10 percent are not shown.) There are two bubbles for each sector—the centerpoint of one measures the share of that industry in imports and the centerpoint of the other bubble measures the share of that industry in exports. The diameter of each bubble is the benchmark TTI of the industry sector, so the size of the bubble is the same for both exports and imports.

How should we interpret these charts? Consider first the export data in the example in Chart V.10, Example 1: High Exposure. The prototype economy has larger bubbles in the upper part of the chart, indicating that the industries that have the largest share of trade are those undergoing the greater transformation through technology (higher TTI). Therefore, this prototype economy has an export pattern biased toward industry sectors that are rapidly being transformed by networked ICTs. This is an economy exposed to the forces of the New Economy through the export trade channel. If its exporters cannot employ the networked

---

[91] Data on trade for PNG and for Viet Nam were not available in sufficient detail for this exercise. Measures of policy conditions for PNG and Brunei were not available either so no Charts are prepared for them.
[92] The industry sectors shown are major SITC categories compiled to match the categories for which research underpins the TTI indexes. "Foods" is the sum of SITC 0 and 1; Energy, natural resources, and chemicals is the sum of SITC 2, 3, 4, 5; Metals&metal mfg is the sum of SITC 67, 68, 69; Consumer goods and Textiles is the sum of SITC 65 and 8; Industrial equipment and supplies is the sum of SITC 71, 72,73, 74; Electrical products is the sum of SITC 75, 76, 77; and auto is SITC 78. All data on trade come from the United Nations and are for 1998 (except Thailand where the trade data are for 1997). For all the economies except Russia, the coverage of trade flows is at least 90 percent.

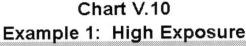

Chart V.10
Example 1: High Exposure

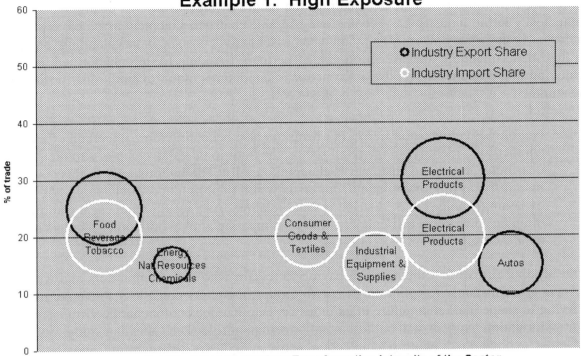

Bubble size is Technology Transformation Intensity of the Sector
(larger is undergoing more transformation)

technology because the domestic policy environment is unconducive, and its competitors can because their policy environment is better, this economy may lose trade competitiveness as information technologies become more pervasively used.

We can use this example to indicate the potential for benefits and challenges to come via the trade channel into the domestic economy, in this case, through imports. Consider again Chart V.10 and look at import bubbles. Sectors with high shares of trade and high TTI (e.g. large bubbles in the upper part of the chart) will be sectors where the forces of the New Economy are transforming firms and the sectors are important for the economy's trade.

The import channel offers two possible avenues for the New Economy to affect the domestic economy: imports as competition for domestic producers and imports as inputs to domestic production. Industries with high TTI (large bubbles) are those where information technologies are reducing costs. Therefore, economies with high exposure to these industry sectors can benefit greatly from using these imports in the domestic production process, if the economy has policy conditions that are conducive to the use of ICTs so that the domestic producers can use the transformative technologies of the imports. On the other hand, domestic producers of products similar to these imports will need to upgrade their own operations through the use of ICTs and through changes to organization behavior to remain cost-competitive with the imported substitutes. Through both of these channels, imports of sectors that are intensive in the use of transformative technologies will raise productivity growth in the domestic economy, although domestic transformation is necessary to gain the productivity benefit.

In contrast, consider Chart V.11, Example 2: Low Exposure. In this case, the economy has smaller bubbles in the upper parts of the chart and most large bubbles are in the lower part of the chart. This indicates that the industries that have the largest share of trade are those with low TTIs. Therefore, this prototype economy has a trade pattern biased toward sectors that are not intensively being transformed by the use of ICTs. This is an economy that is less exposed to the forces of the New Economy through the trade channel. Therefore, if this economy's firms cannot employ networked information technologies, say because of a poor policy environment, the trade channel is not going to force the issue.

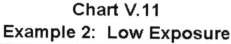

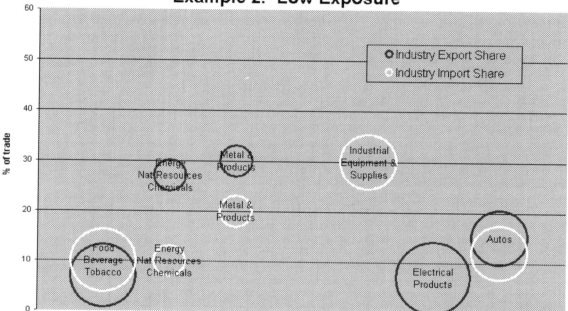

Now consider several of the APEC economies, which present much more complex situations. (See charts in Appendix 3.) Several economies are highlighted simply to show how to read the charts given a full set of data. As an example, Peru might be less affected by the forces of the New Economy coming through the trade channel because most of its trade is in metals/metal products and energy/chemicals which have a low TTIs. Note, however that the high share of export trade in foods, which is a high TTI sector, represents an opportunity for this industry if the policy environment is facilitating. A similar picture emerges for Chile. In contrast, Mexico, Thailand, and Korea, with large trade shares in high TTI, such as industrial equipment and supplies, electrical products, and autos will be more exposed to the forces of the New Economy through the trade channel.

Note that these forces come through different channels. In Thailand, the high share of imports of industrial supply and equipment suggests that the cost reductions associated with high TTI could benefit the economy...if it has the right policy conditions to use these products. And Mexico, with substantial export exposure in electrical products exports could gain trade competitiveness and international market share vis-à-vis other electrical exporters in this high TTI sector—if it has the right policy conditions to support those exporters.

This line of reasoning, which focuses less on the economy and more on the sector, suggests a second presentation of the relationship between trade patterns, intensity of technology transformation, and policy conditions.

Charts in Appendix 4 shows all of the APEC members for each industry sector. Each chart shows economies whose share of exports (imports) in that sector is greater than 15 percent. Example 3 in Chart V.12 is a prototype.

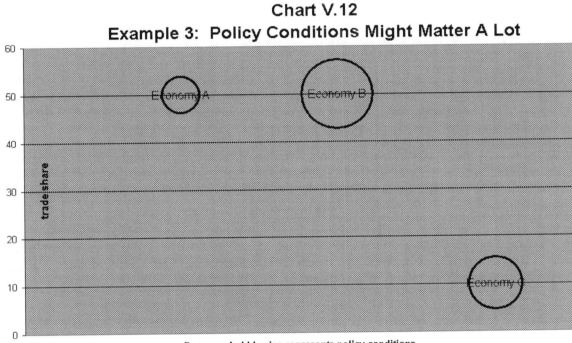

Chart V.12
Example 3: Policy Conditions Might Matter A Lot

Economy bubble size represents policy conditions
(small is a more facilitating policy environment)

The vertical axis measures share of the sector in exports (imports) of the economies, which are arranged along the horizontal axis ordered by per capita GDP. Each economy is represented by at most two bubbles (it depends on whether the trade shares are greater than 15 percent, here in this example, only one trade bubble is shown). The centerpoint of a bubble measures the importance of the sector for that economy's exports (imports). The diameter of the bubble is the classification of the economy's policy conditions (recall that the smaller bubble represents superior policy conditions). So the size of the bubble is the same for each economy's exports and imports, if both are shown. Since each chart shows a sector, which by definition has the same TTI for all economies, these charts gauge how export competitiveness of a sector might be affected by policy conditions, and how imports of a product might enhance efficiency of domestic down-stream sectors and/or yield increased competition to competing domestic sectors.

How should we interpret these charts? Consider Example 3: Policy Conditions Could Matter A Lot in Chart V.12. In this simplified presentation there is only one trade bubble for each economy to represent, alternatively, exports and imports shares. Suppose we know that the industry has a high TTI, such as electrical products. Two economies (A and B) have bubbles in the upper parts of the chart, indicating that these economies have large shares of trade that are exposed to a sector that is undergoing substantial transformation on account of technology (high TTI). Economy C has a smaller share of its trade in this industry. Economy A has a small bubble, indicating that its policy conditions are superior to those of Economy B with a large bubble.

Firms in Economy B have problem. They are exposed to a high TTI sector, but their policy environment at home is not conducive to the uptake of these technologies. The firms in Economy B may lose export competitiveness and market share as the uptake of transformative technologies becomes more pervasive. And, economy B is less able to benefit from the cost reductions coming through the import channel. Note, that although Economy C is not particularly exposed through the trade channel, its policy conditions are superior, indicating that its firms might possibly take advantage of the trade channel, and, in any case, the domestic benefits of a more conducive environment are clear.

Finally, Chart V.13 summarizes all these dimensions: the policy conditions, and export and import exposure weighted by trade shares and transformation intensity. The three fully pointed cones to the left show the archetypal case where 100 percent of export and imports are in the sectors experiencing the greatest transformation due to the forces of the New Economy (the greatest technology transformation intensity index) and where policy conditions are most conducive to supporting an environment where the technologies and information of the New Economy can be most transformative. These three summary measures are shown for members of APEC are shown ranked by GDP per capita.

The more "squat" are the trade-weighted cones the less an economy's trade is in sectors that are being transformed on account of the New Economy. The more squat are the policy cones, the less positive is the policy environment to support the transformation. Thus, when the trade cones are tall and policy cones are squat, there could be a problem in terms of competitiveness and productivity growth in that in the international arena, transformation will be underway, but firms in the economy might be unable to undertake needed changes because the domestic policy environment is not facilitating. Some economies have trade flows that are highly exposed to sectors which are undergoing substantial transformation on account of New Economy technologies (the weighted export and import cones are quite tall), yet do not have overall policy conditions that are particularly supportive (the policy cones are rather short). Other economies have policy environments that are out ahead of their trade patterns, perhaps

Chart V.13
Overall policy conditions and weighted trade exposure

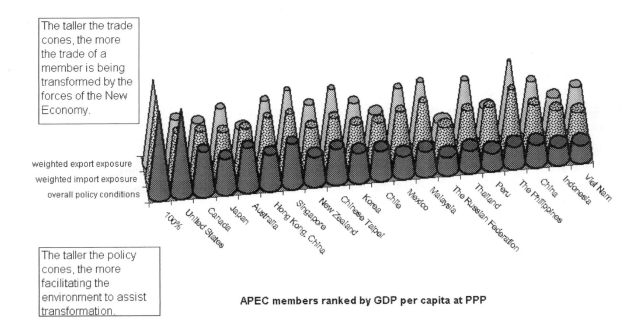

The taller the trade cones, the more the trade of a member is being transformed by the forces of the New Economy.

weighted export exposure
weighted import exposure
overall policy conditions

The taller the policy cones, the more facilitating the environment to assist transformation.

APEC members ranked by GDP per capita at PPP

creating new opportunities in the international marketplace (for example, Australia). Others are currently relatively more insulated from the New Economy (for example, Russia). Economies can judge for themselves whether their policy conditions are likely to support international competitiveness and the productivity growth that comes with it in the New Economy or not.

In sum, the future for international trade increasingly will depend on networked information and communications technologies. Potential changes in competitiveness, productivity, and growth depend on the relationship between the policy environment and the sectoral exposure of trade for an economy. Policymakers, when looking for allies in the reform process should consider the matrix of trade and TTI by sector since this is where the pressures and opportunities will be created.

Other Aspects of Differential Progress

Our analysis points to a widening "productivity divide" within APEC coming from differences in improvement in productivity from ICTs due in large part to underlying structural policy conditions. The "digital" part of this divide is a narrower construct than broader productivity factors which underpin prosperity, but the digital and non-digital are increasingly intertwined.

Thus far, we have focused on specific economic consequences of this divide, such as trade competitiveness, in as quantitative an analysis as possible. There are many social and political facets of the potential divide however, that are deeply tangled with the economic factors.

This study cannot catalogue the whole spectrum of non-economic issues associated with divergent productivity growth. But below it briefly reviews three issues that are implicit in and related to the economic arguments because they deserve special consideration by policymakers and leaders.

Brain drain:

"Brain drain" concerns both highly skilled individuals and the promising enterprises they are often associated with or create. It is an international phenomenon involving two civic players: an unattractive economy and a more enabling one with alluring incentives for wealth creation and prosperity. And it is a phenomenon that is greatly augmented by the heightened transparency of opportunity, greater openness to high-skill migration, and greater economic return to knowledge that characterize globalization generally and the operating modes of the knowledge-intensive New Economy specifically.

Economic analyses of the New Economy trends all highlight the increased "frictionlessness" of markets for goods and services, which benefit consumers, and for foreign direct investment, which benefits reforming policy environments. But with these come brain drain, the dark side of low barriers to economic activity that is increasingly hard to prevent without simultaneously shutting out the benefits.

The social and political lens on this problem is worrisome. Already there are arguments against investing public funds in training professionals for government service for fear that trainees will forthwith migrate to the private sector or other economies. There is little antidote to this concern other than to work toward a creating a domestic economy with good incentives via sound structural policy foundations.

The political challenges abound. In some economies, the very right of entrepreneurs to be represented directly in political decision-making is still debatable. In others, business people are blamed for every social-ill with each new wave of political unrest. In many, their rights to manage their businesses are heavily constrained by political committees and considerations.

The New Economy is not creating this problem: it has existed forever. We believe, and we think it is increasingly evident both from casual and empirical appraisal, that the power of human talent to determine economic outcomes through the choice of their movement is now an order of magnitude greater. The political and social underpinnings of the solution are profound, and as yet not fully appreciated or understood. This much is clear however: the desire of highly-skilled individuals and firms to stay put is a key validation of the policy conditions leaders are responsible for, and likewise their departure is a sign of domestic negligence no less than foreign allure.

Reactions from civil society:

In the domestic sphere, at the more macro level than the choices of the high-skill elite, the New Economy brings the potential for – more, the likelihood of – far more active expectations from broad civil society about the opportunities and potential of their economies and polities. This is a potential wellspring of growth. Higher expectations can mean a higher degree of self-motivation and preparation to capitalize on opportunity, as opposed to the sense of inevitability and conservatism that accompanies narrow horizons on the broader world. But the more information rich community of the New Economy also brings greater demands and assertiveness and the need for government to be demand driven.

Popular reactions to economic under-performance from civil society are likely. What are the consequences of greater citizen awareness of the price they pay for slow adjustment in terms of foregone opportunities for private initiative, lost current markets, lower rates of domestic growth, higher costs of capital, higher rates of unemployment, and so on? Technology makes it increasingly easier to calculate the costs and the comparisons in the neighborhood will be much easier to make. For example, in the United States economists were able in the early 1990s to determine that textile jobs cost consumers $200,000 a year on average to sustain against competition from lower cost producers overseas and, in 2000, that pending steel protection would cost $3.5 billion.[93] These facts do not always alter policy outcomes, but the US did agree to phase out the Multi-Fiber Agreement (MFA) under the WTO and has not yet responded to pleas from the steel lobby. In India today, activists are stirring up a furor simply by publicly posting lists of civic projects for which monies were allocated and disbursed, but which never appeared because of rampant corruption. IT is dramatically abetting such efforts to quantify inefficiencies and expose corruption.

This study provides no easy answers for Leaders or policymakers on how to handle the political and social implications of this trend. This much can be said: the trend is inevitable (without shutting down all the benefits of economic development); it is empowering and fosters prosperity as much as it is politically challenging; and it cannot likely be quarantined in the economic realm and out of the political.

International relations and new alliances?

In the international sphere, in the macro context, divergent productivity performance engendered by differential policy reform achievements and associated uptake of ICTs will have implications that go beyond economic competitiveness. More to the point, changing economic competitiveness will have implications for international affairs beyond the economic realm to include political and security considerations.

Most international economic bodies, the WTO, the World Bank and IMF, the UNDP for examples, are rooted in dichotomies between developed and developing nations. Shifting productivity trajectories will likely alter the alliances and blocks within these groups that have

---

[93] See "Steel: Big Problems, Better Solutions" by Gary Clyde Hufbauer and Ben Goodrich, International Economics Policy Brief 01-9, July 2001, Institute for International Economics, Washington.

become expected. Reform oriented developing economies may have more in common with developed economies than they do with erstwhile colleagues in the caucus of the poor. Shifting interests can be expected to generate institutional tension during a transition period.

The first reaction from laggard economies may be to insist on rich world financial contributions to help bridge the development gap, as though financial shortfalls and not policy problems lay at the root of the problems. This will intensify traditional debates over whether such resource transfers promote or preempt development, and in any case the appropriate role of conditionality for ODA. Since this debate will happen against a backdrop of heightened economic performance in advanced and adjusting economies, the argument that wealth transfer is the ethical position will be sharpened.

Debate about who should pick up the tab for financial, telecommunications, transport and other infrastructures that have not appeared in the laggard on account of the failure to reform is the recipe for continued work by the international financial institutions, but also will engage the WTO because of commitments made in the Uruguay Round.

The tendency to blame successful economies for the performance of low growth economies has undermined international cooperation before. In addition to strife between advanced and less advanced economies over the proper flow of ODA, however, there will likely be increasing strife among less advanced economies, as market shares in advanced markets shift from developing laggards to developing adjusters. This discord may translate into a temptation to pursue deeper international economic liberalization in alternative venues to all-inclusive clubs such as WTO.

VI. Analytical Conclusions

A full understanding of the implications of the New Economy is a long way off. Even economists and Wall Street strategists have not put it all together yet. Irrational exuberists and irrational pessimists alike fail to take account of history and the cycles of innovation and utilization that characterize technological change. Only a few major opinion makers have offered an analysis that fully reflects the medium term productivity enhancements likely to derive from broad diffusion of new technology in an environment that encourages transformation set on a foundation of pro-growth policy.

It appears that a contentious and fundamental debate remains necessary to assert the role of policy in the New Economy model. The mantra of "private sector leads" is not misdirected – but it is only meaningful once government has done its policy job. In addition to "getting out of the way" in some respects, in others it means that policymakers face the very hefty job of deepening and managing the process of structural adjustment.

The goal of this study was to better quantify the upside so that reformers can depict the opportunity costs of inertia and clarify the consequences of a temporarily widening productivity gap. The goal of the recommendations is to help deepen consensus on the political economy of policy reform in each APEC economy, identify what can be done to make everyone a *transformer*, and determine what role APEC as an institution may play.

Challenge to Reforms: Spanning the Four Policy Domains

The New Economy develops best in an environment of comprehensive policy reform, which goes against the structure of most government bureaucracies where separate agencies each has a Minister, Director, staff, and priorities. Second, technological dynamism means that the private sector—including in particular, the foreign private sector—must be given a major role to play in the domestic transformation process. Managing the relationship between the public and the private sector is not easy. Third, the current macroeconomic climate for reform (both at home and in global markets) is not especially auspicious. Finally, many economies are used to financing reform and adjustment through international resource transfers, which have been reduced scale and scope in recent years. How can economies move toward meeting these challenges?

"Stove-pipe" government bureaucracy and public-private alliances:

No government is going to change structure over-night and no Minister will give up power and prestige. But the New Economy with its cross-cutting policies and economic benefits needs a voice at the table. Although not needed by all, some economies that appoint a high-level and charismatic individual or team may do better. This party has vision, charisma, and stature and can broker deals among agencies finding allies and common ground to yield comprehensive policy reform. Such a person or team can fashion pro-active alliances among government agencies and businesses that wish to promote liberalization, deregulation, and competition to achieve the benefits of New Economy transformation. Such a position can help ensure that private sector competitors—both domestic and foreign—actively engage in creating the new environment in which both they and new firms can flourish.

Poor domestic and global economic and political environments:

The US economy slowed dramatically, in large part due to a down-shift in investment in information technology and very quick adjustment by firms and workers to changes in demand. Most prognosticators believe that, on account of the rapid adjustment, the US economy is poised for a resumption of faster growth in Fall 2001. In some economies, adjustment by large industries – politically and economically important – to trade liberalization, domestic changes, and the forces of the New Economy has been difficult and prolonged. Some take these examples—the wrenching nature of the US down-shift and the difficult approach to big-industry change—as evidence that adjustment to the New Economy should be slowed. However, the essence of the New Economy *is* transformation, so its benefits come only when activities can adjust to new information. A measured pace will tend to magnify the costs, solidify the vested interests in the old activities, and delay the introduction and growth of new businesses and methods. Enabling, indeed speeding up these transformations should be the objective of policymakers.

Resource transfers and liberalization:

Economies wishing to enjoy a New Economy boost in productivity and resulting economic gains must make a habit of inducing transformation: the New Economy is not a "one-time" thing. Some resources truly support the process of opening by making skills and technical capacity available—but too often the effect is to blunt adjustment. Where the dependent variable for New Economy success truly is a matter of "bridge financing" to help defray the cost of adjustment, then resources need to be made available in whatever manner is appropriate. But without conducive policy conditions, the transfer of resources will be no more helpful than the transfer of high-technology into an environment where it cannot be utilized. Accordingly, to better understand where resource transfers might achieve additionality, economies would do well to catalog policy standing and progress toward reforms in each of the four policy domains_so that policymakers take advantage of policy synergies, make better use of technology to reform, and can more effectively use neighborhood comparisons to support domestic reform. Programs for capacity building should reflect the imperative of making coherent progress on all policy domains.

Challenges for Trade and Cross-Border Investment Liberalization

APEC has made important contributions to trade and investment reform in the past decade. The Bogor Goals of free trade by 2010/2020 and the Declaration's emphasis on inclusiveness and 'open regionalism' were a powerful signal to the world that the era of protectionism was giving way to an era of individual, collective, and concerted reductions in trade distortions. The Information Technology Agreement (ITA), catapulted from APEC to the WTO level, freed trillions of dollars of global trade in the essential ingredients of the networked information technology revolution. However extensive impediments to cross-border trade and investment remain.

Based on the analysis in Section V, differences in the pace of external (as well as internal) reforms among members are likely to be amplified by changes induced by the New Economy. The APEC community could be pushed apart by the differential productivity gains that result. The remedy to this threat, and the promise of shared prosperity, is redoubled effort on trade and information opening.

We recognize a number of impediments to that objective, both economic and political including absence of an on-going round of multilateral trade talks to help catalyze deeper regional opening and support domestic reforms; incomplete fulfillment of existing commitments; and the temptation of sub-regional arrangements.

Absence of on-going multilateral trade round:

In the past, APEC has been a motivator for global trade and investment liberalization. If APEC renewed its commitment to both the goals and principles of Bogor and the specifics of the Osaka Action Agenda, it would send a very strong signal to its own membership as well as to the global community. The empirical work is clear on the gains to the membership of broad-based multilateral liberalization of trade in goods and services and of complementary cross-border investment. Trade and cross-border investment liberalization, most prominently in the services sectors that support and augment networked information technologies, are key to gain the benefits of the New Economy. Were APEC to endorse wrapping WTO's "built-in agenda" for agriculture and services into a broader agenda for a New Round that includes complete liberalization of manufactures and extensive liberalization of cross-border investment, it would equal or surpass the value APEC provided in catalyzing the Information Technology Agreement.

Incomplete fulfillment of existing commitments:

Voluntary non-binding commitments have been the centerpiece of APEC's strategy of liberalization. Although valuable, particularly to bind together the membership toward common Bogor goals, this approach perhaps has run its course as the guiding method for liberalization with APEC. Within APEC, because the incomplete fulfillment of existing commitments challenges further liberalization, the APEC forum would do well to extend the institutionalization of transparency, monitoring, and assessment of commitments (e.g. e-IAPs and more extensive review as broached by members at SOM II/2001), which would support further liberalization. This is part of the "cataloging" effort broached in a broader sense in the previous conclusion. After all, it is difficult to deepen and broaden liberalization and face adjustment when existing statements and actions with regard to reform are non-transparent or can be called into question.

Challenges for Banking and Financial Market Policies

Reforms to the financial sector are critical for it to play its role in financing innovation and New Economy firms, and the transformation of the economy towards a superior allocation of resources. Economies will do better when they embrace the notion that transparency in financial relationships makes them stronger, that market discipline, (including through foreign participation and competition) of corporations improves corporate governance and behavior, and that a culture of private finance and competition which depends on credit analysis, pricing, and the notion of risk, return and failure will yield a superior outcome for their economies because it creates one that can grow fast and yet be resilient in the face of economic shocks.

But many APEC members see true challenges to reforming this sector, particularly with the recent crises in mind. The challenges have deep institutional roots and the process of reform will have ramifications for macro policy choices and financial market structure. APEC members should continue to work on domestic reforms that enhance performance and institutionalized capacity building in the APEC forum could assist that process. At the same time, progress on trade and investment liberalization has very strong links to the success of the reforms of the financial system.

Challenges to reforming the domestic financial system fall into three categories: Poor supervisory oversight including the inability of regulators to keep up with financial technology; Lack of financial skills among local institutions such that performance poor and the competitive threat from foreign institutions hinders commitment to external openness; Thin non-bank financial (for example, limited bond, equity, or venture) markets such that innovative approaches to raising capital are hampered and foreign capital inflows are (often, particularly now) seen as more of a threat than a benefit

Poor Supervisory Oversight:

The importance of a solid foundation for prudential supervision is now obvious. The Basle Core Principles[94] outline what should be the objectives of the supervisors and the BIS Capital Adequacy Guidelines put numerical measures on these objectives. However, domestic supervisors often are unfamiliar with or untrained in new financial techniques. And supervision will remain an ever-changing challenge as financial institutions and transactions change in response to the demands of the marketplace. To ameliorate these conditions, economies should develop on-going relationships with established supervisory training and exchange mechanisms (IMF, WB and central bank-to-central bank). The APEC Financial Institute could be a focal point to ensure that all APEC members have training in these critical aspects of the New Economy to ensure that all APEC members have access to this critical aspect of the New Economy.

Lack of Financial Skills:

It is not enough to have supervisors, however. Performance of the financial system depends on having a set of trained credit analysts who can spot good risks and lend to them appropriately. Here, technology transfer, global linkages, and international best practice in finance are key ingredients to enabling the New Economy. These can best be obtained by encouraging participation in the local market by foreign financial institutions. Research makes

---

[94] Morris Goldstein, The Case for an International Banking Standard (1997) Policy Analyses in International Economics, Washington: Institute for International Economics.

clear that domestic institutions change, but are not eliminated completely.[95] Technology and knowledge transfers are important to improve domestic activities. Moreover, the partnership between international institutions with technology and local institutions with local expertise brings the domestic institutions into the global network of financial institutions. Early and priority attention to liberalizing barriers to cross-border investment for financial transactions and institutions will allow the learning and application of international best practice.

Thin non-bank financial markets:

The problem of thin non-bank financial markets has two dimensions. The first is that these non-bank financial markets (such as bond, venture, and equity) are particularly important avenues for financing innovative efforts and new firms.[96] Moreover a robust financial system, with multiple channels to allocate resources is also more able to productively allocate inflows of capital, and to withstand the sometimes volatile nature of those flows. Transparent public listing requirements, along with strong accounting standards will help deepen financial markets because they improve the ability of investors to judge credit and improve the ability of firms to present themselves to investors.

Challenges for Fiscal Policy and Reform of Fiscal Activities

The forces of the New Economy, and its benefits, demand the same kinds of transformation within government as within business. We can think of the "business" of government as raising and redistributing revenues and providing public services. Just as private businesses are reaping efficiency gains from the New Economy, so too can government increase the efficiency of what it does. Just as private firms are examining how the New Economy affects the focus and method of their business activities, so too should government consider how the New Economy affects both what it does and how it does it. Moreover, in many economies, the government can play an important role in leading the way and paving the way for uptake of transformative technologies by the private sector.

APEC government have been embracing some of the aspects of the New Economy through the Electronic Commerce Steering Group, e-APEC, and the TelWorking Group. But members face real challenges to reforming both the internal workings of government as well as the external activities of government.

In many APEC economies the government is a large employer and a big spender in the economy. To significantly rationalize and redirect the domestic activities of government (for example, to reduce subsidies or close down state enterprises) can be seen thought to add to the cost of adjustment to the New Economy. Of course, in some cases, these activities are

---

[95] See Mann, Eckert, Knight, Global Electronic Commerce: A Policy Primer, chapter 4; See also World Bank. Finance for Growth: Policy Choices in a Volatile World, A Policy Research Report
[96] See O'Shea, Margaret and Candice Stevens, "Governments as Venture Capitalists," The OECD OBSERVER No. 213 August/September 1998 and Baygan, Gunseli and Michael Freudenberg, "The Internationalisation of Venture Capital Activity in OECD Countries: Implications for Measurement and Policy," OECD STI Working Papers - 2000/7, December 2000.

politically sensitive and are a source of patronage. With respect to the internal activities of government, reform at the federal level may be uncorrelated with reform at the local level, leaving governmental presence and activity fragmented and uneven throughout the economy.

There are significant challenges to the transparency of and flow of information which are crucial to gain the benefits of the New Economy. Tax evasion is a significant problem throughout APEC and stymies the transformations toward the New Economy technologies: on the one hand, incentives that promote evasion tend to undermine the use of electronic transactions methods; as well, digitization could facilitate further evations. Taking stock now makes sense.

However, if government embraces the concept and transformative nature of the New Economy, as well as uses its ICT tools effectively, the net fiscal position of the government can be improved so that spending will help the adjustment process move forward, not just help ride out the storm.

Redirecting internal operations and external activities:

Research points out that the dynamism of the New Economy means that governments should be more careful of their choice of economic activities. Economies pursuing New Economy outcomes should focus activities on areas where the private market is least successful (education and basic research) and carefully evaluate the cost vs. benefit of keeping state-owned enterprises and activities functioning. And, consideration should include the cost vs. benefit of alternative strategies that promote transformation, including social safety nets which can either encourage workers to leave to join new businesses or be a constraint on them doing so.

Transforming inner workings of government:

Research suggests that government agencies can enjoy the same type of productivity gains from the New Economy that businesses do. Getting this expertise into government agencies is the issue and requires both hardware and software (that is, capacity building). Building on elements of e-APEC, E-government teams that are composed of foreign, domestic, and government entities can bring productivity enhancing ICTs as well as transformation into members' government operations. These e-government teams could partner international technology consultants, domestic private sector firms, and personnel within each government agency. These teams could undertake a needs-assessment, affect technology transfer and best practice, and help ensure inter-operability among ICT systems throughout government agencies.

The operations of government can play an important role as a "litmus test" for policy conditions in the economy as a whole. If the government cannot present information to its citizens, or process tax payments through the financial system, or receive procurement through the distribution system, then most probably neither can the private sector. And, the transformations of activities of the New Economy could be slowed.

Challenges for Pro-competitive Market Policies and Legal Regime

Based on some of the case studies, some APEC policymakers may be concerned that competition policy is too sophisticated and the environment is changing too rapidly to enshrine a regime. They worry that legal reforms are time consuming and the relative roles of central and periphery authorities often unclear and evolving. Some see that the transparency associated with the information flow of the New Economy will undermine (or the New Economy will be held back by) corrupt practices. Others think that adjustment within the New Economy paradigm actually will be enhanced by command and control and that letting market forces work will take too long and be too costly and disruptive.

Sophistication and rapid evolution of competitive environment:

The role of competition policy is to create an environment which preserves the private sector's incentives to innovate. Sometimes this implies government intervention to level-the-playing field for new entrants. Sometimes this implies government intervention to ensure that property rights are respected. Sometimes this implies government intervention to act as an advocate for the minority (say with regard to privacy of personal information) that otherwise might be disregarded. In other words, competition policy implies a balance between individuals, firms, and society. There is no particular set of rules that will do this; any particular set of rules to do this would be quite complex; and the rapidly changing environment means that any particular set of rules is likely to be overcome by change. These observations taken together imply that competition principles should be the objective of a competition regime. Therefore, APEC members should discuss how the APEC Principles to Enhance Competition Policy and Regulatory Reform operate in the marketplace of the New Economy where more and more transactions cross international borders.

Difficulty of scope and nature of legal reforms:

Specific reforms to legal code and new model laws that create an environment of certainty in which the New Economy can develop are being undertaken by many economies and international bodies. The UN Committee on International Trade Law (UNCITRAL) has put forward model contracts, the OECD and WIPO are working on electronic signatures. APEC members should look to these international efforts for legal precedent and models. However, individual APEC members will have to embody these laws in the various jurisdictions of their governance structure. Moreover, it is important to recognize that laws alone do not create an environment in which the New Economy can flourish. The "rule of law"—the transparency of law, the belief that the law applies to all, and will be enforced, is necessary.

Lack of a trusted environment:

Fraud, an environment of perceived unfairness, and uncertainty are costly—and are even more costly in the environment of the New Economy where arms-length transactions, digital delivery, and obtaining and using information are key. A trust environment raises productivity gains by expanding the activity of transformation that businesses undertake. APEC members should recognize that the technologies of the New Economy (such as secure transactions) can be used to improve trust in the environment, when those technologies are underpinned by law.

Command and control will speed adjustments right now:

Regardless of the legitimacy of such a statement at a point in time, the New Economy depends on a complex, rich web of information and reaction by many entities. Domestic private enterprises and firms must learn to recognize opportunities themselves, otherwise the full benefits of the New Economy will not accrue. Failure is a part of learning and therefore a precursor to success. The pace of technological change and the dynamic nature of adjustment to the new demands of the marketplace mean that government policymakers have no hope to achieve the "right" outcome through command and control. APEC's knowledge network will catalog private-sector 'success stories'_which will help other governments pursue a better strategy to achieve the transformation to the New Economy.

A Final Word

This Report has been prepared by economists for the Economic Committee of an economic forum. It has been narrowly focused on the policy requirements to achieve the benefits of the New Economy. But the fullest understanding of the New Economy paradigm, just as with previous technological shifts, must involve a far more universal analysis. The nature of society, government, security, culture and individual experience are all being impacted by the tendency toward globalization that is inseparable from the New Economy economic trends described herein. The parsimony of analysis here is not an oversight but a necessary sacrifice to stay within the mandate for this Report and the purview of the economic policymaker audience for whom it is prepared. Clearly however it must be examined in a larger context, and hopefully it will make a contribution to that context as well.

Appendix 1
Research on Transformation of Industries by ICTs Technologies

	Goldman Sachs	Litan and Rivlin	Forrester			NAM Ernst & Young				EITO (Europe)		
	Cost Savings Percent	Cost Savings Percent	Product Fit Score	Industrial Readiness Score	Average	Zero (percent)	e-Info (percent)	e-Interaction (percent)	e-Commerce (percent)	Internal (score)	External (score)	Total
Industry												
Food Ingredients	3-5		4.8	3.4	4.1							
Consumer goods			3.5	2.9	3.2	1	21	42	36			
Textiles										1.4	2.5	3.9
Energy, Chemicals, Natl Res						7	32	29	28			
Coal	2											
Chemicals	10											
Pharmaceuticals			3.9	3.1	3.5					2	2.4	4.4
Forest Products	15-25											
Paper	10		3.8	3	3.4							
Steel	11											
Machinings (Metals)	22					9	29	40	21			
Heavy Industries			2	1.5	1.75							
Industrial Eqpt & Supplies			2	4	3	6	22	47	25			
Technology & Electronics						0	25	40	35			
Computing & Electronics		5 (Cisco)	4	4.8	4.4							
Electronic Components	29-39											
Computing	11-20											
Aerospace Machinings	11		1.5	1.5	1.5					2.6	2.2	4.8
Autos	..	11	3.3	1.5	2.4	3	24	47	26	2.7	3.2	5.9
Shipbuilding										2	1.6	3.6
Shipping/Warehousing			4.4	4	4.2							
Freight Transport	15-20	xx										
Utilities			4.4	4	4.2							
Communications/Bandwidth	5-15											
Health Care	5	xx										
Life Science	12-19											
Construction			2.2	4.5	3.35							
Media and Advertising	10-15											
Retail		xx										
Finance		xx										
All		0.25-0.5				4	26	42	27			

Sources:
- Goldman Sachs (2000) *The Shocking Economic Effect of B2B*
- Robert Litan and Alice Rivlin (2001) Beyond the Dot.Coms; The Economic Promise of the Internet (July draft); **XX** means research has been done on these sectors, but classifying the importance of the Internet for saving costs or increasing efficiency has not been completed by the authors/editors.
- Forrester Research (2001), *The B2B Opportunity Index from Forrester Research*, www.ebizchronicles.com/backgrounders... (as of June 26, 2001)
- The National Association of Manufacturers and Ernst &Young (2001); *E-Commerce Trends Index*
- EITO (2001), *European Information Technology Observer Millennium Edition*

Appendix 2
Trade Exposure Charts for Each Economy

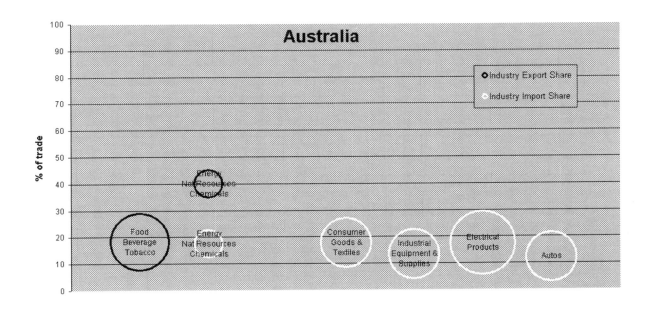

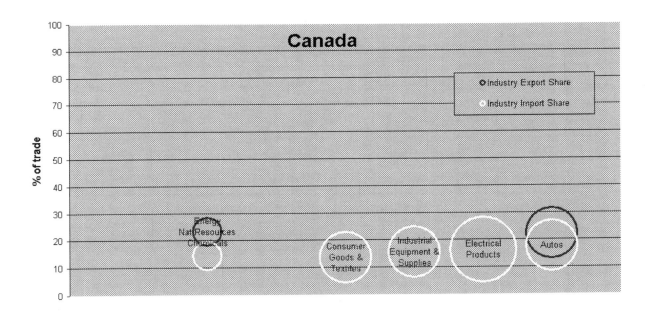

Bubble size is Technology Transformation Intensity of that sector (larger is undergoing more transformation).

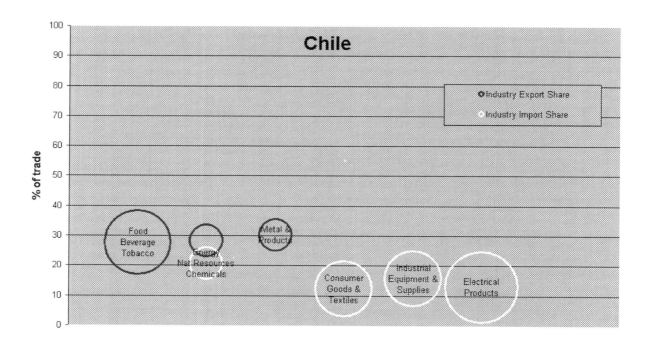

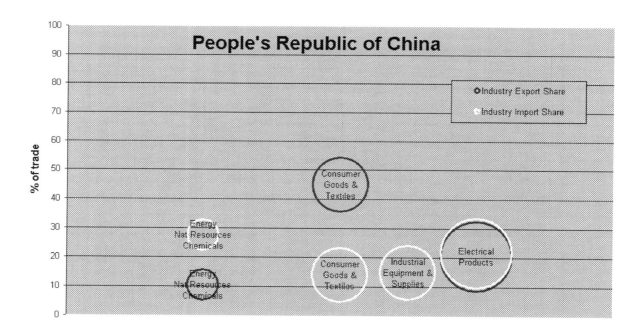

Bubble size is Technology Transformation Intensity of that sector (larger is undergoing more transformation).

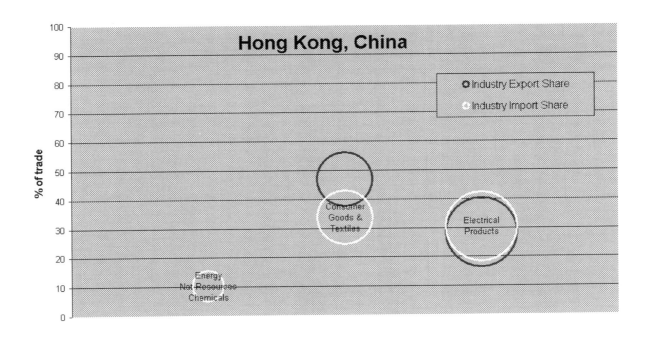

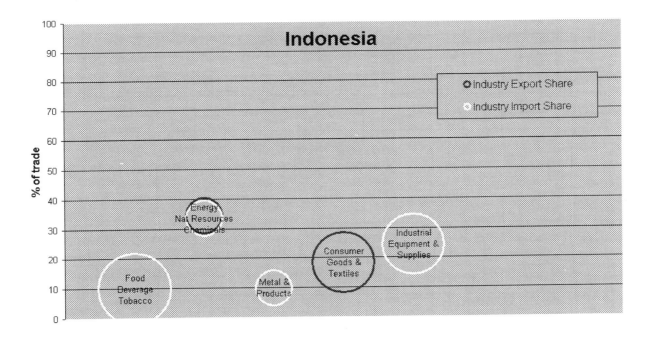

Bubble size is Technology Transformation Intensity of that sector (larger is undergoing more transformation).

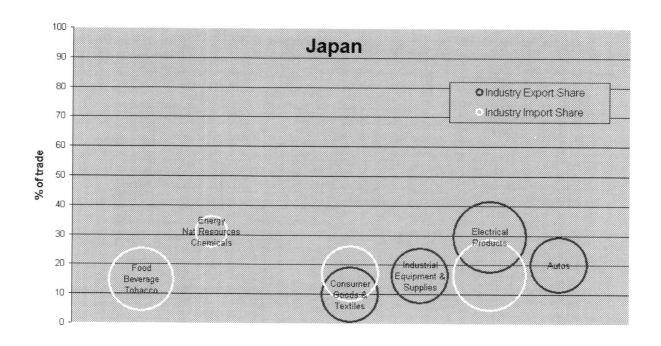

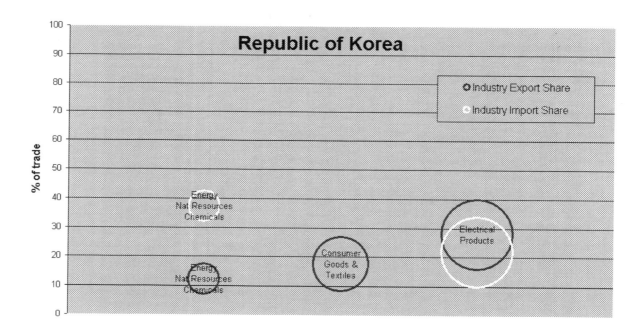

Bubble size is Technology Transformation Intensity of that sector (larger is undergoing more transformation).

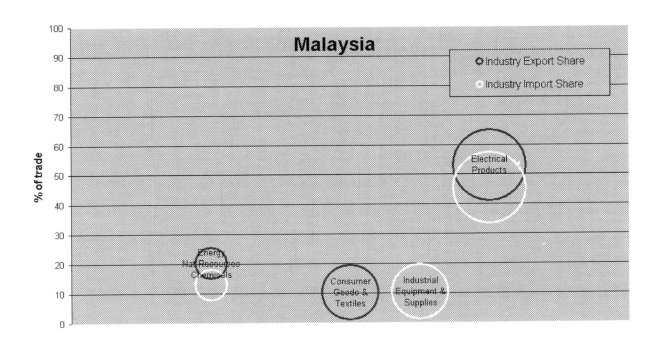

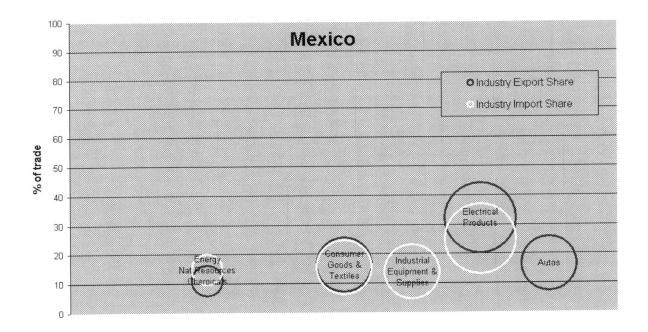

Bubble size is Technology Transformation Intensity of that sector (larger is undergoing more transformation).

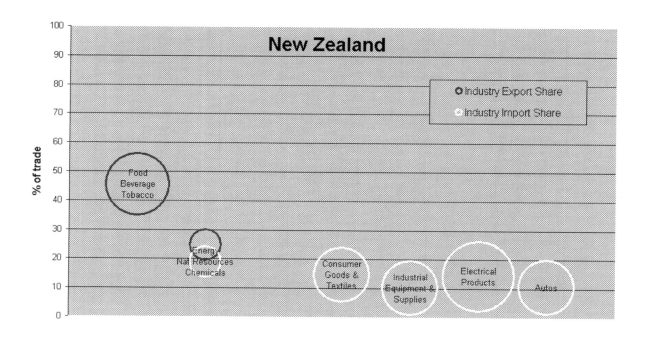

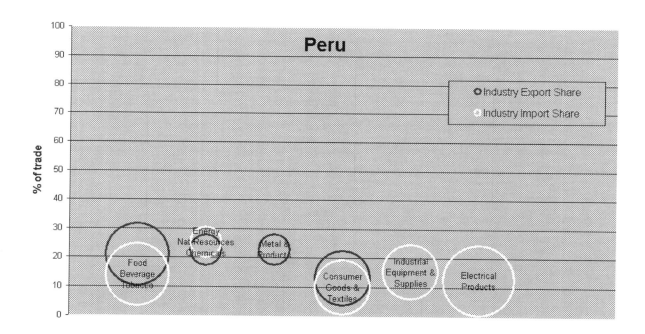

Bubble size is Technology Transformation Intensity of that sector (larger is undergoing more transformation).

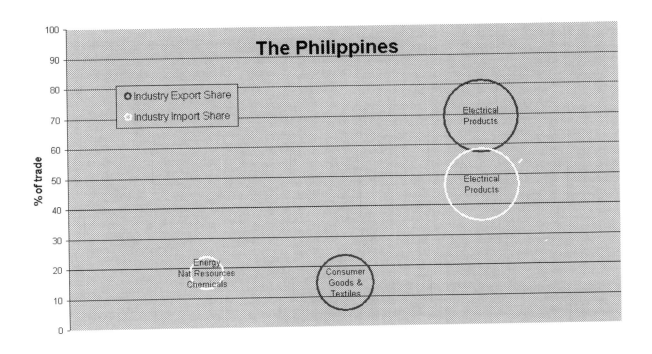

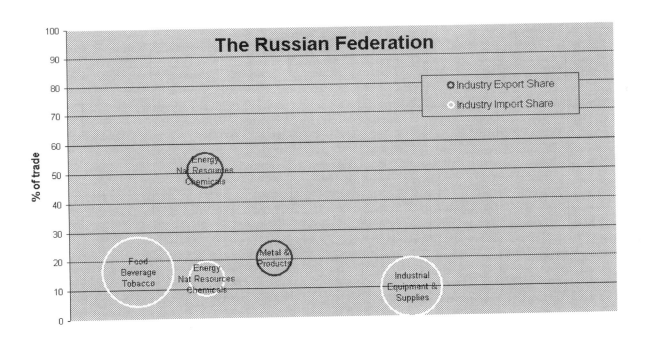

Bubble size is Technology Transformation Intensity of that sector (larger is undergoing more transformation).

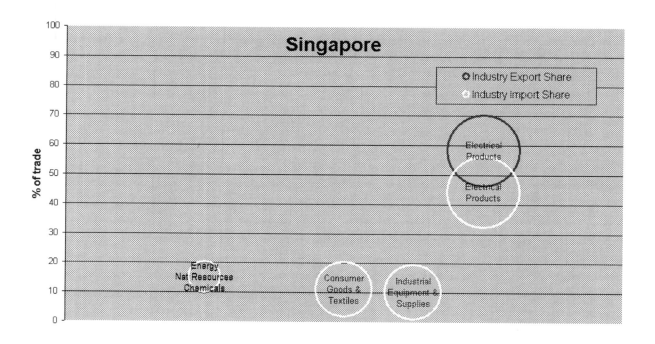

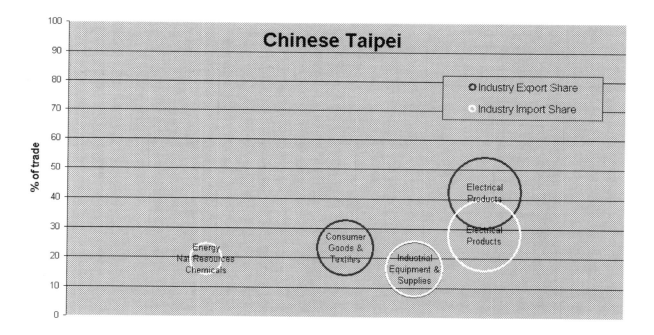

Bubble size is Technology Transformation Intensity of that sector (larger is undergoing more transformation).

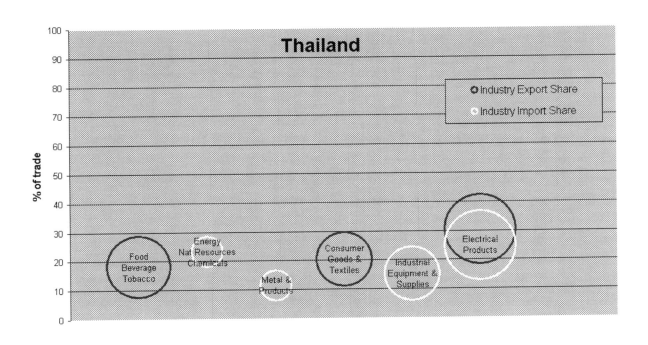

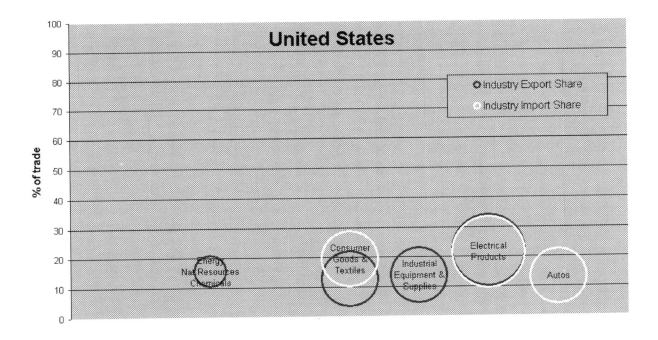

Bubble size is Technology Transformation Intensity of that sector (larger is undergoing more transformation).

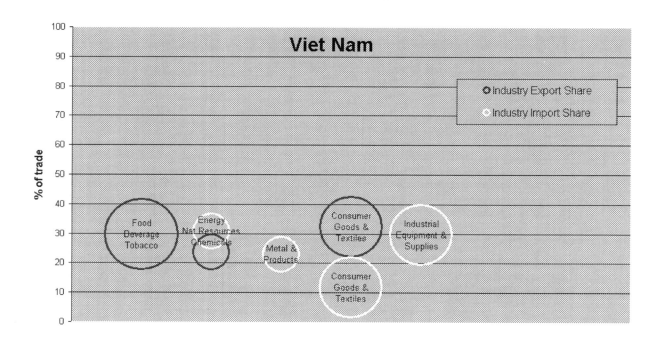

Bubble size is Technology Transformation Intensity of that sector (larger is undergoing more transformation).

Appendix 3
Trade Exposure Charts for Each Sector

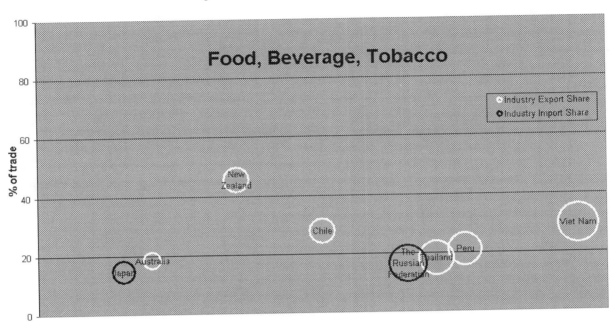

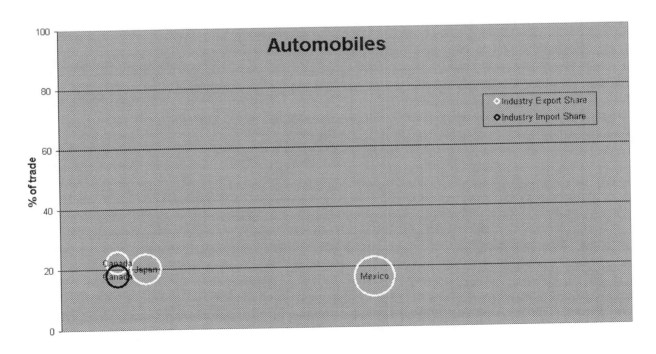

Bubble size represents policy conditions of the economy. The smaller the bubble the more facilitating the policy environment. Economies are ordered left to right by GDP per capita. Economies with trade share less than 15% are not shown.

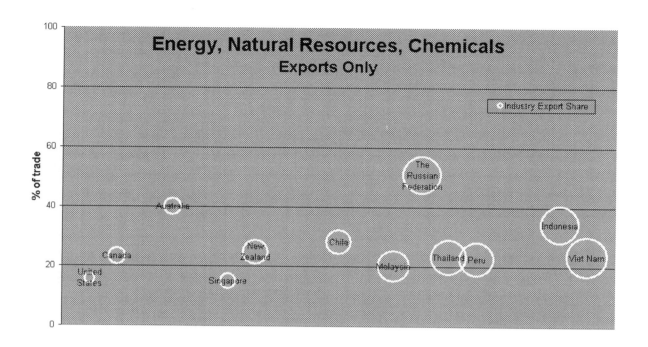

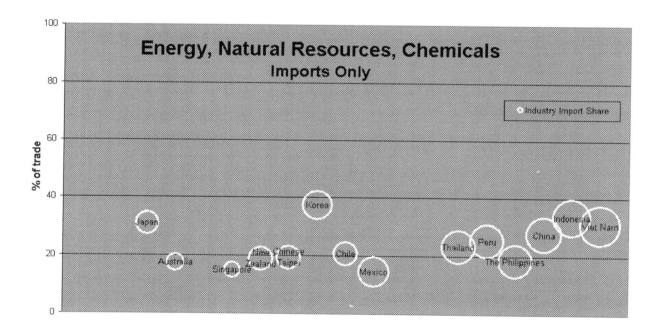

Bubble size represents policy conditions of the economy. The smaller the bubble the more facilitating the policy environment. Economies are ordered left to right by GDP per capita. Economies with trade share less than 15% are not shown.

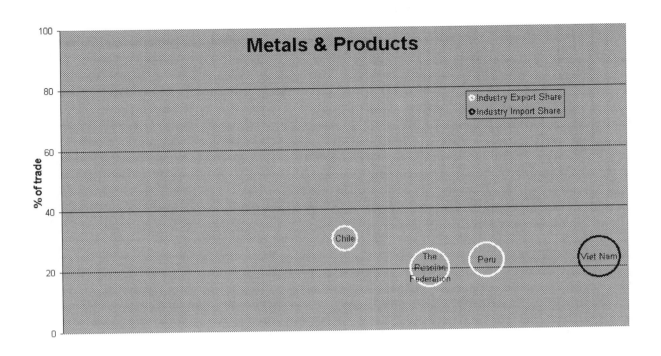

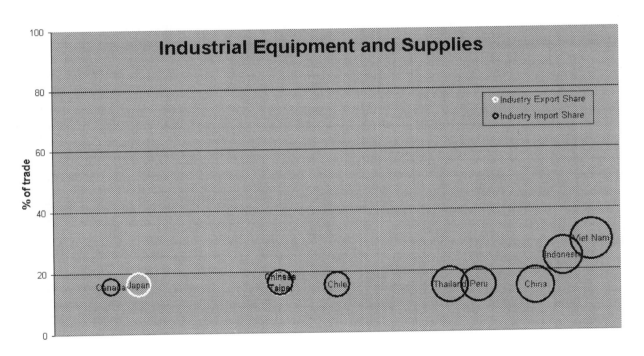

Bubble size represents policy conditions of the economy. The smaller the bubble the more facilitating the policy environment. Economies are ordered left to right by GDP per capita. Economies with trade share less than 15% are not shown.

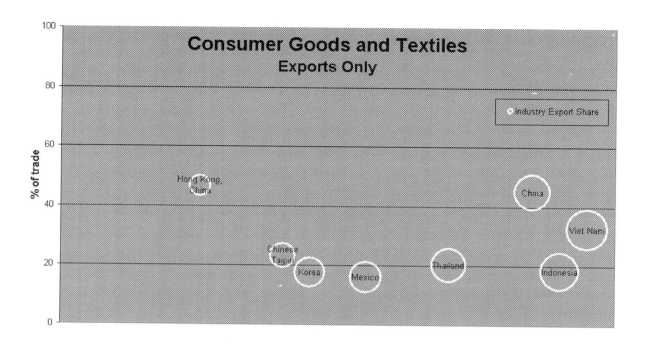

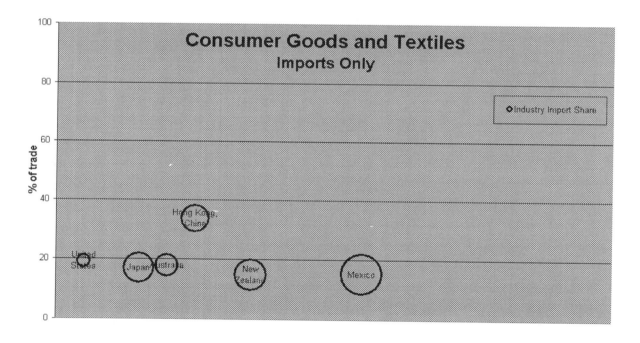

Bubble size represents policy conditions of the economy. The smaller the bubble the more facilitating the policy environment. Economies are ordered left to right by GDP per capita. Economies with trade share less than 15% are not shown.

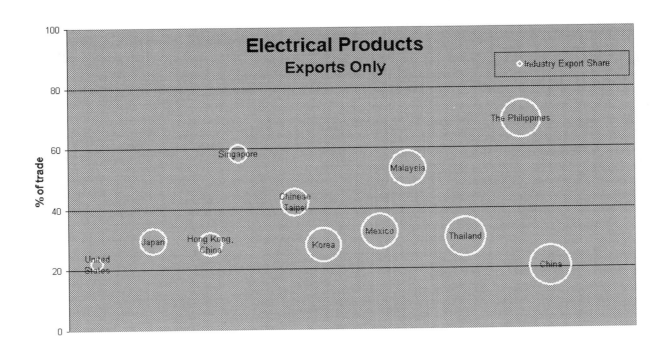

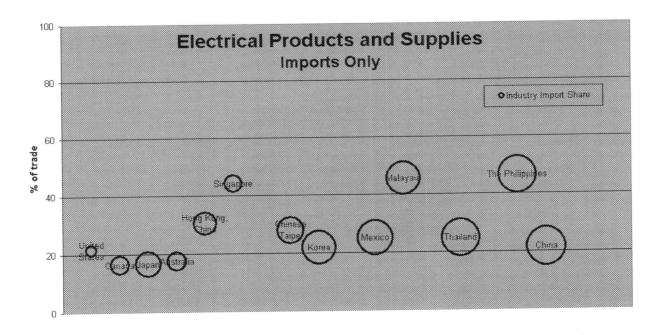

Bubble size represents policy conditions of the economy. The smaller the bubble the more facilitating the policy environment. Economies are ordered left to right by GDP per capita. Economies with trade share less than 15% are not shown.

APPENDIX 4

A key component of the New Economy and APEC report is the distillation of common themes from case studies. Sixteen case studies from twelve APEC members were prepared especially for this Report. Nominally following a "template" (reproduced below) these mini case studies come from both official APEC sources as well as independent researchers and address how businesses, civil society, and governments are being transformed by the technologies of the New Economy—or are being held back from that transformation by the state of the domestic and international policy environments. The case studies are very short (thus the term "mini"-case studies) and represent only a sketch of the situation and response of the specific entity reviewed

Template

Short overview of the client.

This section should tell us about the firm, civil group, or government agency that is being reviewed. This section should be no *more than one-quarter* of the total length of the study.

- Sector (e.g. type of business activity, or focus of civil activity, or agency of government)
- Size (e.g. earnings, employees, number of separate business offices or entities if a conglomerate)
- Age
- Type of governance
  - Business: (e.g. privately headed and controlled, stock-holder control, separate governing board)
  - Civil groups: (e.g. single head, consensus group)
  - Government agency: (e.g. independent agency, reports to some other government body)

"New economy" narrative

This section should tell us about how the client is being affected by new economy forces—to change the way it does business, interacts with its civil or social objectives, or the manner in which it interacts with the public. The specific focus here is on whether and how the client uses information technologies, broadly defined, in the conduct of its activities. These technologies can be taken to include any networked two-way information and data communication device (such as computers, mobile phones, personal digital assistants) as well as the software that runs and networks them. The client could be a user or creator or both of these technologies.

- How did the client come to use these technologies?
  For example,
  - Did the client itself initiate the use or creation of information technologies
  - Was there an outside force (such as a multinational firm or international agency) that precipitated the use of the new technologies?

- Has APEC played a role (such as through the e-IAP process or through the readiness assessments, or e-government pilot projects for example?)

- How have the technologies changed what the client does or the way it does it? For example:
  - These information technologies and the new economy environment have: Reduced costs, sped-up operation times, expanded the set of suppliers or buyers, created new business ideas and operations, generated more transparency, achieved greater reach to civil society....
  - Specific anecdotes would be helpful, such as these: "We were able to find a new buyer for our product through the Internet." (Vietnam) "We were able to reach rural health clinics and improve information exchange using mobile phones." (Bangladesh) "We have reduced the cost of procurement by 10 percent using information technologies." (US) "We were able to improve the daily process of pricing and transport of the product by moving from fax to Internet." (Thailand) "We are using networked information technologies to improve tax administration." (Morocco) "With the same budget, we were able to tell more people about what is going on in the legislative process." (Chile)

<u>New Economy and policy</u>

The objective of this section is to explore the extent to which policies and or the policy environment stand in the way or have aided the client in its uptake of new economy technologies.

- *Macroeconomic policy and environment*:

  How has the client's experience with new economy technologies and activities been affected by the macroeconomic environment, including:
  - Inflation and interest rates (level and volatility),
  - Exchange rate volatility,
  - Economic growth generally (level and volatility).

  For all clients, these factors will be relevant, but the key issue to explore is the impact of these macro factors on the development and uptake of new economy technologies.

- *Services infrastructures, policy and environment*.

  How has the client's experience with new economy technologies and activities been affected by the:
  - Cost, quality, density of communications infrastructures:
  - Cost, timeliness, and overall performance of financial intermediaries, including international financial exchange;

- Cost, speed, mode-integration (air-land-sea) of various distribution capabilities, including cross-border capabilities.

- *Micro business and labor environment including rule of law.*

  How has the client's experience with the new economy technologies and activities been affected by the:
  - Regulatory environment for engaging in new activities
  - Labor market environment for both hiring and separation
  - Rule-making environment, including rules for electronic contracting, verification.

How services infrastructure and the business environment affect a client will differ substantially depending on the type of client. What we would like the researcher to explore is whether the client thinks that policy changes to improve performance and/or the environment (such as, for example, through changing ownership, more competition, increased amount of or access to infrastructure, appropriate regulation, eased licensing, more flexible labor market, improved body of cyber laws) would affect how they produce or use new economy technologies.

- *Human resource capability*

  How has the client's experience with the new economy technologies and activities been affected by the quality and availability of workers to:
  - Produce new economy products or services
  - Use new economy technologies
  - Has there been any policy focus on the issue of human resource development, e.g. through pilot projects, awareness, education programs or curriculum changes, community focused access and uptake?

<u>Summing-up and looking-forward:</u>

This section should be one paragraph or so and should sum-up what the new economy means to the client, what the client plans to do in the future, and what three specific policies changes it would recommend to the policy authorities.

111

AN AUSTRALIAN BANK ADAPTS TO DEREGULATION AND INFORMATION TECHNOLOGY

Tony Weir
New Economy Branch
Department of Industry Science and Resources
Canberra, Australia [1]

Introduction

There was a dramatic deregulation of Australian banking in the early 1980s, which included the opening of the market to foreign competition. The interplay of this with the parallel widespread adoption of information technology makes an interesting case study of a service industry in the new economy. Table 1 summarises the history of these parallel streams in Australian banking.

Table 1. Chronology of developments in policy and ICT in Australian banking

Date	Policy framework	Technology development
1981	Campbell report on Australia's financial system recommends opening to foreign competition	
1982		First public ATMs
1983	Australian dollar floated	
1984	ANZ purchase Grindlays' Bank, giving it representation in 45 countries	EFTPOS systems started
1985	16 foreign banks granted banking licences. Competition encourages "loose" lending.	
1987-91	Stock market crash and recession, many loans defaulted	
1990	ANZ proposal to merge with National Mutual Life vetoed by Government	National (inter-bank) EFTPOS system in operation
1997	Wallis report on financial services recommends regulatory regime based on functions (rather than institutions or products)	Phone banking introduced
1999	*Electronic Transaction Act* facilitates e-commerce	Internet banking introduced
2000	Sale of Grindlays' Bank - ANZ no longer so international as a group	ANZ strongly involved in e-commerce, setting up a B2B portal and other facilities

---

[1] The opinions expressed in this paper are the sole responsibility of the author and do not necessarily reflect those of the Department of Industry Science and Resources or of the Australian Government.

To make the case study more specific, we have focussed on one particular bank, namely ANZ Bank[2]. ANZ is one of the "big four" Australian banks. In 1999, it had assets of A$149 billion (approx US$97 bn)[3] of which 69% was in Australia, 13% in New Zealand, and 18% elsewhere. The bank employed 23000 staff in Australia and New Zealand and 8000 elsewhere in the region. Part of the special interest of ANZ is its efforts to expand internationally as one of its responses to foreign competition in its home market. (See Figure 1 for the history of these figures.)

We pay special attention to more recent developments relating to electronic commerce and the use of the internet and the recent policy framework, as they are the focus of the IIE report for the APEC Economic Committee.

The Policy Framework

Banks have been an important part of the Australian landscape since the early days of European settlement. In particular, strong bank involvement in the development of an export-oriented Australian agriculture through the nineteenth century and the gold rushes of the 1850s left almost every Australian country town dominated by the imposing buildings of several rival banks. With consequent expansion into the suburbs of the growing cities, most Australian Banks including ANZ possessed an extensive national network of branches. All were companies owned by a wide range of shareholders, rather than family owned as is more common in some other countries.

From the 1950s to the 1980s, the entrenched banking oligopoly was protected from foreign and new domestic competition by a policy of not granting new banking licenses. The Reserve Bank applied strict regulation, but also effectively guaranteed bank deposits. A parallel non-bank sector grew up that was subject to far less regulation, and which therefore often made riskier loans than the banks but at higher interest. ANZ (and the other major Australian banks) set up subsidiary finance companies to operate in this market.

By the late 1970s, technological change and greater integration of world financial markets led to widespread acceptance, including by the banks themselves, of the need for broad ranging financial deregulation in Australia. In anticipation of this, the larger Australian banks embarked on some key mergers, so that by the early 1980s there were four major Australian banks, of which ANZ was one.

---

[2] The full name of the company is Australia and New Zealand Banking Group Limited; ANZ is the trading name. The name correctly implies that the bank has substantial operations in New Zealand, which it has done since 1839 (under various earlier names).
[3] Unless noted all financial figures are given in Australian dollars. Over the period, the A$ varied from US$1.14 (1980) to US$0.56 (2000).

The Campbell Report of 1981 on the Australian financial system[4] spurred Australia to embark on a relatively rapid transformation from one of the most regulated financial sectors in the world to one of the more liberal. Key steps included

- floating the Australian dollar in December 1983,
- granting 40 new foreign exchange licences in June 1984,
- granting banking licences to 16 foreign banks in February 1985,
- removal of interest rate ceilings (1985-86) and restrictions on the range of activities in which banks can engage,
- Liberalisation of reserve requirements (1985, 1988).

Consequently, from the 1980s, the Australian banking system has transformed from one consisting of a small number of major banks, four State banks, and a very small number of minor ones, to a system with open entry where though the four major Australian banks still dominate, they are open to competition from subsidiaries of foreign banks[5] and from small and regional banks (and other deposit-taking institutions, such as building societies[6]).

Most of the new local banks were formed by consolidation of existing financial institutions such as building societies and "savings banks". Very few of the foreign-owned banks attempted to compete with the established local banks by setting up or acquiring a large branch network. Instead they went for niches such as merchant banking or personal banking to very rich customers. (The introduction of ATM networks in the early 1980s by the major local banks can be seen as an attempt to discourage competitors in the "retail" market.)

The major exception to this was the National Mutual Royal Bank, formed by National Mutual (one of the largest local insurance companies) and Royal Bank of Canada. This rapidly built up a retail network of nearly 200 branches across Australia by acquiring local building societies. In 1990, ANZ perceived that "deregulation" offered scope for synergy between traditional banking and the previously segregated life insurance and superannuation business, which looked likely to become a more favoured savings medium than traditional savings banks, as government encouraged (indeed compelled by legislation from 1992) workers to save for their retirements. ANZ therefore proposed a merger with National Mutual, but the Government refused to allow it, citing "national interest grounds" – essentially, too great a concentration of financial institutions within Australia was seen as anti-competitive.

This raises the question: about what "market" should competition policy be concerned? Table 2 shows a matrix of possibilities. Competition policy in Australia has been largely concerned with the bottom left quadrant, as indicated by the very title of the main regulator, the Australian Competition and Consumer Council, set up in 1975. But the management of ANZ and the big local banks are most strategically concerned with the top right quadrant: their concern is whether ANZ is big enough to fight off foreign companies who wish either to

---

[4] *Final Report of the Committee of Inquiry into the Australian Financial System* , Australian Government Publishing Service, Canberra, 1981.
[5] In strict legal terms, there are no "foreign" banks in Australia- rather, foreign-owned banks operate through subsidiary companies.
[6] Roughly equivalent to the "savings and loans" institutions in USA.

compete across the spread of ANZ's domestic market or even to attempt a take-over (a prospect which looks more tempting with the fall of the A$ since 1980).

Table 2. Matrix of concerns for competition policy

	Domestic	International
Producers		
Consumers		

In this case, though the cross-sectoral merger was blocked, ANZ was allowed to take-over the banking subsidiary (in late 1990), with the upshot that no foreign bank currently has a branch network in Australia remotely comparable in size to ANZ.

One response by the bigger Australian banks to increased competition at home—including from foreign banks—was to themselves expand overseas. In particular in 1984 ANZ acquired Grindlay's bank, and thus became overnight the most international of Australian banks, with branches in 45 countries. (Grindlays' was a British-owned bank, with a substantial network in India, and branches in many other Asian and African countries.)

In the late 1980s, competition and deregulation made banks much more willing to lend than before. As interest rates rose and recession set in the early 1990s, the level of non-performing loans soared. Some of the newer banks went out of business. In 1992 ANZ made its only recorded loss for decades, largely because of provision for $1600m of bad debt. The bank acknowledged that "there was some imprudent lending in the boom of the late 1980s, particularly to small and medium enterprises where market share was most contested following deregulation". This "imprudence" reflected the change in the role of a bank manager from allocating scarce credit under regulation to actively seeking loans business and consequently having to assess more dubious risks—many old-style managers lacked the skills to adapt to this new environment. The problems in the financial sector were a major factor in the introduction of a new set of prudential requirements on banks, based on capital adequacy requirements, that continue today largely unchanged.

That ANZ did not make more extensive overall losses in the late 1980s and early 1990s was due to steady profits from its overseas operations, which in all except one year offset its domestic losses. However, the bank was beginning to rationalise its overseas operations, to better fit a strategic concentration on those parts of the Asia-Pacific region where its Australian customers aimed to do business. In 1992, it sold the Grindlays' operations in Africa.

By 2000 ANZ, having steadily built up its business banking operations in East Asia, North America and Europe, sold off what had once been its overseas "flagship", the Grindlays' business in India where it was the largest foreign bank. This left ANZ without a substantial retail operation outside Australia and New Zealand, though it still has substantial assets (14%) overseas, and is supposedly "contemplating acquisitions in East Asia".

Technological Developments and Their Implications

The 1980s and 1990s featured a remarkable and steady increase in the technological sophistication of the bank's operations. Notable steps included:

- Back office computerisation—even by 1980 more than 90% of branches had their accounts processed by a centralised computer sections, even though the raw data was sent on paper by courier.
- Computer-linked teller terminals (from 1985)
- Improved telecommunications between branches and the corporate centres, including the international outposts. By 1985, the group had a private packaged worldwide telecommunications network, which has been steadily upgraded technologically. Moreover liberalisation of telecommunications policy in Australia in the 1990s and consequent increased competition enabled the bank to negotiate cheaper contracts, with savings of tens of millions of dollars p.a.
- Automatic Teller Machines (ATMs) - first introduced in 1980, by 2000 on the outside of every branch and also independent of the (decreased) number of branches in places like shopping malls and airports; altogether Australian banks have over 9000 installed ATMs.
- Electronic Payment at Point of Sale (EFTPOS—special terminals in shops, service stations etc, first introduced in 1984 and rapidly expanded. By 2000 there are over 300 000 "cash access points" in Australia.
- Telephone transaction banking (from 1996)
- Internet banking (introduced in 1999, with 100 000 customers registering in the first year)
- Use of expert systems software to assess lending risks (from 1989)
- A common computer banking system throughout the banks international system (phased in from 1996)
- In the late 1990s the bank also became a significant supporter of and player in e-commerce (see below).

The main driver of these developments, all of which involved substantial up-front costs, was competitive pressure from other banks and financial institutions. These forced ANZ and the other major banks to seek efficiencies and productivity gains wherever they could. ANZ sought "to optimise use of our electronic as well as our traditional branch delivery channels, to serve customers better and to provide ANZ with a permanently lower cost base" (1994). Plus it could not afford to look old-fashioned compared to its competitors, as information technology rapidly evolved.

The readiness of most Australian consumers to accept new technology, the technical skills base available to the bank (including its subsidiary software company in India!), the quality of ICT infrastructure and early adjustment of some regulation all contributed to Australia being among the first countries to adopt the technologies listed above.

Figure 1: ANZ performance over period 1980-2000 (indexed to 1990=100). Since 1990, Business (assets) have increased but staff and branches have decreased. In 1990 ANZ had 2700 branches world-wide (of which 1300 were in Australia), 48000 staff worldwide (30000 in Australia), and assets of A$99bn.

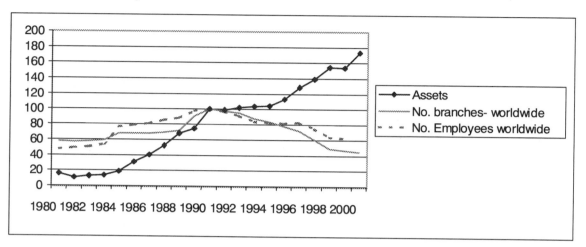

As in many other industries, new technology and "productivity improvements" can mean that either the same number of staff have greater output or that the same output is achieved with fewer staff. Both of these applied in ANZ at different times (see Figure1). Staff numbers grew continually through the 1980s (from 23000 in 1980 to 48000 in 1990) as the bank grew by acquisitions at home and abroad. But as regulatory prudential restrictions on lending were eased, many existing and new customers also did greater volumes of business with the bank. However, in the 1990s, numbers of both staff and branches decreased by around 50%, even as business increased (assets rose over 70%). The decline in rural branches, which paralleled the decline in rural earnings, attracted much public and political criticism.

While an over-the-counter banking transaction today costs about $1 to process, an ATM transaction costs around 10c, and an online transaction costs 1 cent. By shifting existing customers into electronic banking, banks can consequently benefit from substantial cost reductions. While many customers have moved in this direction because of the convenience to them, ANZ, like other banks in Australia, has re-inforced the trend by charging higher fees for across the counter transactions. Consequently, not only are most transactions now electronic in some form, but some 15% of customers already use internet banking—one of the higher rates in the world.

Modern E-Commerce

Banks have been leaders in the uptake of electronic commerce in Australia. They have used e-commerce to streamline their operations and been heavily promoting business-to-business (B2B) e-commerce. Through e-commerce banks have cut operational costs such as transaction processing, distribution and procurement.

To boost its strength in e-commerce, the ANZ embarked on several acquisitions and eagerly sought alliances during 2000. These included 10% of the Hong Kong, China online broker Boom.com and a joint investment with the Overseas Chinese Banking Corporation in an online bank for Asia. ANZ has owned 10% of online broker E*Trade Australia since early 1999.

ANZ describes itself as "a new breed of bank" for the e-commerce environment. ANZ provides e-commerce solutions from production development and conception through product rollout to on-site implementation. ANZ eGate is a secure Internet-based payments gateway offering deferred trade terms settlement, comprehensive reporting and reconciliation for both buyer and seller, and the convenience of online authorisations for any major credit card, charge card or 'on account' purchase.

ANZ's internet-based procurement service, anzebiz.com, brings together buyers and suppliers in a virtual marketplace and provides access to a broad-based catalogue listing a range of indirect supplies. It is a supply chain solution designed to provide cost savings, increased flexibility and greater market reach. One high profile procurement project is the bank's membership of the CorProcure buyers' portal, which includes some of Australia's largest companies.

Successful implementation of e-commerce is to a large extent dependent on the security and efficiency of incorporated payment systems. According to several surveys, security rates as the major obstacle for e-commerce uptake by SMEs, followed by privacy concerns. Banks can bring their strong reputations for security to B2B exchanges, thus encouraging B2B uptake. Their credibility enables markets to function more efficiently and provides greater confidence to SMEs. Entry by banks into B2B exchanges may also help to encourage the development of interoperable systems for B2B. The major Australian banks have recently begun to implement a joint digital signature certificate framework that is interoperable with worldwide banking systems, and has been accepted by the Australian government for dealings with it.

The development of e-commerce is greatly assisted by an appropriate extension of the regulatory framework to cover the "virtual economy". In particular, *the Electronic Transaction Act* (1999) facilitates the development of e-commerce in Australia by broadly removing existing legal impediments that may prevent a person using electronic communications to satisfy obligations under Commonwealth law. It is complemented by privacy legislation and various codes of conduct designed to enhance consumer confidence in e-commerce and electronic communications without placing unnecessary burdens on business.

Other important roles of government that have facilitated e-commerce include encouraging competition in telecommunications (and thus innovation and lower costs) and a strong education and training system to give the necessary technical and commercial skills base.

International harmonisation of regulation, such as through the APEC paperless transactions agenda and the APEC Finance Ministers' initiative on electronic financial transaction systems, should further facilitate electronic commerce in the region.

Conclusions

Banking in Australia is an example of a service industry in which new technology and policy liberalisation have exposed the incumbents to substantial competitive pressure. However, through acquisitions at home and abroad, and through greater operating efficiencies from the adoption of new technology, ANZ and the other 3 banks who dominated the Australian market when it was "deregulated" in the early 1980s still do so. The reluctance of customers to move their accounts, unless strongly provoked to do so, has given the incumbents a major advantage. However the advantages of incumbency are being rapidly eroded by the technological and business developments of the "new economy", as summarised by the CEO of ANZ in Table 3.

Table 3. Old protections from competition are being neutralised in the new economy

Incumbent's historic advantages	...Neutralised in some (most) cases
Government regulation limits competition , especially foreign competition	Liberalised ("deregulated") market allows open competition
Privileged access to customers, technology, labour and capital - hard for others to compete	Access available for everyone - easier for new competitors to enter and for customers to compare and switch
Familiarity with local ways of doing business needed	Regional (or global) standards and protocols become common - local familiarity becoming less important
Vertical integration the best model	No real need for integration within the company - can be accomplished with external parties
Protection from capital market pressure	Capital market rewards the strong and punishes the weak

Source: J McFarlane, CEO of ANZ Bank, "The Australian Banking scene - competing in a globalising world", October 2000 [on the web at //www.anz.com.au/]

Those banks (especially some overseas ones new to the Australian market) who chased market share through rash loans to business speculators lost out badly when the business climate soured in the late 1980s and early 1990s; several such banks failed, which further consolidated the position of the incumbents.

As part of its response to this competition, ANZ itself expanded overseas. Its ventures overseas have been reasonably successful in financial terms, but the most publicised of them – Grindlays' Bank – has recently been sold, as ANZ, under competitive pressure , has been forced to tighten its strategic focus to countries where its domestic customer base looks for banking support.

Looking to the future, ANZ sees e-commerce as perhaps the greatest challenge and opportunity for business today, and especially for the banking business. E-commerce will bring competition—from online banking and financial services firms which are now beginning to enter traditional bank markets, but without the overheads of a traditional branch network. Already, the Dutch bank ING has established a "virtual" bank in Australia with 50,000 customers but only one physical branch.

ANZ believe that globalisation, the Internet, and changing customer expectations will accelerate the disaggregation of traditional integrated financial services companies into a set of loosely linked specialist businesses. At a strategy seminar in July 2000 the CEO of ANZ said "These forces will impact financial services at different rates in different countries, but their long-term impact is inevitable". In response, "ANZ would use technology to transform its existing businesses and focus on creating new growth opportunities". It aims to become "an e-bank with a human face".

Acknowledgments

I thank my colleagues Dimitri Markotsis, Albert Dessi, Stephen Joske, Rob McKeon, and Andrew McCredie for helpful contributions to this paper.

References

ANZ Banking Group annual reports (1980–2000) [many on the web at //www.anz.com.au/]

Supriya Singh "The bankers: Australia's leading bankers talk about banking today", Allen & Unwin, Sydney, 1991

Trevor Sykes "Australia's Banking History", talk on ABC Radio (2000) [on web at //www.abc.net.au/money/currency/features/feat3.htm]

Treasury "The Capital Account and Financial Sector Liberalisation Process in Australia", a case study for part one of a report to APEC Finance Ministers on the "Voluntary Action Plan for Promoting Freer and More Stable Capital Flows". Canberra September 2000.

THE IMPACT OF E-BUSINESS AND E-COMMERCE ON THE CANADIAN GENERAL MERCHANDISING RETAIL SECTOR[*]

Philippe Richer, Service Industries Branch (Industry Sector)
and Raymond Lepage, Electronic Commerce Branch (SITT Sector)

Introduction

Businesses today are under increasing pressure to make tangible productivity gains and to hold costs in check, just to remain competitive. The evolution of a variety of hardware and software technologies is fundamentally changing the economics for technology investment. The integration of e-commerce into business models will have an increasingly positive impact on productivity growth, better manufacturing-distribution co-ordination, reduced time to market, improved or "just-in-time" manufacturing, improved inventory management, lower procurement costs, reduced processing errors, extended business reach and better customer service.

All sectors of the economy, both old and new, can gain considerably from more extensive use of information and communication technologies (ICTs). To realize these gains, however, firms must ensure that all components of their value chain operate smoothly and seamlessly.

This study focuses on the impact of electronic business and electronic commerce on the retail operations and logistics systems for the Canadian general merchandising retail sector.

Approach of the study

The information contained in this study is based on extensive interviews with a number of key firms in the merchandising retail sector regarding the use of e-commerce and information technology. Three prominent Canadian department stores are featured in this study. For confidentiality purposes, we renamed these companies as company A, B and C. Each organization participated in an extensive interview where they discussed their experience with electronic commerce and Internet-based technologies in considerable detail. The interviews took place during the summer and fall of 2000. In addition to the primary interviews, a number of discussions took place with various players in e-commerce, the Internet and logistics.

The study was developed in the context of an ongoing OECD project called "Electronic Commerce Business Impact Project (EBIP), which involves participation from ten countries including Canada.[17]

---

[*] This study does not necessarily reflect the view of Industry Canada or of the Canadian Government.
[1] The industry consultations follow an interview guide developed by the OECD regarding the impact of electronic commerce on specific industries in a number of countries.

Overview of the Canadian Retail and Merchandising Industry

Canada's retail trade industry is a dynamic and vital component of the services economy. In 1999, the sector employed over 1.7 million persons, representing approximately 12 percent of Canadian employment and generating $48 billion (1992 constant dollars) or 6 percent of the Canadian GDP.[28]Major constituents of the retail industry sector include food and beverages, drugs and patent medicines, apparel, household furniture, appliances and furnishings, automotive and parts, and general merchandising.

Canada's retail trade industry is highly competitive. At the same time, the industry is undergoing deep-rooted changes with the onslaught of "Big Box" stores and fierce competition. Retail sector is under constant pressure to increase productivity, reduce costs and improve the quality of service.

New Technologies and The Retail Industry

The retailing industry has made strong capital investments in machinery and equipment, e-commerce and new technologies designed to improve business efficiency. Competition is especially fierce in the discount department store market where larger retailers are placing a great deal of pressure on less efficient and independent retailers. The number of department store firms has steadily declined over the past two decades.[39]

The highly competitive nature of retailing sector and pressure to cut costs and gain efficiencies in product flow should continue to drive new investments in hardware and software technologies,[410]in spite of high initial costs, as electronic data interchange (EDI) systems, either proprietary or Internet-based, provide the glue or information infrastructure to hold the value chain together.

With the emergence of electronic commerce and integrated logistics management concepts, supply chain management and logistics, is becoming an integral part of this fast paced and changing new economy.[511]The explosion in ICTs is driving the integration of operations with

---

[28] Statistics Canada, *Gross Domestic Product*, CANSIM, Matrix No. 4677 and Statistics Canada, Labour Force Survey, CANSIM Matrix No. 3472.

[39] In 1979 there were 28 firms in the department store business. In 1990 there were 14 firms. In 1997 there were 6 firms. Similarly, department store sales as a percentage of total retail sales have steadily declined. In 1979, department store sales represented 11.2 percent of total retail sales. In 1990, this share was 7.3 percent. In 1997, it was 6.8 percent. Strategic continental approaches are being developed by retailers, wholesalers and manufacturers in order to manage the key links of their chains of supply such as sourcing and marketing.

[410] Note that the Canadian general merchandising industry shows a low return on capital employed, thus it is strategic reasons not cost of capital issues which are driving these large investments.

[511] Industry Canada, *Logistics and Supply Chain Management: Sector Competitiveness Framework*, 2000.

suppliers and customers. The availability of very powerful information systems, based upon personal computer networks utilizing local networks, Extranets and the Internet, provide distribution firms of all sizes with the ability to streamline their business processes, especially in their logistics systems. In the 1980s and 1990s, there was a substantial growth in logistics information systems in such areas as electronic data interchange (EDI) with transportation carriers, EDI with vendors, radio frequency applications, inventory control and warehouse management systems. Today, these proprietary systems are beginning to use web-based technologies, which offer considerable cost savings over proprietary EDI systems. Internet-based technology solutions are used to link carriers, suppliers and retailers to a central logistic centre. [6]

Computer and Internet Usage

According to the 2000 Survey of Electronic Commerce and Technology conducted by Statistics Canada, 75.5 percent of retailing firms used personal computers when conducting their business operations.

However, 47.7 percent used e-mail and 52.7 percent used the Internet. In spite of these relatively low figures regarding e-mail and Internet usage, the general merchandising industry, especially the larger department stores, are extensive users of proprietary EDI technology. Many chain stores are developing electronic systems using Internet technology with leading software vendors including Oracle, IBM and Microsoft.

An even smaller set of percentages described the retailing industry web presence and usage. For example, 22.9 percent of firms had a web site in 2000. Only 13.5 percent of retailing enterprises used the Internet to purchase goods and services. A smaller percentage (8.7 percent) used the Internet to sell goods and services. In 2000, the retail sector generated $889.9 million of Internet sales, which represented only 0.4 percent of total revenues (Statistics Canada, April 2001).

Case Study Presentations

The three department stores selected for this study each have sales of about $5 billion (CDN), with employees ranging between 30,000 and 50,000 and hundreds of retail locations, suppliers and customers. Two of these companies are publicly traded on the Toronto Stock Exchange while the third one is not publicly traded in Canada, its US based parent company is traded on the New York Stock. Two of them have been in business for many years, while the third one has just entered the Canadian market in recent years.

---

[6] Logistics is a very important function for the retail trade sector. Logistics related activities include: transportation services, postal and courier services, storage and warehousing, packaging materials, gasoline and diesel fuel, business travel for purchasing supplies, business services costs, and inventory carrying costs etc.

Company A

Company A is one of Canada's largest retailers focuses primarily in hardline categories such as automotive parts and accessories, hardware, home improvements, housewares, sports and leisure, and lawn and garden. These products can be shipped directly from suppliers to stores, or through distribution centres operated across Canada.

Electronic commerce is a critical enabler for many processes across Company A. E-commerce plays a role in: business to consumer (B2C) initiatives such as Company A online and electronic flyers; business to business (B2B) with each of its stores for such activities as replenishment, product information, store planning, promotional planning, point of sale, shipping and billing; and B2B with its suppliers for activities such as purchasing orders, planned order forecasts, inbound planning, invoices and point of sale data.

Company A continues to invest aggressively into a variety of electronic commerce technologies, and is migrating more and more to Internet-based solutions. Three examples of how company A takes advantages of these technologies are: (1) sharing retail level data, over an Extranet, with suppliers; (2) collaborating on replenishment for promotions, in addition to sharing a six-month view of future orders with suppliers; and (3) e-learning to train and educate employees in stores with respect to product and application knowledge, and customer service.

A proprietary EDI transaction processing connection links Company A to its stores. In addition, Company A continues to leverage traditional EDI technology to process transactions with suppliers.

In all areas of application, Company A continues to invest in e-commerce to improve productivity by reducing costs, improving cycle times and contributing to improved customer service levels.

Company B

Company B is a major department store which generates over 6 billion dollars in revenues and employs over 40,000 people. It receives more than one thousand orders on its web site per day. In 1999, Internet sales exceeded $ 22 million.

It has largely replaced its paper-based systems with e-commerce solutions. The firm uses a proprietary EDI network to place orders, pay suppliers and track the shipment of goods. The firm also communicates with suppliers through the Internet and e-mail. These collaborative information systems provide suppliers and its retail operations with key information on markets and completed transactions. Suppliers must do one of the following: buy and/or build their own solution and integrate it with existing system; use a value-added network (VAN/) or third party service provider; or buy a package solution. Company B also publishes comprehensive general merchandise catalogue and has a comprehensive B2C web site that provides product information to consumers and facilitates orders via the Internet.

125

As a result of a major restructuring initiative of all its procurement practices, Company B has streamlined its wide range of supplier payment processes into four categories. Company B has provided suppliers with password-protected access to a secure on-line server that they use to share two-way interactive specification sheets, big-ticket forecasts; inventory by store; and catalogue. Company B has also consolidated a considerable number of its warehouses (distribution centres) over the past few years.

Electronic commerce is a critical enabler for many processes across Company B. For example, Company B maintains an electronic database of its retail store and catalogue products and electronically provides product information and prices on each product. All of these new initiatives focus on collaboration and visibility through the whole supply chain execution.

Company C

Company C, a part of the foreign-owned chain, is a large department store which employs roughly 40,000 people across Canada. Company C value chain is based largely on dealing with Canadian suppliers (manufacturers). It also deals with wholesalers. While the basic relationship with suppliers has not fundamentally changed in terms of price and service, there is a significant priority on quick response and flow. Flow management is an integral part of the value chain. Internet-based systems provide market and other information to suppliers regarding how well and how fast their products are selling. Company C's philosophy is to drive information fast; speed and quick response rates are critical.

Application of e-commerce technology is key to Company C's management practices, as it has helped save logistics costs considerably. While just-in-time shipments have resulted in increased trucking costs, these are more than offset by reduced inventory and other logistics costs. All transportation logistics are outsourced to a company Z, which is part of a chain of logistics companies operated by third party logistics group. Contracting out logistics services to the company Z has allowed Company C to focus on its main strength, which is retailing. Company Z is tied to Company C's electronic system that communicates data with each of the stores.

Company C switched to an Internet-based e-commerce system in the late 1990s to communicate orders and exchange critical information on product flow and inventories with its suppliers. Company C uses its network to place orders, submit invoice, track shipments of goods and pay its suppliers. Its collaborative information systems provide suppliers and its retail operations with key information on markets and completed transactions and facilitate better decisions on product flow.

The firm has an information program, which is used to supply critical information to suppliers, that vendors or suppliers can use to see how their products are selling. It shows performance indicators for inventory and market share status, thereby taking the guesswork out of analysis. Suppliers pay no upfront costs to use the information program software. All they need is access to the Internet, a browser and a computer. Product flow is timed very closely to the time of sale at the store level. Company C keeps a low inventory in its distribution centres, with only up to three to four weeks of supplies on hand. Orders go directly to the manufacturer and data is sent to the stores for replenishment.

Towards a New Economy - How Have the New Technologies Changed What These Companies Do or The Way They Do It?

Implementation of Technologies

The participating general merchandise firms have embraced e-commerce for their B2B operations for both EDI and Internet technologies. Each organization began its e-commerce system based on proprietary EDI technology and to some extent is migrating to Internet-based systems (Table 1). These players are using the Internet to exchange critical product information between suppliers and/or consumers. Suppliers and retailers are able to collaborate on product forecasts and product flow decisions.

Inventory Management

Inventory management is a critical part of the logistics systems for each of the participants. The emphasis is on product flow rather than on price when ordering supplies to be sold in stores. Internet-based systems communicate information to suppliers in order that the best production and inventory decisions are made. These collaborative systems, based largely on Internet technology, allow suppliers and retailers to share in the risks and opportunities regarding product flow and
inventory management. Critical decisions and costs are being passed down the supply chain. The end result is improved efficiency, better flow and lower costs. These major retailers keep inventory levels to a minimum (e.g., 3 weeks supply) as many products become rapidly obsolete, in addition to inventory carrying costs and administrative expenses.

Each participating organization reported that their inventory turns have improved substantially over the past several years. Similar gains in efficiency are expected to occur in the future.

In addition to reducing costs, e-commerce solutions permit customers to custom order products based on individual needs and preferences. Retailers are able to allow customers to mass customize orders based on virtually thousands of choices. Internet-based systems are more efficient in communicating customized product information to suppliers.

Table 1: Electronic Commerce and Supply Chain Management Processes

Company	Paper	EDI	Internet Collaborative Systems	E-mail	Web site	Online Sales
Company A	P	E	E	E	E	E
Company B	P	E	E	E	E	E
Company C	P	E	E	E	F	F

P= Past Effect; E= Present Effect; F= Future Effect

Relationships Between Retailers and Suppliers

Each of the participating firms stated that e-commerce and Internet solutions have strengthened existing relationships with their suppliers. E-commerce improves the flow of information between the parties. The entire value chain makes better decisions collaboratively with the end result being vastly improved performance throughout the entire chain.

The next step will be to implement collaborative tools with end-to-end solutions that will integrate forecasting, planning and execution capabilities with complete visibility across the supply chain. The objective essentially consists in accelerating processes through better planning and execution among partners. The main challenge to achieving seamless integration is one of cost, as significant investments will be needed both within the major firms and at the supplier level.

Investment Decisions

Investment in machinery and equipment and other infrastructure has been growing rapidly. The emergence of "Big-Box" stores and other players on to the retail market has driven firms to make large investments in technology in order to maintain or strengthen their competitive advantage. Some existing players are concerned that the retailing industry will experience more consolidations, mergers or exits from the marketplace.

Not only is competition fierce, but firms are also becoming more uncertain of their competitors' identity. In the retail sector, the traditional value chain of supplier, distributor, retail and customer is changing rapidly. The Internet adds to this insecurity, as prominent manufacturers now sell their products directly over the web - bypassing whole sellers, distributors and retailers. As a result, retail organizations are often faced with the difficult situation of competing among both other retailers and their own suppliers in certain cases.

Logistics Services

Internet-based technologies are changing logistics from being a packaging and moving function into an information business. Electronic business integrates carriers with shippers via electronic ordering, inventory decisions and product flow. Electronic systems have been instrumental in streamlining the supply chain and logistics operations of the retail sector. Inventory costs are being passed down the supply chain, as manufacturers are able to make better decisions on product flow, based on collaborative Internet-based networks between suppliers and retailers.

Logistics managers are placing greater emphasis on external functions and demand-pull systems that are customer-oriented. In the past, they concentrated exclusively on internal logistics functions such as warehousing and transportation.

E-Tailing

Of the participating general merchandise firms, one organization has a large established e-tailing site, another has just launched a comprehensive consumer web site and another has not identified any immediate activity in this area.

For those players using an e-tailing (B2C) site, it was believed that a B2C and a B2B presence were interdependent

Advantages of the Internet Over EDI Systems

The firms participating in the study are migrating from EDI to Internet-based systems. Internet technologies are used to collaborate information between suppliers, retailers and other players. It is not practical to exchange substantial product flow and other demand-driven data between various players using proprietary EDI networks. The Internet is extremely well suited for this type of information exchange, and thus, it is being heavily used for this purpose. It is expected that these collaborative exchanges of information will continue to accelerate in the future.

It is likely that the Internet will continue to gain favor amongst retailers. The up front costs are lower for suppliers (a computer and a web browser are all that is needed) and data can be exchanged amongst a number of players more quickly in real time [7]. The problem retailers are facing in migrating from EDI to Internet systems is that large investments by both suppliers and retailers have already been made in EDI technologies. As Internet-based systems also involve large capital investments, major improvements in efficiency and costs over the longer term need to be demonstrated. Some companies may be reluctant to invest in new technologies until the original investment in EDI technologies has been fully depreciated. Furthermore, retailers may wish to protect investments their suppliers have already made in older EDI technologies. The substantial competitive nature of the retailing sector and the

---

[7] B2B Internet systems also involve large up-front costs for the retailer. The main cost advantage is for suppliers that do not have to purchase costly EDI hardware and software.

pressure to cut costs and gain efficiencies in product flow should continue to drive massive new investments in Internet technologies, in spite of high initial costs.

<u>Web-Based Auctions</u>

While the firms interviewed were generally not in favor of web-based auctions to source goods for their retailing operations, everyone interviewed agreed that the use of the Internet to lower costs will become more prevalent in the future. Relationships with suppliers will continue to be important. Market forecasts and inventory decisions are made more efficiently and effectively in a collaborative environment. Global Internet systems that are able to strengthen relationships and offer a comprehensive suite of services, in addition to lowering costs, will likely have the best chance of succeeding.

Mapping the Effects of E-commerce

Significant innovations have been accomplished by the participating firms that use the Internet These areas include:

Transaction Preparation - for advertising, catalogues, and information services and for negotiating with suppliers. These innovations have taken place for both B2B and B2C processes and have encouraged greater customization of products as well as geographical expansion and market segmentation.

Transaction Completion – the participating firms that use the Internet for placing orders, billing and payment, finance and delivery of orders placed have made significant innovations. These innovations have taken place for both B2B and B2C processes and have encouraged increased customization, improved logistics, better co-ordination, integration, geographical expansion, market segmentation, trust and loyalty.

Product Support – significant innovations have been accomplished by the participating firms by providing support for the Internet transactions for information capture, information management, and market analysis as well as for market development. These innovations have encouraged increased customization, improved logistics, better co-ordination and integration, geographical expansion, market segmentation, trust and loyalty.

Future Innovations – future innovations in the transaction structure are expected to occur in the customization, diversification and bundling of retail products. These innovations are being driven by the increased use of the Internet as a collaborative tool to exchange information between the value chain players.

Policy considerations

Key messages from the Canadian retail and merchandising industry in general are that government should allow markets to work efficiently without over regulation. However, government has a role to play in continuing to raise awareness of e-commerce benefits, as success will engender more success. The firms also believe that there is also a major role for the government education system to develop adequately trained personnel and programs to support firms' capacity to engage in electronic commerce.

Successful national strategies for the new economy depend very much on rapid adoption and use of networks and e-services within all sectors of the Canadian economy. Supply change transformation, e-marketplaces and globalization have become significant determinants of competitive positioning for all firms. Government can indeed play a strong role in making the business community aware of these unprecedented changes, including the enormous advantages of using electronic commerce. The competitiveness of industry will increasingly depend on the ability to undertake targeted, strategic investments in the promotion of sectoral e-market initiatives. As electronic marketplaces begin to determine the competitive positioning of firms, the challenge is to ensure that firms have access to key Internet markets on a global basis and are able to realize significant benefits in marketing efficiencies and improvements in supply chain productivity. Measures are thus needed to assist in creating electronic platforms that will enable transformation and competitiveness of industry supply chains.

Creating and maintaining a high level of expertise in, and understanding of, the networked economy is critical to spurring innovation and to obtaining brand recognition internationally. Not only does advanced research provide the technologies and insights that underlie the grow the networked economy, it also produces the highly qualified personnel needed to propel international recognition and leadership.

In addition to providing training, education, e-awareness and communications infrastructure, it is important that the government provide a sound fiscal framework, low inflation regarding stable price as well as stable interest rates. It is especially true for retail sector as the large merchandising firms must be convinced that the economic environment is conducive to sustaining economic growth before they make large capital investments.

Acknowledgements

This study was prepared jointly by Philippe Richer, Service Industries Branch (Industry Sector) and Raymond Lepage, Electronic Commerce Branch (SITT Sector). Surendra Gera provided helpful contributions to the paper. Thanks are also due to Someshwar Rao, Bev Mahoney and Larry Murphy for their insightful comments.

MINI-CASE STUDY: CHINA

Christine Loh
Chief Executive Officer
Civic Exchange, Hong Kong

Overview

China has 1.25 million kilometers of optical fiber cable, 39% of urban areas are served by telephones (national average is 20.1%), the rate of mobile phone users is about 6.7%, and cable TV has reached 100 million viewers. Although there were some 9 million host computers connected to the Internet and 26 million Internet users in Mainland China as of March 2001, that accounted for less than 2% of its 1.3 billion population. The number of users in all sectors is growing rapidly, although in national terms, percentages remain low. Nevertheless, outside of Japan, China's Internet users in 2000 represented 26.3% of all of Asia's. By 2005, that figure is expected to reach 41.9%. After the US and Japan, China's base of Internet users will be the third largest in the world.

For Chinese policy makers, there is a serious digital divide that needs urgent correction. For example, user disparities between regions are stark - 37.87% of the users are in Beijing, Shanghai and Guangzhou, whilst users in 10 backward provinces in central and western China accounted for only 4.35% of the total. The divide can also be seen in terms of gender, age and education attainment. According to UNDP, China's Internet user profile shows that 69.6% are men and 30.4% women; 75% of them are under 30 years old; and 70% of the users have university degrees.

China has over 300 Internet Service Providers (ISPs) and more than 600 Internet Content Providers (ICPs). There are now more than 123,000 domain names registered and over 265,000 websites, of which 370 are estimated to be B2B and 677 B2C sites. As in other countries, most Chinese surf the Internet from home, while others log on-line at work, or in Internet cafes. The main services used are e-mail (95%), search engines (67%), software downloading (51%), news (45%), and chat lines (37%). Just under a third of the users had purchased anything on-line – mostly books or software, paid by means of cash and carry or postal money orders. Credit cards and direct debit cards in China are not widespread.

Bank of China, the largest bank in the country, has issued about 10% of the bankcards in use. So far, the bank has issued about 4 million Great Wall Renminbi credit cards and 19.4 million Great Wall electronic debit cards. Over 20 online portals (such as sina.com, sohu.com, 8848.net) and a number of large e-commerce companies (like Zhongtian, Jitong, and CYTS on-line) accept on-line payment from these cards.

Official figures show that in the year 2000, e-commerce was valued at US$9.32 billion, of which B-to-C transactions reached US$47.1 million and B-to-B US$9.28 billion.

Foreign and domestic manufacturers of multimedia PCs, servers, network products and Internet accessing devices see big opportunities in equipping the Chinese web. Content providers of value-added e-commerce services are also keen to jump in. Decreased costs of purchasing computers and telecommunication links to go on-line will spur demand. The exponential growth in Chinese-language content and the government's own use of the medium will further fuel expansion.

Still, the urban penetration of home PCs is only about 3.3% at this point. But unlike the global outlook for PC market growth, forecast to go below 12.5% in 2001, China is expected to sustain average growth rates of 30% per year for the foreseeable future. The growing demand for PCs in China is due to increased personal usage, popularity of the Internet, and lower costs. Last year, 6.45 million PCs were sold, an increase of 42.4% over 1999. In 2001, a further increase of 32.6% is expected, to 8.55 million PCs.

Government Policy

The Chinese government has created the word "informatization" to express the process to develop an IT infrastructure, industry, and applications in the country's quest for modernization. It has identified the Internet as a crucial part of the development. However, for a country that still feels it has to regulate information tightly, the Internet presents both opportunities and threats.

On the one hand, the government knows that access to all types of information by its citizens is crucial to the country's development. The Internet also provides an excellent tool to disseminate laws, government information, policies and propaganda. The government's site - (http://www.gov.cn/) - has a vast amount of information. More and more government agencies are posting useful and timely information on-line. Even chat rooms serve a useful purpose – they help the government to gauge popular feelings and provide the public with a safe channel to vent their frustrations.

On the other hand, the government deems certain types of information to be undesirable. The Ministry of Information Industry (MII) regulates access to the Internet, while the Ministries of Public Security (MPS) and State Security (MSS) monitor its use. In order to control information, the government issued regulations governing ownership, content, and other aspects of Internet use. For example, the *Internet Information Services Regulations* bans the dissemination of any information that might harm reunification of the country, endanger national security, or subvert the government. Promoting "evil cults" is banned, as is providing information that "disturbs social order or undermines social stability". There are regulations requiring chat rooms service providers to monitor content and restrict controversial topics, and for Internet café patrons to register with "software managers" and produce a valid ID card to log on.

Yet another example is that from May 2001 in Beijing, there is a requirement that all Internet banner advertisements must be submitted to the Beijing Administration for Industry and

Commerce (BAIC) – www.hd315.gov.cn - for approval before being placed on commercial sites. The "hd" of the website refers to the *hong dun* (red shield) of consumer protection and the "315" refers to March 15, which is Consumer Protection Day. This move has aroused concerns among advertisers and content providers about being able to continue responding quickly to market demands – the Internet's inherent strength.

As commercial ventures, China's Internet businesses face major difficulties. Network connections, increasing costs, regulatory uncertainty, and competition from the telephone monopolies are often a problem. Despite the risks and difficulties, China's Internet businesses are growing rapidly and gaining attention from overseas companies with the technological and financial resources to bring to the local market.

Case Study: TCL Holdings Corporation Ltd. (TCL)

TCL, a leading manufacturer and marketer of branded household electronics products, is a good example of a Mainland Chinese conglomerate in the process of being transformed by the new economy. It has used its successful brand on the Mainland to form aggressive alliances with international players to strengthen its new IT-related products and services to meet new needs.

Established in 1980, TCL started out as a state-owned electronics enterprise in Huizhou, about 90 kilometers north of Hong Kong, China. Over the last 20 years, it has grown into China's third largest electronics conglomerate. It has one of the strongest distribution and after-sale networks in the country - with 34 branches, 198 sales offices, 87 representative offices, over 3,000 service centers, and more than 20,000 distributors.

In 2000, TCL had total assets of US$1.2 billion, over 30,000 staff, and turnover of US$2.5 billion – with US$500 million in exports. It's compound annual growth rate of over 50% in the last 10 years places it as China's fastest growing major electronics group. The TCL brand name – with nationwide recognition – was ranked 5th in China in 2000 by the Beijing Brand Name Asset Appraisal Firm, valued at US$1.3 billion.

Initially, TCL was a traditional state-run electronics company, among the earliest to enter into a Hong Kong, China joint venture, contract-manufacturing cassettes at the outset. From there, TCL developed its first branded product (telephones) becoming the best-selling brand in the country within several years. But it was in 1992, when it introduced its first wide-screen color television that it became a major domestic player in household electronics. It was the first company in its field to list on the Shenzhen Stock Exchange in 1993, enabling TCL to raise capital and invest in other television manufacturers - the Henan Meile Electronic Group and Luk's Industrial in Hong Kong, China. In 1999, TCL International Holdings Co. Ltd. raised US$128 million with an IPO on the Hong Kong, China Stock Exchange. Today, TCL's products include a range of household electronics, such as audiovisual equipment, air conditioners, refrigerators, and washing machines, mobile phones. WAP-related products, personal digital assistants (PDAs), computers and IT related products).

Televisions remain the mainstay of its business today, and represented 79% of its total turnover in 2000. TCL color televisions now alternate with Sichuan Changhong as being the Number 1 and 2 brands in China, with TCL having about 18% market share. In 2000, TCL sold 5.8 million TVs, representing growth of 29% over the year before. TCL had export sales of US$71.4 million in 2000, up 85% from the previous year. Over 50 new models were launched in 5 series of new concept TVs, targeted to the middle to high end of the market. In this segment – wide-screen, super-thin, high-resolution digital, rear projection, and Internet-accessible Home Information Display (HiD) TVs – TCL has cornered 95% of China 's domestic market.

According to China's Ministry of Information Industry, the total production of televisions in China decreased in 2000 by 2.8% over the previous year. There are signs that the market is becoming saturated. Whilst overall domestic sales are predicted to grow at about 8% in urban areas and 10% in rural areas over the next few years, sales for TCL had slowed and with margins also being eroded, a decision was made to diversify quickly. As early as 1998, a strategic move was made into Internet-related IT products and value-added services, which is expected to grow by 20% over the next 5 years in China.

The TCL IT Industrial Group was established in 1999 to spearhead all of TCL's computer and Internet related businesses. A substantial investment in capital and resources has been devoted to this effort. TCL's goal is to decrease dependence on television sales from the current 79% of total turnover down to 30% in the next few years. Although only 4% of its revenues came from IT-related sales in 2000, TCL hopes that by 2003, there will be substantial strides made. To achieve its goal, TCL has moved aggressively into IT products and services. TCL formed a series of strategic alliances with international players to enhance its market positions.

For example, in 1996, the TCL Group set up a research and development team in the US for developing digital television products. A cooperative relationship was established with Lotus Pacific, and then an equity joint venture company was set up in 1999, to engage in the design, development, and manufacture of cable set-top-boxes, cable modems, and routers for sale in China and abroad. TCL also established a new company - TCL-GVC Computer Technology Company - with Chinese Taipei's GVC to manufacture PCs. In an alliance with Intel, it became the first Mainland China company to launch the Pentium 4 computer. TCL also has cooperative agreements with Microsoft China and Oracle.

A further investment of US$45 million was made into TCL Computer - now the third largest PC maker in China, having sold 260,000 units in 2000. The company is expected to achieve more than 60% revenue growth in 2001. The computer division has an annual production capacity of 600,000 units and is targeted to achieve 3 million units annual production volume in three to five years. Internet-accessing PDAs are also designed and manufactured in this division.

The ejiajia Net Technology Company was created in May 2000, with an initial investment of US$2.4 million, to develop information services platforms and an e-commerce model for TCL products. An e-commerce portal – www.ejiajia.com - was launched in October 2000 with information on various family lifestyle subjects and value-added customer services. It was designed to support TCL terminal products like Home Information Display (HiD) TVs, Internet computers, PDAs and mobile phones. A household electronic appliance "virtual shopping mall" for TCL products was added to complement TCL's national network of dealers. Again, according to the China Internet Network Information Center (CNNIC) survey done in January 2001, a lot of people are interested in this concept of browsing and shopping on-line: computer appliances (46%), AV equipment (31%), delivery of gifts (29%), and household electrical appliances (19%).

In November 2000, a TCL Education Web joint venture teamed up with China Central Radio and Television University in Shanghai to develop interactive long distance learning programs in teacher training, graduate studies, and MBA degree courses. The university will provide education resources and will be responsible for planning and operation. Students are now being recruited. US$8 million has so far been invested, with this Internet services initiative expected to breakeven in three years. Like other e-learning projects, the path to profit remains unclear. But based on the latest survey of web users done by the CNNIC, 33% of people are interested in receiving educational on-line services.

APEC's Policy

The Internet is part of a wider trend of China's embrace of communications technology and the information age. The Internet itself does not create a voice for the people but it provides a vehicle for people to communicate. Indeed, the Internet needs to be seen as part of a convergence package with telecommunications, wireless communications, cable television, and a software industry.

A sound mix of regulation and non-regulation is needed in order to promote the development of the Internet and wireless services, put it more within reach of the majority of the population and tap its economic potential. For developing countries, such as China, APEC's policy should be to:

1. Assist in the construction of "informatization" overall;
2. Obtain assistance from developed countries to provide IT and IT management training in China;
3. Enable developing countries to share more information and knowledge resources;
4. Lobby developed countries to provide public data for developing countries free of charge or at reasonable cost;
5. Encourage the authorities to establish on-going dialogue with key stakeholders (ISPs, ICPs, foreign investors, telecommunications and wireless service providers, etc.) to help develop and promote policies and self-regulation.

In China, new laws and rules from the central, provincial and local governments seem to be announced every week, from e-commerce taxation to regulations on employment Web sites, to restrictions on news sites. And the national government is now formulating new regulations to clarify the licensing regime for ISPs and content providers. The resulting regulatory environment of these vague, uncoordinated, arbitrarily enforced rules is not helpful to development of the Internet. APEC can help share development experiences from across the region, and promote sounder policies.

CASE STUDY OF CIECC

China International Electronic Commerce Center
of the Ministry of Foreign Trade and Economic Cooperation

China International Electronic Commerce Center (CIECC), founded in February 1996, is subordinate to the Ministry of Foreign Trade and Economic Cooperation, PRC. CIECC is to establish the electronic management framework for foreign trade, to realize online governmental administration on trade business under the principles of fairness, openness and efficiency, and to promote paperless trading development. Till now, it has branches in 97 cities throughout China, with over one thousand employees.

CIECC's foundation and development are in line with the development and improvement in China's macroeconomic environment, foreign trade and IT technology. As computer and Internet-based e-commerce development and EDI application in developed countries for decades have successfully established a series of international standards for electronic trade, trading companies in other countries are required to adopt these standards. Facing challenges from fast development of Internet, E-commerce and new economy, Chinese enterprises must take full advantage of information technology to promote efficiency, decrease cost and increase their portions in the international market.

One of the major tasks before APEC, the largest economical and cooperative organization in the Asia-Pacific area, is to realize the paperless trading among developed economies by 2005 and among developing economies by 2010. The date of fulfillment has thus been settled before APEC member economies. In order to catch up with other organizations in the world, Chinese government highlights the role of IT and E-commerce in national economy and start its State Golden Gate Project to enhance electronic administration and trading and accelerate China's accession to the international market.

With five years construction and development, CIECC has established China International Electronic Commerce Network (CIECNet), the backbone network of the State Golden Gate Project, and made CIETNet an integrated platform of communication, information and data exchange platforms, and a starlike network with 97 nodes covering China. CIETNet has complements full link and data-sharing with trade management organizations at various levels, the General Administration of Customs, the State Administration of Foreign Exchange, the State Bureau of Taxation as well as banks, and it is also connected with networks (such as Hong Kong, China Trade-Link Network) in other countries and regions. Enterprise can access the nearest nodes for necessary technical support and service.

On the safe network infrastructure, CIECC constructed the international e-commerce platform of government trade management and enterprise e-commerce application (incl. e-government affairs platform and e-commerce platform).

The e-government affairs platform consists of a series of governmental application systems on trade administration, such as the Quota License Management System (QLMS) and the

Processing Trade Network Management System (PTNMS). It has realized dynamic governmental administration in various aspects: namely, online bidding for import and export commodities, online applying for import and export quotas, online approving of import and export certificates as well as online applying for and approval of processing trade contracts. This platform highly improves the quality and efficiency of the government work. Taking the processing trade system as an example. With over 300 units authorized by CIETNet as approval agencies and over 20,000 member enterprises, the system helps realize online inquiry and management at any time, gives a heavy strike to smuggling and the illegal activities in the foreign exchange, and protects the rights and the interests of the enterprises. It also makes the governmental administration on trade more efficient and more transparent, eradicates low efficiency arbitrary and bureaucracy and helps to build an administration-service system of standard, efficiency, justice and transparency. CIETNet enables the Chinese government to realize the online verification with customs of major quota-setting countries and regions, such as the United State, Canada, EU and so on. Consequently, no more trade frustration or argument caused by false license occurs between the United States and China since 1998.

Up to date, all major governmental affairs on foreign trade and economy administration of all levels have been made on-line accessible. In domestic, office automation has been fundamentally achieved, and all overseas economic and trade institutes have been web-linked. In 2000, about 40 billion U.S. dollars export transactions used CIETNet to transmit export documents. A global, advanced, safe and practical CIETNet will further improve the transparency and efficiency of the foreign trade administration on all levels, and it will greatly adapt to the requirements of the more open-up policy and to the rules of WTO.

The e-commerce Platform is a collaboration platform between enterprises, where numerous enterprises can work in coordination, share resources and manage their production and trade through network.

The platform integrated the management system of supply chain jointly developed by the CIECC and Sino-Foreign Transportation Group, adopted the EDI technology that is internationally standard and achieved the network-based management of logistics, e.g. the network-based management of important services including shipping space booking, transportation documents transmission, container management, ship management, goods tracking, finance and settlement.

The platform is highly extendable, compatible and reliable. Enterprises can integrate their internal ERP system with the Platform. By making use of the Platform, enterprises can optimize trade partners dynamically in the world, integrate and optimize the industrial supply chain including manufacturers, suppliers, purchasers and users, so that the link between enterprises in the supply chain can be more close and harmonious, and enterprises can focus on their own core advantages, create agile supply chain, promote their core competitiveness and enhance the speed of response to market and clients.

In order to promote e-commerce application in enterprises involved in foreign trade and to realize critical changes in trading methods, CIECC will strengthen cooperation with international organizations especially in the aspects of E-commerce policy, laws and standards. Its cooperation with e-commerce organizations in the Asia-Pacific area (like Singapore Network Service Ltd., Hong Kong, China Trade-Link Ltd., Taipei Van-Trade Network Co., and Korea Trade Network) focuses on extensive research and exchange of trading documents standards and information security technology to achieve joint promotion on multinational e-commerce.

MINI-CASE STUDY: HONG KONG, CHINA

Christine Loh
Chief Executive Officer
Civic Exchange, Hong Kong

Overview

The up-take of IT usage in Hong Kong, China in recent years has been impressive. The city has 6.8 million residents and 2.6 million registered Internet accounts, compared to around 600,000 in 1998. There are around 240 Internet Service Providers, with a wide range of services at competitive prices. The city has laid enough fiber optic cables to enable all commercial buildings and most homes to be wired for the Internet thus providing a solid platform for broadband services.

IT penetration among households is relatively high – as of March 2000, 50% of all households had PCs at home, and 73.3% of them had Internet connection. Moreover, 30.3% of all persons aged 10 and over had used the Internet at home that year.

Despite its size, Hong Kong, China is the 9th largest trading economy in the world. However, it is not yet using electronic means to do business in any substantial way. Although 51.5% of business establishments had PCs and 37.3% of them had Internet connection by March 2000, according to government information, only 7.3% of them had websites, and only 0.3% of them had made e-sales, although 35.3% of them had received e-products, services or information. In 1999, official information showed that business receipts from e-sales amounted to only US$590 million. However, industry sources think e-commerce today could be around US$2 billion – still modest for a substantial trading economy like Hong Kong, China. However, some industry optimists believe that the total value of transactions (both business-to-business and business-to-consumer) could grow to over US$70 billion by 2004.

It should be noted that 79% of the population have mobile phones and Hong Kong, China phone services are among the cheapest in the world. Mobile phones and other handheld devices will become important tools to access the Internet. Furthermore, there are 7 million "smart" cards in use in the city mostly for making e-payments for public transport and a growing range of retail services.

Government Policy

The Hong Kong, China Special Administrative Region Government has made a significant push to promote IT since 1998 with the announcement of the *Digital 21 Strategy*. In April 1998, it established the Information Technology and Broadcasting Bureau – the equivalent of a ministry – to chart policies, whose function is supervised by the Financial Secretary, the equivalent of the finance minister. The bilingual (English/Chinese) government site, www.info.gov.hk is up-to-date on the latest government information and press releases, and contains useful information about departmental structure, functions and policies.

The government is implementing a 5-year IT strategy in education involving significant capital and recurrent spending to equip schools with computers and programs to encourage teachers to learn IT skills. Furthermore, its *IT Hong Kong, China Campaign* aims to promote the wider use of IT at all levels of society. For example, the first round of an IT awareness program took place from October 2000 through March 2001 and provided about 18,000 places for different sectors of the community to attend 4-hour awareness course run by a private sector training agency.

The *Digital 21 Strategy* includes a range of initiatives for on-line government information and services. For example, a dedicated e-Government Coordination Office will be established to continue putting most public services and procurement tenders on-line. It also targets to provide an e-option for 90% of public services by end 2003 (65% of services now have an e-option). The government has passed the Electronic Transactions Ordinance to provide a clear legal framework for the conduct of electronic transactions. It plans to conduct the auction of 3G mobile licenses in September 2001.

To drive the use of new technologies, Hong Kong, China plans to be among the world's first in issuing mobile digital certificates to support secure mobile commerce, and earmarked over US$385 million to roll out smart identity cards with multi-application capacity to the entire population. It will also establish linkage between local universities and the Internet2 network for conducting research in the next generation of Internet technologies over a high-speed network.

Case Study: Hong Kong Trade Development Council (TDC)

Although trade is Hong Kong, China's lifeblood and local traders are nimble and entrepreneurial, e-commerce is still more talk than reality among the 290,000 small and medium-sized enterprises (SMEs), who account for the bulk of Hong Kong, China's US$479 billion trade in goods and services in 2000. Indeed, SMEs, who account for 98% of all business establishments in Hong Kong, China and employ 60% of the workforce, form the backbone of Hong Kong, China's trade network.

The TDC, a statutory body, provides a useful case study of the Internet challenge for Hong Kong, China business. The TDC was set up in 1966 to promote international trade for local companies, especially the export-oriented SMEs. The TDC's database is the largest of its kind in Asia with details of 100,000 companies in Hong Kong, China, 120,000 in Mainland China, and 380,000 overseas. It also contains over 18,000 brand names, and their agents, licensees, and owners in Hong Kong, China.

The TDC has a 19-member governing body, the members of which are appointed by the government. Membership is a mixture of government officials and business leaders. The TDC has a professional staff of around 900 people and 48 overseas offices. It has an annual budget of approximately US$180 million, of which approximately 22% is derived from declaration charges for imports and exports collected by the government. The balance comes mainly from organizing trade fairs in Hong Kong, China and from advertising revenue. In 2000-2001, it organized 330 promotional events around the world and 15 major international trade fairs.

Affects of the "New Economy"

The Internet enables the TDC to have a much closer relationship with Hong Kong, China and overseas companies, and better coordinate with its own global network of offices. It allows more frequent contact as well as instant service - saving time, effort, and cost. Without the Internet the quantity of information, frequency of exchange, and volume of contacts would not have dramatically increased.

Between 1995 and 2000, and despite the severe economic downturn in Asia between 1997-1998, the TDC invested over US$23 million to upgrade its internal IT system and provide more comprehensive, user-friendly, on-line services. The move was made to stay on top of rapidly evolving technologies to ensure Hong Kong, China's continued success as a business information hub.

The first step was the installation of an Internet e-mail system in 1995, linking the TDC with its global network of offices and to enable easier trade contact. The annual number of business inquiries processed each year jumped to 350,000 after e-mail was introduced.

An on-line version of *Hong Kong, China Enterprise*, the TDC's flagship product promotion magazine, was launched in 1996. Furthermore, *TDC-Link*, the on-line text-based trade information service was upgraded and re-launched. Business inquiries to the TDC jumped to 750,000 per year - more than double that received previously.

Free services on *TDC-Link* include access to the Hong Kong, China database as well as an electronic marketplace of bids and offers for the sourcing and supplying of products and services. Local corporate subscribers, for a nominal fee, can access Mainland Chinese, Chinese Taipei, and overseas business opportunities and company contacts.

In 2000, the TDC home page was transformed into trade portal *tdctrade.com*. Users can access a lot of useful information in both English, and for the first time, in Chinese in both traditional and simplified characters, to suit Mainland China, Hong Kong, China and Chinese Taipei audiences. It features five industry-specific vertical portals – electronics and electrical appliances; garments and textiles, gifts and household wares; toys and sporting goods; timepieces and jewelry; and optical goods – reflecting Hong Kong, China's major export sectors. The daily hit rate for *tdctrade.com* has been steadily climbing to an average of 1.4 million per day – more than four times the hit rate of the TDC's old website.

The TDC has partnered up with others to increase exposure of *tdctrade.com*, including the Microsoft Network and China's Ministry of Foreign Trade and Economic Cooperation (MOFTEC). It has also forged alliances with many IT service providers in developing its capabilities. Among them is Tradelink Electronic Document Services, and together they promote IT awareness among SMEs and provide training seminars. Tradelink, working with the government to automate commonly used forms like trade documents and export licensing, is also helping TDC develop electronic data interchange (EDI) on-line services for *tdctrade.com.*

Tdctrade.com also launched TDC webcast, a multimedia broadcast platform, and a cyber SME center serving SME needs. Visa applications forms and requirements of around 100 countries are also available for local users using the portals Visa-On-Demand service.

TDC joined forces with Dialog, a leading provider of Internet-based business information services to provide information on market research, competitive intelligence, business directories, corporate financials for US and international companies, and worldwide patent, trademark, and copyright developments are available for secure on-line purchase.

Trade enquiries handled by the TDC have now reached 1 million per year as a result of having a better presence on the Internet. Many print publications have been phased out as they are now available on-line, which has reduced costs and increased circulation. The TDC believes that the Internet has helped it to have greater impact in promoting its work and enabled it to serve its local and overseas customers better.

Reasons for Slow IT Up-Take among SMEs

Despite clear government policy and public sector encouragement, Hong Kong, China businesses are still slow in embracing e-commerce. This can be seen from the results of a survey conducted by the Hong Kong, China Productivity Council and IBM in September 2000. The following chart shows the e-commerce adoption rate among the 1,122 Hong Kong, China companies, mostly SMEs, interviewed.

e-business Adoption Index

Levels 0-5	Identifiable features	%
0: No intention	No e-mail address and no intention in next 6 months	54.4%
1: Show intention	Plan to set up an e-mail account and/or a website within next 6 months	45.5%
2: Basic adoption	E-mail usage only	42.4%
3: Prospecting	Well-established web page and e-mail communication	15.3%
4: Business integration	Web application for online transaction or basic integration with internal operational systems or with external business partners	3.8%
5: Business transformation	On-line transaction, on-line payment, internal and external integration, web page, email	0.3%

There are a number of constraints as to why Hong Kong, China SMEs have been slow in developing IT capabilities. Firstly, Hong Kong, China starts from a relatively low technological base. It has a strong trade and weak technology tradition. In order for local traders to catch-up on technology to enhance their business, they first need to become more familiar with the use of computers and software applications.

Secondly, even among the SMEs who use the Internet, most of them take a conservative approach to fully embracing e-payment capabilities, as do their bankers. There are over 20 banks in Hong Kong, China offering various forms of Internet banking but HSBC's experience is instructive since it is the bank with the deepest penetration in Hong Kong, China. HSBC indicated that whilst many of its SME customers use the Internet for e-mail and information gathering, only the "early adopters" are using it for banking functions. While its Personal On-line Banking services – enabling the checking of account balances, transferring of funds between accounts, and making payments to third parties over the Internet – have been available since August 2000, these services will not be fully available to business customers until later 2001. Because the investment for banks in developing depth and breadth of e-banking services is substantial, they are reluctant to offer such services until their own research shows broad-based usage.

Thirdly, many SMEs were wary to invest in IT over the last few years at a time when the region was in recession and their profit margins slashed. For example, in the 1998-1999 tax year, less than 5% of the companies contributed more than 80% of the corporate profits tax, and 80% of the companies contributed 7% of the corporate profit tax yield. Even though Hong Kong, China's economy has improved, profitability remains an issue for many SMEs, who remain reluctant to make investments in IT up-grade.

Fourthly, in the catching-up process, there is a lack of the right kind of personnel to assist with everything from general computer maintenance services, to programmers, systems analysts, database administrators and project managers. According to a government study, there were over 60,000 IT practitioners in Hong Kong, China in 2000, with average annual growth of 11.8% expected through 2005. Hong Kong, China local tertiary institutions are offering around 19,000 full-time degree-level places in IT-related fields annually. Over 30 new programs at the diploma, graduate or post-graduate levels on e-commerce and related subjects are on offer. The Vocational Training Council is offering around 17,000 sub-degree level IT places annually, while the Employees Retraining Board is providing over 44,000 IT related training places each year.

However, there is a shortage of experienced personnel today. Like elsewhere in the region, the government has set-up special visa schemes to attract overseas technologists, including from Mainland China.

APEC E-Commerce Readiness Assessment Guide – Hong Kong, China

APEC's *e-Commerce Readiness Assessment Guide* provides a self-assessment tool that can be used by economies to assess their readiness to participate in the digital economy. Results can help governments identify steps to be taken in improving the e-commerce environment, and facilitate dialogue between governments and businesses on policies.

The Hong Kong, China authorities conducted a self-assessment in October 2000 and found that the city has a solid foundation from which to build an information society. It already has an advanced telecommunications infrastructure in place and wide consumer choices. The use of the Internet has become an integral part of the daily lives of Hong Kong, China people. Mobile penetration is already very high and more people will be able to access the Internet and conduct m-transactions as mobile services continue to grow. Indeed, Hong Kong, China's m-services are far better than those in the US and Europe. Hong Kong, China's challenge is to help its SMEs to become more IT savvy.

ELECTRONIC FINANCIAL TRANSACTIONS IN HONG KONG, CHINA

Financial Services Bureau
Government of the Hong Kong Special Administrative Region

Introduction

Hong Kong, China, China is a major international financial centre in the Asia Pacific region. Its integrated network of financial institutions and markets is characterised by a high degree of liquidity. The institutions and markets operate under effective and transparent regulations which meet international standards. The Government of the Hong Kong, China, China Special Administrative Region encourages market liberalization to enhance competitiveness, product innovation and efficiency. The Government also encourages the use of information technology (IT) to further integrate the full range of financial services – securities, futures, clearing – through an open and secure electronic network. These measures are a good pointer to Hong Kong, China, China as a market with increasingly attractive investment potential.

There are over 150 licensed banks in Hong Kong, China, China. There are also about 120 representative offices in Hong Kong, China, China representing banks from over 40 different countries. The volume of the banking system's external transactions is about US$780 billion, the tenth largest in the world and third largest in Asia. In foreign exchange, Hong Kong, China, China is the world's eighth largest centre in terms of total foreign exchange and derivatives transactions, with total average daily net turnover at US$82 billion. Hong Kong, China, China's stock market is the tenth largest in the world and third largest in Asia. Total market capitalisation of the main board is about US$570 billion, with average daily turnover at about US$1.14 billion. The second board's total market capitalisation is US$8.2 billion and average daily turnover is US$17 million.

Electronic Transactions in the Banking Sector

E-Banking Services for Retail/Personal Customers

Over 20 banks or banking groups, which consist of the majority of retail banks in Hong Kong, China, China, have introduced Internet banking services for retail or personal customers. In addition, a number of other retail banks are planning to introduce Internet banking services in the near future. The Hong Kong Monetary Authority (HKMA) is processing a few applications for setting up Internet-based banks in Hong Kong, China. Regarding the services offered over the Internet, many banks have introduced investment services, apart from banking services, over the Internet. For instance, these include Internet stock trading services and other investment services (e.g., FX margin trading, e-IPO, unit trust) over the Internet.

As regards the use of mobile phones or other electronic channels for offering e-banking services, around 10 banks or banking groups have launched mobile phone banking or stock trading services (over mobile phones using SIM Toolkit technology), through which their customers can transfer funds or trade stocks using certain types of mobile phones over designated mobile networks (e.g., networks of PCCW HKTelecom, Orange). A few banks have used other channels to offer e-banking services, such as through the kiosks or intelligent telephone sets installed at non-branch outlets, and the households' television sets with Internet connection.

E-Banking Services for Business Customers

Several banks have introduced Internet banking services (e.g., trade services, cash management and payment services, FX trading, custody and clearing services) for their business customers. A few banks plan to offer bond trading services to their business customers. Many international banks have formed alliances or joint ventures to develop portals for bond trading.

Many banks have introduced e-commerce related services for business customers. For instance, a number of banks have launched Internet payment processing services for their merchant customers. Some banks have introduced online shopping malls or electronic marketplaces.

While there are no relevant statistics about the exact extent of banks' reliance on outside vendors or other third parties in Hong Kong, China, banks in Hong Kong, China generally have been working with outside vendors and other relevant service providers (e.g., Internet service providers, mobile network operator) in developing their e-banking systems so as to acquire the expertise for operating and maintaining the systems. Some banks will make use of the expertise of their parent banks or overseas head offices in introducing e-banking services. Banks have been reminded of the importance of developing their internal expertise to manage the risks associated with the e-banking services.

E-banking raises the challenges of risk management particularly in respect of strategic risk, operational risk (including security risk), legal and reputation risk. Moreover, e-banking could raise customer protection issues. For instance, the ability for banks to collect personal information of a customer through an open network (e.g. the Internet) raises privacy issues.

Electronic Transactions in the Securities Sector

The Securities and Futures Commission (the Commission) conducted a survey with all registered dealers in April 2000 in relation to the use of online trading facilities. It was found that 28 brokers offered online trading facilities at that time. Most of them offered online dealing in Hong Kong, China listed securities. A few of them offered online dealing in overseas listed securities (predominantly US securities) and online trading in futures contracts. In addition to online trading, these brokers also offered services like research information, real time price quotations for financial instruments, provision of investment advice, securities offers including initial public offerings and placements, and funds dealing. By December 2000, the number of online trading services offered by brokers registered with the Commission has increased to 86, a three-fold increase since April 2000.

An On-line Trading Working Group was established in early 2000 to study the growth of online trading in Hong Kong, China and make recommendations to facilitate its development. The Commission, in the process, has consulted various securities firms that offered or intended to offer online trading services and identified issues of consideration for future development. In December 2000 the Commission issued a "Consultation Paper on the Regulation of On-line Trading of Securities and Futures" to solicit market comments. The consultation paper has identified problems faced by existing online brokers. These include heavy influx of competition, small population of users compared to other Asia countries, decreasing brokerage commissions, costs of ongoing compliance, and shortage of experienced management, traders, information technology personnel and technicians. Regulatory issues were identified which include the security, capacity and contingency of the online trading systems.

Impediments and Challenges to the Development of Electronic Financial Transactions

For the Banking Sector

Hong Kong, China Infrastructure

Hong Kong, China has a good infrastructure to support the continued growth of the development of e-banking businesses. Hong Kong, China has one of the finest telecommunications infrastructures in the world. Over 80% of households and more than 90% of business buildings are covered by broadband network. Its external connectivity is also amongst the highest in Asia. In addition, penetration rates for electronic delivery channels in Hong Kong, China are among the highest in the world:

- about 50% of households have PCs;
- about 36% of households have Internet access;
- 74% of the population use mobile phones.

Regulatory Framework of E-Banking

The HKMA's regulatory approach tries to strike a balance between dealing with the risks of e-banking services while promoting competition and innovation. A number of guidelines have been issued on electronic banking since 1997.

Impediments and Challenges to the Development of E-Banking Services

While we are not aware of any major impediments facing banks regarding e-banking services in Hong Kong, China, there are several major challenges that the banks may encounter when providing e-banking services:

(a) Cost savings through e-banking services have proved to be difficult to realize. The potential of the Internet to reduce operating expenses for banks depends on their ability to migrate customers onto the new low cost channel and to close the resultant surplus branches or convert them into sales outlets rather than transaction centres. While this process is going on, the banks will have to increase their spending on front & back-end IT & associated expenses such as advertising;

(b) Revenue growth through e-banking has been difficult to achieve. Ability of banks to cross-sell products is unproven, and margins will come under pressure from greater price transparency;

(c) Banks need to handle increased competition from new, low-cost new entrants (e.g. virtual banks, e-lenders, and aggregators). They may need to differentiate themselves from existing players through image, culture, products, service, integrated and personalized approach to customers;

(d) The Internet also poses new challenges to the banks on security risk because of its open nature. If the security issue is not properly managed, it will damage the banks' reputation and their customers' confidence.

As for system failures of Internet banking services, there were several such occurrences, which had minimal impact on the banking services to their customers, because the Internet is not the only channel for banking services.

For the Securities Sector

To facilitate electronic trading, Hong Kong Exchanges and Clearing Ltd has undertaken a number of projects to further automate the trading processes since its official establishment in March 2000. They include:

(a) the launching of the Automated Trading System (the "HKATS") (an electronic trading platform for the trading of futures and options contracts) by its subsidiary Hong Kong Futures Exchange in June 2000; and

(b) the rollout of the third generation of the Automatic Order Matching and Execution System (the "AMS/3") (an electronic trading system for securities trading) by its subsidiary the Stock Exchange of Hong Kong since October 2000.

Both the HKATS and the AMS/3 are equipped with access functions to enable investors to trade online via brokers. Investors can place orders through the Internet or a broker's proprietary system. Both the HKATS and the AMS/3 allow direct connection of a broker's proprietary system to its trading engine through a defined API (Application Programming Interface) to facilitate straight through processing of orders. According to SEHK statistics, about 10 % of its participants have proprietary systems which are developed by outside vendors.

The Steering Committee on the Enhancement of the Financial Infrastructure in Hong Kong (the "SCEFI") was established in early 1999 to examine and recommend ways to enhance the financial infrastructure. The Steering Committee completed a report in September 1999 with a full range of recommended measures to reduce the cost of transactions, increase efficiency and facilitate better risk management. Among the key recommendations are the establishment of an open and secure electronic network that will allow straight through processing of securities and derivative transactions and the development of a scriptless securities market. Good progress has been made in the implementation of these recommendations.

Legal/Policy Framework

The Electronic Transactions Ordinance (ETO), which was largely based on the United Nations Commission on International Trade Law Model Law on Electronic Commerce, was enacted in the Hong Kong Special Administrative Region (HKSAR) in January 2000. The ETO provides legal recognition of electronic records and digital signatures as that of their paper-based counterparts. It provides a framework for the establishment of local public key infrastructure (PKI) and recognition of certification authorities (CAs) operating in Hong Kong, China. With the use of CA services and digital signatures, the four major concerns of electronic transactions, i.e. authentication, integrity, confidentiality and non-repudiation can be addressed. The ETO and establishment of a local PKI have provided a favourable and reliable environment for electronic transactions and led to the development of applications to facilitate electronic transactions in different service sectors.

For the Banking Sector

Policy Framework of E-Banking Services

The HKMA's role is to provide a regulatory environment in which banks will properly manage the risks arising from electronic banking, while not standing in the way of these developments. Given the rapid pace of development in this area, the HKMA has been keeping its supervisory policy for e-banking under review. Since 1997, the HKMA has issued a series of guidelines and guidance notes to set out its regulatory approach on electronic banking services and to provide authorised institutions with recommendations on the risk management for these activities. Existing banks seeking to offer an Internet banking service should consult with the HKMA in advance.

In 2000, the HKMA issued a Guideline on the Authorization of Virtual Banks (available at http://www.info.gov.hk/hkma/eng/guide/guide_no/20000505e.htm) under the Banking Ordinance. The main principle is that virtual banks, which deliver banking services primarily through electronic channels, should satisfy the same prudential criteria that apply to conventional banks. Moreover, the HKMA issued two guidance notes to provide authorized institutions with recommendations on the security aspects of electronic banking.

While HKMA will continue to issue guidelines and guidance notes when appropriate in relation to the latest development of e-banking and emerging technologies, the HKMA established a specialist team of examiners with the necessary skills and technical knowledge to conduct more focused examinations on e-banking activities of banks.

Customer Protection Issues

As e-banking simplifies the collection and sharing of personal information, it may raise customer protection issues such as privacy. The increased risk for unauthorized transactions conducted over e-banking leads to the need for a fair allocation of liability between banks and customers for such transactions. The HKMA and the banking industry are in the process of reviewing the Code of Banking Practice to issue more guidelines, such as on customer protection and electronic disclosures, pertaining to e-banking.

<u>For the Securities Sector</u>

The Electronic Transactions Ordinance provides that:

- Where a rule of law requires information to be given in writing, that requirement is met by electronic records;
- Where a rule of law requires information to be retained; or retained or presented in the original form, that requirement is met by retaining or presenting the information in the form of electronic records;
- Where a rule of law requires the signature of a person, that requirement is met by a digital signature; and
- Contracts shall not be denied legal effect solely on the ground that electronic records are used in their formation.

The Commission has issued the following regulatory guidance in relation to Internet regulation and online activities. They include:

- Guidance Note on Internet Regulation;
- Circular on Provision of Financial Information on the Internet – Licensing Requirements
- Guidelines for Registered Persons Using Internet to Collect Applications for Securities in an Initial Public Offering
- Guidance Notes on the Application of the Electronic Transactions Ordinance to Contract Notes

These guidance notes set out and clarify the Commission's regulatory approach towards various issues or concerns raised by market participants in relation to the offering of online trading services. Electronic copies of these guidance notes are available on the Commission's web-site (http://www.hksfc.org.hk).

Cross-Border Supervisory Issues

For the Banking Sector

While we have not encountered any specific cross-border supervisory issues with respect to electronic banking in Hong Kong, China, we recognise that cross-border e-banking may increase the potential for jurisdictional ambiguities with respect to the supervisory responsibilities of different authorities, which might lead to insufficient supervision of cross-border e-banking activities. In particular, customers in Hong Kong, China may be able to gain access to financial services or advertisements for financial services provided by overseas organisations that may or may not be subject to supervision. The HKMA has studied the issue of Internet advertisements for offshore deposits and completed the proposed legislative amendment to regulate such advertisements. The HKMA will then develop a guideline to set out the factors that the HKMA will take into account in determining whether an Internet advertisement for deposits is targeted at the general public of Hong Kong, China.

For the Securities Sector

The Commission has set out the basic regulatory approach towards Internet trading in its "Guidance Note on Internet Regulation". It stipulates that *"the fundamental principles of regulation for activities over the Internet are not premised on the use of a particular medium of communication or delivery. Regulated activities should be uniformly regulated irrespective of whether such activities are conducted via paper-based media or electronic media. .... As a general principle, The Commission will not seek to regulate securities dealing, commodity futures trading and leveraged foreign exchange trading activities that are conducted from outside Hong Kong, China and over the Internet, provided such activities are not detrimental to the interests of the investing public in Hong Kong, China."*

However, if a person or an entity who uses Internet technology to induce people residing in Hong Kong, China to trade in securities, commodity futures contracts or leveraged foreign exchange, or holds himself out as carrying on such business activity in Hong Kong, China, such person or entity will be subject to registration requirements and other regulation imposed on traditional brokers. The Commission, in determining that, will consider the totality of the facts of each case, including the actual physical location or presence of the business, the manner in which and nature of the activities that have been carried out in Hong Kong, China, and the motives for and circumstances surrounding the conducting of such activities.

Payment and Settlement

For Commerce/Trade Sector

Electronic Financial Transactions (EFT), e.g. through Real Time Gross Settlement (RTGS) system, autopay instructions, SWIFT payments, PC banking, is widely used for B2B (business to business) and B2G (business to government) transactions. We have noticed a recent trend that more banks have introduced Internet payment services for their business customers. However, paper-based payment instructions such as cashier orders and paper cheques are also used by corporations for making payments to the Government or businesses. We understand that the service providers normally implement security policies, apply security technology in the processes and have their own ongoing audit and monitoring arrangements. For B2B transactions, Secure Socket Layer (SSL) protocol or Secure Electronic Transaction (SET) technologies have been widely used.

Specifically for B2G transactions, we have launched various initiatives where businesses and citizens can now pay almost all the Government bills via electronic means, including via the Internet, a tone phone, bank autopay system and a bank Automatic Teller Machine (ATM). For instance under the payment by phone service, registered users using a tone phone can pay for a wide range of public services including Government services, utilities, telecommunications service, any time and any where. The Electronic Payment Service (EPS) enables all citizens and businesses to pay for all kinds of services via a bank ATM. Recently, our banking sector has embarked on various new Internet banking services. For instance, subscribers to Jetco-online, an online service of a local bank network, will be able to pay their bills online via the Internet.

In our recently launched Electronic Service Delivery (ESD) scheme which is a portal providing a wide range of public services online, electronic payment can be made in public information kiosks and at home or office through their personal PCs.

One good example showing the extent of the use of EFT is the payment of tax via electronic means. Taxpayers are well receptive to electronic payments. Earnings and profits tax paid by electronic means during 1999-2000 reached 19% of the total payment in the previous two years.

Our Customs and Excise Department will adopt an EFT approach in collecting duty payment for the dutiable commodities via the Electronic Data Interchange System for Dutiable Commodities Permits (EDI-DCP) project. It is expected that the EFT will be implemented by mid-2001 in line with the roll-out of EDI-DCP. This will serve as an additional facility to the over-the-counter duty payment.

In all these EFT applications, service providers have delivered their service by using widely recognised technologies e.g. the encryption using Secure Socket Layer (SSL) protocol or Secure Electronic Transaction (SET) technologies, digital certificates, to address the security concerns.

In Hong Kong, China, EDI is a type of electronic service involving computer-to-computer exchange of information electronically in a standard format. The application of EDI in commerce in Hong Kong, China has resulted in improved efficiency and a significant reduction in paperwork. Since 1997, the Hong Kong Government has adopted the EDI service provided by a private sector service provider to allow businesses to submit trade-related documents electronically. As far as we are aware, the EDI technology is not directly used for payment and settlement.

There is a wide range of electronic payment and settlement infrastructure provided by the private sector in Hong Kong, China. They include PPS, ATM, multi-purpose cards, internet banking, phone banking, etc.

For the Securities Sector

The Central Clearing and Settlement System (the "CCASS") of Hongkong Clearing is the key settlement infrastructure for B2B transaction in the securities market in Hong Kong, China.

Trades concluded in the Stock Exchange of Hong Kong are transmitted electronically to the CCASS for clearing and settlement. Trades are currently settled on T+2. Securities settlement is effected either by scheduled daily batch settlement runs or immediately on-line by the input of Delivery Instructions on settlement day.

During each batch settlement run on settlement day, the stock account of the delivering participant is debited and that of the receiving participant is credited. However, a delivering participant may choose, or be requested by its counter-party, to settle a position or transaction on-line by initiating Delivery Instructions. Each Delivery Instruction takes immediate effect upon input, if there is sufficient stock balance available in the delivering participant's stock clearing account.

Hongkong Clearing provides money settlement services for all transactions settled on a DVP basis. Each participant is required to establish an account at a designated bank and authorise Hongkong Clearing to initiate electronic instructions to debit or credit its designated bank account. Book-entry money records are generated for a participant in its money ledger with respect to its settlement and other financial obligations due to or from Hongkong Clearing. Settlement is processed through the clearing system of the Hong Kong Interbank Clearing Ltd. against participants' designated bank accounts.

Trades settled under the Continuous Net Settlement system of CCASS are always settled on a day-end DVP basis. The money positions arising from a broker participant's trades settled under the Continuous Netting System in each stock position are netted, resulting in a single net amount due to or from the participant. This is settled by direct debit or credit instruction issued by Hongkong Clearing to the designated bank of the participant at the end of settlement day.

Hongkong Clearing acts as a facilitator for Isolated Trades, Settlement Instruction and Investor Settlement Instruction transactions settled on a DVP or Real-time DVP basis, and issues electronic payment instructions to the designated banks of the participants concerned to effect money settlement. For Isolated Trade transactions, participants can choose to settle on a DVP or a Free of Payment basis. For transactions settled on a Free of Payment basis, participants make their money settlement outside CCASS without involving Hongkong Clearing. Participants can also elect to settle Settlement Instruction and Investor Settlement Instruction transactions on a Real-time DVP basis. Under the Real-time DVP system, shares are delivered to the stock account of paying participant upon receipt of payment confirmation from the Hong Kong Interbank Clearing Ltd.

Electronic Payment System for Business to Government

As one of the key initiatives to develop electronic Government and promote electronic commerce in Hong Kong, China, the Information Technology and Broadcasting Bureau (ITBB) has launched the Electronic Service Delivery (ESD) Scheme which provides a one-stop-shop portal of online services 24 hours a day and seven days a week. The public can now access these services through a common interface via the Internet using their personal computers and public information kiosks installed at various convenient locations like subway stations, supermarkets and major shopping malls. The ESD infrastructure is open to the private sector to deliver online commercial services to the community.

The ESD Scheme accepts a wide range of electronic payment methods, e.g. debit card (EPS and JETCO), credit card (Visa, Mastercard and Diners) and smart card (Visa Cash). Advanced technologies such as SSL (Secure Socket Layer) and SET (Secure Electronic Transactions) will be used to ensure secure electronic payment. Examples of electronic services for which electronic payment is supported by ESD include renewal of driving and vehicle license, application and renewal of Business Registration Certificate, application for search or copy of Birth/Death/Marriage Certificate etc. Moreover, citizens can also pay various types of Government bills electronically via ESD, e.g. rates and rent, water and sewege charges, tax etc.

There is no Customs tariff in HKSAR. Excise duties are levied on four groups of commodities irrespective of whether they are imported or manufactured locally. These commodities are hydrocarbon oil, tobacco, liquor and methyl alcohol. The Customs and Excise Department will introduce an electronic duty payment system for dutiable commodities in mid-2001. Under the proposed system, traders can opt to pay the duty via Internet banking services. They can also pay the duties by making transaction at a computer installed with the electronic fund transfer software.

Importers and exporters of other general cargoes have to pay trade declaration charges which are notional in nature. The traders can lodge the import or export declaration of their goods via the electronic data interchange (EDI) system provided by a specified electronic service provider (SESP). SESP is entrusted for the payment of the relevant charges to the HKSAR Government on behalf of the traders.

Real Time Gross Settlement (RTGS) System

Hong Kong, China's interbank payment system successfully changed to the RTGS system in December 1996. Over the past four years, the system has provided smooth and efficient settlement for interbank payments. The RTGS system in Hong Kong, China is a single-tier settlement structure with all banks maintaining settlement accounts with the HKMA. All RTGS payments are settled in real time, transaction in transaction basis across the books of HKMA. The banks' settlement accounts are not allowed to go into overdraft. Intraday liquidity can be obtained by the banks through the use of their Exchange Fund Bills and Notes for intraday repurchase (repo) agreements with the HKMA.

Coordination in the Development and Promotion of the Use of Electronic Payment Systems

The policy objective of Information Technology and Broadcasting Bureau (ITBB) is to provide the necessary legal and physical infrastructure to facilitate developments of electronic commerce (e-commerce) in Hong Kong, China. While ITBB's focus is on infrastructural developments to facilitate electronic transactions in general, it has no policy oversight nor the expertise over the institutional framework for the coordination and development of electronic payments systems in Hong Kong, China. As part of the electronic government initiatives, ITBB is liaising with the Treasury for the provision of the electronic payment gateway for the electronic settlement of fees and charges payable by the public to various Government bureaux and departments.

One of the main functions of the HKMA is to develop Hong Kong, China's financial infrastructure to enable money to flow smoothly, freely and without obstruction. This function has been facilitated by the introduction of the RTGS in 1996. In the context of the development of electronic payment systems, and insofar as interbank fund transfer are concerned, the HKMA continues to play the role as the overseer in this area.

There exist a number of policy initiatives by the various bureaux and departments of the government to promote the use of the electronic payment systems. At the same time, the government endeavours to accommodate, as it has been successfully doing so, the market development with a free market environment, so that the private sector is able to conduct business using electronic payment systems and to carry out researches on technical innovations.

Summing Up and Looking Forward

Hong Kong, China is well-poised for the new opportunities in the New Economy. With a good infrastructure in IT and telecommunications, business-friendly policies, up-to-date legal and regulatory framework meeting international standards, Hong Kong, China stands ready to meet the challenges in electronic financial transactions. The geographical compactness of Hong Kong, China and the presence of a large number of banks, brokers and financial services intermediaries provide easy access and a high degree of convenience to investors. Hong Kong, China is also well connected not only electronically and geographically but also in terms of movement of goods, people, and capital. Such characteristics are valuable assets for Hong Kong, China in the New Economy.

E-TRANSACTIONS IN HONG KONG, CHINA

John Ure
Director of the Telecommunications Research Project
www.trp.hku.hk
University of Hong Kong

Introduction

Various estimates of e-commerce by research organizations place Hong Kong, China around the Asia-Pacific average of 1 percent of GDP, of which 96 percent is estimated to be business-to-business (B2B) or government-to-business (G2B) and the rest business-to-consumer (B2C). Other data suggests less than 4 percent of individuals have ever purchased online in Hong Kong, China. Such fragile figures indicate the age of electronic commerce is still very much at its inception.

Undoubtedly one reason for the dominance of B2B and G2B is the fact that many business transactions are doing no more than transferring existing business from offline to online to streamline supply chain management and reduce transaction costs. By contrast, B2C is largely about forging new business, growing new markets and creating new distribution channels that are in competition with existing bricks-and-mortar shops and shopping malls. In a clustered urban environment like Hong Kong, China, the genuine benefits of B2C have yet to prove themselves.

Does any of this matter? If the markets operate efficiently and effectively without e-commerce then no, it doesn't, at least not to the functioning of the economy. At this level the test should be whether the markets are sufficiently informed about e-commerce to know when is the right time, the cost-effective time, to adopt electronic transactions, and whether the adoption process is relatively painless. Why then are governments so concerned about promoting and facilitating e-commerce? Clearly the detailed answer will vary from economy to economy, but in principle the answer is fairly simple. E-commerce is seen as a pre-requisite to becoming an effective player in the global economy, and the spread of e-commerce is also seen to be stimulating to local companies innovating in information and communications technologies (ICTs). For example, a 'new media' value chain is emerging which can be layered as follows:

1. Content conception – creative activity
2. Content creation – from drawing board to realization
3. Content packaging – making content marketable
4. Content service provision – distributor of content
5. Content transmission – distribution channel, such as cable TV or mobile phone service provider
6. Content access device – computer, TV, cellphone, handheld PC
7. Content consumer – private, public, business, mass market consumer

Each economy will identify its own strengths and weaknesses along this chain, and there are similar value chains for other elements of the ICT sector. For example, some economies are major producers of IT, others, like Hong Kong, China, are major users of IT. For this reason the Hong Kong government sees a role in facilitating and promoting the use of ICTs to build upon areas of competitive strength and innovation, especially in ICT applications and content. For example, a good test for the future will be the adoption of mobile e-commerce (m-commerce) as packet-switched (Internet) mobile cell phone networks replace second generation (2G) circuit switched (voice and SMS) networks in Hong Kong, China.

Underpinning the successful adoption of ICTs is the information infrastructure. A decade ago this was less true because the adoption of IT was mainly in the form of stand-alone computers or workstations networked internally through a local area network or LAN. Only the larger corporations bought private leased circuits from a telephone company to establish a wide-area network or WAN. Today, computer networking is the essential pre-requisite of e-commerce, and the use of Internet Protocol (IP) has transformed IT systems and brought convergence to the IT and communications worlds, hence ICTs. In this regard Hong Kong, China enjoys an enormous advantage in having a truly world class ubiquitous telecommunications network. In fact Hong Kong, China has several fixed and wireless networks, narrowband and broadband, since the sector was opened to competition in the 1990s.

Part 1: SMEs in Hong Kong, China

Computing and processing technologies, and the underlying physical infrastructure to connect them, are clearly enablers that offer organizations and individuals the opportunity to increase their productivity (output in relation to cost) and their productiveness (their range of outputs) as well as extend their reach to connect to new markets. But Hong Kong, China's economy, like many in Asia Pacific, is dominated by small and medium-sized enterprises (SMEs) and they are naturally reluctant to embrace capital expenditure unless and until the costs and benefits are unambiguously favourable. This is not so much risk-averse behaviour as good commercial common sense. Hong Kong, China's SMEs have shown an agile mobility in being able to change products, or geographical markets or even location – especially to southern mainland China – in reaction to shifts in supply and demand conditions. One aspect of this mobility is the high demand for very portable enabling technologies, such as fax machines, pagers and mobile phones, and an aversion to avoidable sunk costs.

According to a Census and Statistics Department [12] survey of 340,000 establishments in 2000, only 52 percent had computers. While 90 percent of larger establishments had purchased their first computer before 1997, this was true of only 55 percent of all establishments. Perhaps most sobering of all is that 95 percent of establishments without a computer had no plan to install one. 'The major reason for not installing PC was mostly no business benefits to do so, followed by lack of personnel familiar with using a PC.' (p.5)

---

[12] Census and Statistics Department (2000) *Report on 2000 Survey on Information technology Usage and penetration in the Business Sector*, Hong Kong SAR, PRC.

Enterprise type	Percentage with computers	Average number of computers
Large	92	110
Medium	78	8.5
Small	48	1.3
All	52	4

Large defined as having 100 or more staff in manufacturing, or 50 or more staff in other industry sectors; small as having less than 10 staff.

Of these two reasons, the first is clearly commercial, and therefore presumably rational, although it is equally possible that lack of information means missed business opportunities. The second reason is clearly a barrier problem that is likely to diminish as a younger generation of entrepreneurs takes over or replaces traditional family-run businesses. It is also a problem that can be addressed directly by governments in terms of training and assistance programmes, and through the public provisioning of computer access, such as making available computer kiosks in public libraries, malls and community centres.

Having a computer is obviously a pre-requisite for e-commerce, but the percentage of businesses with computers undertaking online ordering or transactions remains quite low.

Enterprise type	Percentage using e-commerce
Large	18.5
Medium	10.4
Small	4
All	4.9

Of those using e-commerce, 73 percent said the major use was 'general online order or purchase of goods, services or information', and of these 93 percent said the major use was 'online receipt, browsing or searching information. Only 2 percent expressed that the major activity was general on-line receipt of digital products and services.' (p.11)

'Regarding the major reasons for not having ordered or purchased through electronic means, 47 percent of the establishments that had not done so considered that there were no business benefits. The opinion was, however, quite different for large establishments. According to large establishments that had not ordered or purchased through electronic means, 39 percent expressed that it was not popular in the industry.' (p.10)

So here we have two distinct market segments. Larger establishments are more prepared for e-commerce but are held back by the general low level of acceptance within their industry. This will obviously vary with the industry in question. For example, the utilities sector (16 percent) and the financial, insurance, real estate and business services sectors (12 percent) showed higher levels of adoption in the Census and Statistics Department survey. As firms get smaller the primary constraint becomes one of perception. The benefits are just not perceived. No doubt this factor is compounded by the lack of experience and know-how with IT among many SMEs. Falling IT prices suggest that cost of equipment may not be a factor, but the – often hidden - running costs maybe. These include the need to upgrade software, the requirement for IT literate and skilled staff, the dangers of viruses, the logistics of management of a web site and of files and backups, and so on. A well known survey in the US in the late 1990s, for example, found that while PC prices averaged US$1,000 business running costs easily reached US$12,000 annually per PC. SMEs may not have these estimates to hand, but they have a pretty good idea that once spending on IT starts it rarely stops.

So the question for governments is how to change the perceptions of SMEs – which should include how to help them master the cost management of IT as well as seeing the advantages of adoption - and how to encourage a greater acceptance of e-commerce in industry. In Hong Kong, China these two tasks tend to be addressed in two different ways. Quasi-autonomous non-governmental organizations ('quangos') such as the Hong Kong Productivity Council, the Vocation Training Council and the Hong Kong Industrial Technology Centre Corporation (now part of the Hong Kong Science and Technology Parks Corporation) devote much of their energy towards promoting and facilitating IT adoption and applications among SMEs.

The surveys of the Productivity Council, for example, found in September 2000 that 54.4 percent of SMEs had no intention of adopting e-commerce, a decline from 60 percent a year earlier. Those using e-mail – nowadays the most basic level of e-communications – went up from 34.5 percent to 42.4 percent, and the trend for SMEs to have web sites – the next rung on the IT ladder - increased from 10.2 percent to 15.3 percent. Almost static over the period were the numbers who had gone further and had begun to integrate their web sites with their front-end sales systems (around 4 percent) or transform their back-end business systems (0.3 percent). Numerous reasons were offered by SMEs for their reluctance, of which the most frequent were: (a) bank support for online payments facilitation was too expensive, (b) the high costs of logistics for the delivery of goods ordered online, (c) lack of IT and web-skilled people, (d) a weak revenue model to support the investment, (e) no convincing examples of successful cases, and (f) information security risk.

Encouraging industry to accept e-commerce as a cost-effective way of doing business that simultaneously widens business opportunities is more the role of the government in Hong Kong, China. Of course, the main driver is the market, and for industries like banking and insurance, transportation and logistics, business consultancy and law firms, the adoption rate is largely a natural progression of trade and commerce. But for the majority of Hong Kong, China companies, and for Hong Kong, China citizens, the experience of e-commerce and e-transactions is very limited. It is in this context that Part 2 examines the efforts of the Hong Kong, SAR Government to go online.

Part 2: New Times in Hong Kong, China

It is often said that Internet time is much faster than pre-Internet time, the clock has been speeded up. The observation known as Moore's Law that the number of transistors on a silicon chip doubles every 18 months, or the cost falls by half, has been driving the ICT sector for the past twenty years, and over the past decade the position of governments has shown similar fast change. It is instructive to recognize just how radical it has been. In 1995 with full confidence I could write that:

little effort has been made by government to encourage the use of on-line information. For example, the Government Information Service (GIS), which is the primary interface between government and the Hong Kong, China media, is not on-line, although file transfer is available, and in 1995 the teleprinter service was replaced with a proprietary standard non-interactive on-line broadcast connection to the media, but not the general public - and only two government services, laws and the land registry, are provided on-line.[13]

By 1998 my assessment was very different.[14]

> Just three years later this view is quite out of date. A check of http://www.info.gov.hk will reveal that just about every government agency is now on the Web as part of the government's efforts to emphasize the importance of IT in building an information society in Hong Kong, China. This is a long step forward from 1992 when two principal members of the government's Information Technology Services Department, which is responsible for promoting civil service efficiency, wrote,

> '...no preferential treatment to the information technology sector has been given. The use of information technology in Hong Kong, China is requirement-driven rather than coordinated and promoted by the Government, apart from promotion through its own consumption. such a stance is welcomed by the community and the IT industry at large.'[15]

The clearest statement of the new commitment came in the Chief Executive's Policy Address in 1997. "Our targets... are:
* The availability of an open common interface for electronic transactions between Government, businesses and individuals
* The extensive use of IT within Government
* Higher computer literacy rate in the community
* High IT take-up rate in businesses and households
* Hong Kong, China's active participation in international and bilateral IT co-operation

The Information Technology & Broadcasting Bureau has been tasked with the implementation of these policy objectives in the strategy document Digital 21. The conceptualization of Digital 21 is set out below.

---

[13] Petrazzini B. and J.Ure 'Hong Kong's Communications Infrastructure: The Evolving Role of a Regional Information Hub'. In J. Burn ed. (1997) *Information technology and the Challenge for Hong Kong.* Hong Kong University Press (pp. 61-90).

[14] J.Ure 'Convergence in Hong Kong' in M.Hukill, R.Ono and C.Vallath eds. (2000) *Electronic Communication Convergence: Policy Challenges in Asia, Sage Publications,* New Delhi (pp. 148-176)

[15] C.C.Greenfield and E. Lee 'Government information technology policy in Hong Kong' in J.King ed. *Informatization and the Public Sector: Special Issue* v.2.2 1992 (pp.125-132)

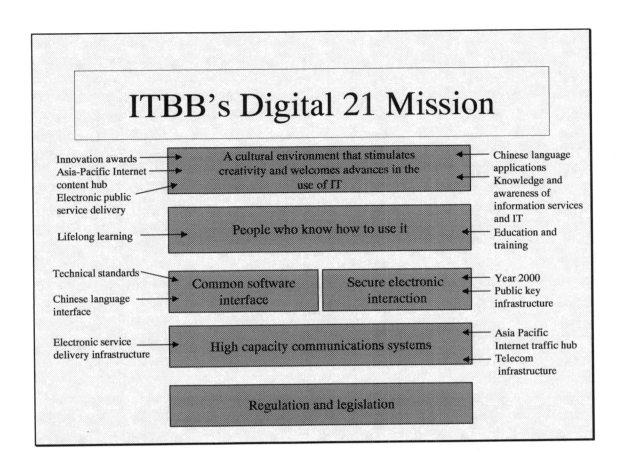

In the 1990s the liberalization of telecommunications policy was accompanied by a transparent and light-handed regulatory regime, and this has since been supplemented with the Electronic Transactions Ordinance, enacted in January 2000, that establishes a legal framework for a public key infrastructure, including digital certificates and recognition of certification authorities. A Personal Data (Privacy) Ordinance and legislation providing for protection of copyright, trademarks, patents and other intellectual property, along with powers against computer crime add to the 'soft' infrastructure supporting e-commerce in Hong Kong, China.

The physical telecommunications infrastructure is now able to provide broadband connectivity throughout Hong Kong, China. The software infrastructure is being built with the promotion of Chinese language interface standards and a supplementary Hong Kong, China character set. In addition to numerous campaigns to spread IT awareness among SMEs and the general public, the initiatives include IT awareness courses for housewives, the elderly, the disabled, new arrivals, as well as IT literacy classes in community college programmes. Over 2,200 public computers have been installed in public libraries, post offices and community centres for the free use by the public. About a hundred kiosks are also installed in subway/train stations, shopping malls, supermarkets, Government buildings etc to facilitate the public to gain access to e-government services under the Electronic Service Delivery (ESD) Scheme.

An important aspect of the Government's strategy has been to enhance the role of the Information Technology Services Department (ITSD) as a champion of IT usage in the economy as well as in government. As we saw above, this is a marked change from the position in 1992 when the ITSD's role was merely to monitor and coordinate government use of IT. For example, under the Electronic Transactions Ordinance it is the director of the ITSD who is responsible for approving certification authorities. The ITSD also runs the Tripartite Forum on Commercialisation of IT Research Results in Hong Kong, China at which technology research and development projects are presented to audiences comprising venture capitalists and IT companies looking for talent and ideas. The ITSD over recent years has presided over the growth in IT usage within government as the following table illustrates.

Year	Civil Servants	PCs	PCs/civil servant
2001 (Q1)	180,600	93,000	51%
2000	183,400	84,000	46%
1999	187,000	73,000	39%
1998	189,300	72,000	38%
1997	185,200	63,000	34%
1996	184,200	50,000	27%

Note: > 70% Government computers are networked. 23% had Internet access, December 2000

Government has gotten smaller and IT larger. But the important development has been how the IT is used. During the 1990s the government began going online, first with some departments but not others developing informational web sites, and this was followed by the Government Information Service (GIS) building a web page for public access to all government agencies. (See http://www.info.gov.hk). Then, in 2000 the Hong Kong SAR government launched the Electronic Services Delivery (ESD) online service for citizens, a portal enabled for interactivity and transactions.

Electronic Services Delivery: G2C

The 'must read' message on the ESD web site (http://www.esd.gov.hk) states

> The objective is to provide more comprehensive services to users and make use of the ESD information infrastructure *to pump-prime the development of e-commerce in the private sector.* (emphasis added - JCU).

So ESD is more than just a community service making good use of IT. It is intended to pump-prime, and by that standard it will need to be judged over the coming years. The service is provided by ESD Services Ltd, a privately contracted joint venture of Hutchison Global Crossing and Compaq. The government is just one of several content providers and is not held responsible for the site. The government estimate the cost advantage of this outsourcing is an average payment per transaction of HK$5.5 (US$0.70) for the five year period of the contract in contrast to an average HK$13 per transaction for 'over the counter' services. Navigation of the site is by means of three channels, 'People', 'Business' and 'City' and a search engine. As of June 2001, 29 government departments were to some extent online, offering 79 services in

9 service categories: citizenship, business, education, employment, finance, household, leisure, transport and tourism.

Visitors per day rose from 35,000 in March to 105,000 in May 2001, but the percentage performing 'transactions' remained hovering around 4 percent. 'Transactions' is defined rather widely to include the booking of appointments as well as making payments. For payment transactions a digital certificate is required, but by March 2001 the number of business certificates issued by the recognized certification authority, the Hongkong Post, was 10,600, or just 1 percent of business establishments in Hong Kong, China. Those issued to individuals represented around 3.5 percent of total households. However, Tradelink, a consortium set up to act as a gateway between government and the importing and exporting sector – but yet to receive recognition under the ETO as a CA – had issued over 150,000 business certificates.

Job search was the most frequently used service with average 43,000 visitors per day January – April 2001, followed by tourist information services. Third came the payment of Government bills, such as rates and taxes, with transactions rising from 630 per day in December 2000 to 1,350 per day January-March 2001. Although these numbers are not yet huge, the trend is clearly encouraging. On a personal note, my observation is that some parts of the portal are not always possible to reach, which may have to do with server congestion, or network congestion, or possible congestion on the LAN that I use to access the site. Whatever the cause, this can be a source of frustration, especially for those less acquainted with IT usage, and governments everywhere must be aware that success implies an inevitable spiral of supply-leads-to-demand which calls for a growing commitment of resources. Outsourcing may reduce costs, but it will not halt the growing demand for electronic resources.

Electronic Tendering and Procurement: G2B

This is the area of most direct impact upon the business community, and upon SMEs in particular, in bringing about industry acceptance of e-commerce. It is particularly relevant in Hong Kong, China's case where less than 2 percent of Government supplies came from the local economy, but 90 percent of the tenders submitted are from local agents. These figures have since risen to 11 percent and 97 percent respectively. The Government's Electronic Tendering System (ETS) which handles contracts below the value of HK$10 million (US$1.3 million) – this ceiling will be raised from July 2001 – encourages local SMEs to submit offers and also widens the scope, and cuts the costs, of sourcing. Just over 70 percent of tenders are sent electronically, and by value around 75 percent. Over the period June 2000 to June 2001 ETS registered suppliers have increased 130 percent to 5,304, still a small number but significant growth.

On the backend of the Government's IT network a **G**oods-**O**n-line **O**rdering, **D**istribution, **S**tock **M**anagement and **A**ccounting **N**etwork system (GOODSMAN) provides remote terminals over two LANS for online goods ordering and inquiries, with a barcode reading system for stock management. Quality monitoring is undertaken by a system known as PMSU (a **P**rocurement **M**anagement **S**ystem Upgrade) that makes evaluations of offers, orders, contracting and supplier performance. For large-scale public works tendering an ETS approach is to be adopted during 2001, and since August 2000 all tender documents go out in CD-ROM form. The use of an ESD system for public works tendering is also under study, which would make possible the exchange of planning and design documentation, feasibility studies, utilities information, tendering and administration.

Planned for the near future is more backend automation, such as ASLPS (**A**llocation **S**tores **L**edger **P**osting **S**ystem) for the automatic replenishment of standard store items, and the use of e-marketplaces for the volume purchase of small value items at the department level. On a grander scale the automation of customs clearances using EDI is foreseen, although this is a huge challenge for an economy that rides on the burgeoning re-export trade from mainland China. Through all these means the Hong Kong Government is widening the opportunities to tender online, which brings benefits to public expenditure and brings equal opportunities to local SMEs and foreign companies to supply the public sector. The learning curve for SMEs who grasp this opportunity is a benefit not just to them but to the whole economy.

Conclusion

E-government in Hong Kong, China is designed to meet certain challenges beyond the simple task of bringing information and - *less simple* - accessible government to citizens. On the consumer side of the economy it is designed to be pump-priming, to stimulate the take-up of inter-active services, such as the payment of taxes and online applications. On the producer side of the economy it faces two principal challenges. At the industry level to increase the level of acceptance of e-commerce as the normal business practice. For SMEs, to bring tangible benefits at low cost with user-friendly systems so as to encourage the adoption of IT leading to e-commerce.

It remains too early to judge the success of the initiatives outlined above, or to identify the lessons to be learned. But one thing is already clear, this is an ongoing process. Success will breed success, and that in turn will increase the demand for electronic resources in the public as well as in the private sector. Managing this will, in turn, require a continued commitment by governments. Although outsourcing will bring tangible benefits in terms of outside expertise and resources, governments, like the private sector, will need internal champions to sustain the commitment. In Hong Kong, China the ITSD has been thrust very much into this role, and it has embraced it with enthusiasm, but will it be enough? Governments are uneven across departments, and in the final analysis it always requires commitment from the top, and that cannot be outsourced.

MINI-CASE STUDY: JAPAN
On the Effects of the New Economy on the Japanese Economy

International Economic Affairs Division
Cabinet Office, Japanese Government

Macroeconomic Effects

Information technology (IT) has a potential to accelerate long-term economic growth by improving productivity, and has to become driving force behind a new economic development worthy to be named "New Economy."

The long-term impact of the latest IT has yet to be known, but we see the growing possibility of the IT as great technological innovations such as the steams engine, electricity and the automobile. The impact not only benefits IT-related manufacturers and telecommunications businesses but also transforms business styles in a wide range of industrial sectors by dramatically cutting costs of communications and information search. New products and services using IT are exerting a great influence on the lifestyles of consumers. The IT impact on the economy is likely to be even greater.

According to estimation (Economic Planning Agency 2000) using the ORANI-G model, a multisectoral general equilibrium model, improvement of the productivity of manufacturing IT-related equipment industries and the spread of e-commerce up to 2004 will have a direct effect of 2.1% (approx. 11 trillion yen) of GDP. The effect on the economy as whole including ripple effect will be 4.2% (approx. 23 trillion yen).

From the trough of the business cycle in the period from April-June quarter 1999 to the period from July-September 2000, IT-related demand and production contributed to economic recovery. Exports had contributed greatly to growth against the backdrop of heightened global demand for IT-related goods of which production centers are located in Asian countries. Electrical appliances and other IT-related industries have also been major forces driving production and business investment. IT accounted for roughly 30% of exports, 50% of production and 80% of business investment (Figure 1—see figures at end of case study). There was also marked growth of job offers in the information services industry and other IT-related industries. Amidst an overall lack of growth in consumption, there was a marked increase in IT-related expenditures, including spending on telephone charges and personal computers. In contrast, growth in production and business investment in the non-IT-related sector was poor, while non-IT-related household consumption also experienced sluggish growth.

Effects on Business Investment

IT-related business investment (hereinafter referred as "IT investment") contributed greatly to growth from the mid-1990s (Figure 2). According to *"Questionnaire Concerning Corporate*

Activities 2000", IT investment accounted for 15.2% of overall business investment over the past three years and was expected to account for 18.3% of the same over the next three years. These results show the aggressive attitude of enterprises toward IT investment despite the recession. A comparison by industry revealed that IT investment ratio of non-manufacturing industries was about twice as high as that of manufacturing industries. Among the former, the particularly high IT investment ratios of wholesale and service industries indicates the considerable weight of information intermediary business in these industries (Figure 3).

IT investment is also becoming specialized. While the ratio of "Acquisition of computers and peripheral equipment" and "Acquisition of software" will fall, those of "Software development" and "System operation and development" are increasing particularly in large enterprises (Figure 4, 5)..

Regarding the status of the introduction of IT-related equipment, PCs (excluding portable PCs), e-mail, LAN and Internet are being introduced on a company-wide scale at 70-90% of enterprises (Figure 6). However, another comparison by company capital shows that large enterprises are generally outstripping medium sized enterprises in this area. In particular, the introduction of LAN Internet and other network infrastructure is not advancing among smaller enterprises. Intranet and groupware introduction ratio is also lower among enterprises with smaller capitalization (Figure 7).

Concerning targeted business areas of IT investments, there has been a shift from the areas of "Human resources and salary" and "Accounting" to areas that greatly affect corporate competitiveness, especially "Management planning" and "Procurement" (Figure 8).

There have also been changes in the objectives of IT investment. While "speed up of operations" is becoming less important, other objectives are getting more important, such as "Strengthening business and sales force," "Organizational reformation," and "Reduction in procurement cost." From this it can be seen that IT investment is being undertaken as an active corporate management strategy (Figure 9).

However, while many companies have experienced the effect of "speed up of operations," the other objectives have not yet to been realized in many companies (Figure 10).

On the other hand, in companies' proceeding with IT investment, their major problems are a scarcity of professional personnel and employee education issues. In addition, pointed out are the rapid obsolescence of technology, the low cost effectiveness of IT investment, and high telecommunications charges (Figure 11).

Many companies choose the option of outsourcing as a measure to resolve these problems. It can be seen that there is a growing trend for companies to seek human resources and capabilities in the IT sector, in which there is a lack of talent, both internally and externally (Figure 12).

One of the reasons for slow expansion of production and business investment in non-IT related industries is the ripple effect of IT-related goods on other sectors. Looking at the ripple effect on the manufacturing industry caused by increased demand for machinery, the ripple effect of IT-related goods on other industries is smaller than those of automobiles and conventional household appliances. The ripple effect of IT-related goods is confined to its own sector is high. Two reasons can be cited for this situation: i) Automobiles and conventional household appliances require parts made by various sectors, such as steel and chemical products, while PCs, mobile telephones and other finished IT-related products use semiconductors, liquid crystals, batteries and many other parts that are IT-related; and ii) Investment in finished IT-related products has a higher import ratio to the input compared to automobiles and home electric appliances.

IT investment has following macroeconomic effects: i) Boosting IT-related demand among enterprises and households; ii) Raising productivity at enterprises; and iii) Effects on employment.

Effects on Consumption

While total nominal consumption has been falling, IT-related spending has served to support total consumption. According to the Family Income and Expenditure Survey, IT-related expenditures reveals continual marked growth, mainly on PCs and telephone charges, amidst year-on-year decreases in overall consumption expenditures. As a result, the ratio of information-related spending to overall consumption expenditures has been rising.

Prices of IT-related consumer goods have been quickly declining. Price decreases have been seen in wider areas of IT-related goods from around 1993. Provider connection rates and other Internet connection-related expenses are also decreasing. These price decreases are likely contributing significantly to expansion of consumption and investment.

Business-to-Consumers (B to C) e-commerce is expanding affected by the spread of the Internet. The introduction of B to C e-commerce is either completed or planned at a very high ratio in the areas of homepage creation and Internet advertisement and direct sales (Figure 15). The most often cited impacts of the increase of these kinds of e-commerce are "Intensifying price competition" and "Elimination of intermediates in the distribution process," while few enterprises cited "Increased sales" and "Increased profitability" (Figure 16). On the other hand, "saving the trouble of going shopping," and "being able to order goods when you like," were cited as benefits that can be derived by consumers through the spread of e-commerce (Figure 17). In addition, there is comparatively high latent demand among consumers for e-commerce. Items that consumers want to buy through e-commerce include "Air and rail tickets," "Hotel reservations," and "Concert and theater tickets." E-commerce for such products fulfills the function of retail sales without having to use a retail store (Figure 18). Conditions cited for the future spread of e-commerce include "Computer and Internet literacy," "Reliable settlement methods" and "Cheaper communications charges."(Figure 19)

Effects on Supply

The effects of technological innovations on supply-side include the improvement of productivity. We have measured the productivity-boosting effect of IT investment by measuring productivity for IT-related and other capital and have confirmed the productivity-boosting effects of IT investment in the latter half of the 1990s (Figure 20).

It is also said that the effects of IT first become evident in cases where there are high levels of IT-related investment and human capital, and where corporate flattening and delegation of authority are advancing at the same time, while in other cases productivity improvement is sluggish due to the mal-adaptation of the enterprise toward IT. It was found that in cases where human capital accumulation and corporate flattening were promoted at the same time as moves toward IT, Total Factor Productivity (TFP) tends to increase. This suggests that changes in human capital and workplace organization are needed in order for firms to reap the benefit of higher productivity from IT adoption. Although firms are mainly responsible for such reform, policy measures to make labor markets more flexible and help enhance human capital will greatly complement individual firms' efforts.

Effects on Employment

Concerning the effects of new technologies on employment, demand for white-collar workers, especially those in the mid-and older-age groups, has apparently declined as the IT revolution has lowered information transmission costs. On the other hand, while IT-related job offers have been increasing, the number of dispatched workers has retained an uptrend since the middle of 1999. This apparently indicates that the IT revolution has led to an increase in jobs that can be undertaken by temporary workers rather than regular workers who are more familiar with their company environment.

When changes in corporate management to respond to the IT movement are examined while focusing on trends in employment relations, until now the most popular example is "Use of temporary employees and part-timers." This is indicative of the strong moves to supplement insufficiencies in personnel involved with IT. Frequently observed are the changes involving employment adjustment such as "Reduction of administrative and management personnel", and "Reduction of manufacturing and sales personnel."

Meanwhile, IT has also influenced labor supply by allowing telework for child-raising housewives who cannot commute. According to a report by the Japan Telework Association, the number of teleworkers in Japan stood at 2.5 million in 2000 and is projected to increase to 4.5 million in 2005.

Employment relations from now on are expected to develop more along the lines of "Treatment based on merit and ability," "Securing human resources with priority on competitiveness and expertise." These responses seem to foresee that enterprises will try to link IT to their competitiveness more strategically by advancing restructuring of the human resources within their organizations (Figure 21).

Effects on Finance

IT development have had great effects on the financial sector as well as the real economy. First, the development of IT has led to more efficient electronic financial transactions. Electronic transactions that have traditionally existed between financial institutions have begun to expand between these institutions and consumers. The introduction of Internet banking and Internet stock trading services indicates that the IT development has improved convenience for consumers as well as financial institutions. Manufacturing companies and long-existing banks are now planning to establish Internet banks without offices.

IT have enhanced the convenience in the financial sector. On the other hand, we cannot deny that IT has served to destabilize financial and capital markets. For example, an increase in the number of the so-called day traders using Internet stock trading has reportedly added fuel to market fluctuations by bringing about an expansion of herd behavior, meaning that some market participants tend to follow the suit of others in trading.

Effects on Business Activities and Business Organizations

Information sharing using IT, and IT management methods like Customer Relationship Management (CRM) and Supply Chain Management (SCM) are expected to be rapidly introduced over the next three years (Figure 23, 24), with a particularly high penetration rate in processing manufacturers.
- CRM: Formulation of marketing strategies based on customer's individual needs, using customer data.
- SCM: Common use of information such as inventory, sales and procurement to optimize operations between business as a whole.

It is forecast that B to B e-commerce will make a transition through the Internet from interaction between individual companies to a marketplace type, with large numbers of buyers and sellers being able to congregate on the web and do business when their individual conditions are met (Figure 25). The influence of the increase in B to B e-commerce is expected to result in, "intensifying price competition," "growing gap between companies," and the "elimination of intermediaries in the distribution process." In addition, "increase in corporate partnerships and mergers and acquisitions," "reduction in long-term sustainable business," and "increasing horizontal division of labor with outside companies," while currently not making much impact in replies to the survey, are expected to increase in significance over the next three years. The increase of B to B e-commerce will therefore not only result in a smaller role for intermediaries, but will also bring about a change in B to B commercial relations as a whole (Figure 26).

In the 1980s, the organization of Japan's big companies responded to economic environment changes very flexibly. It has been frequently noted that these companies' cooperative relations with subcontractors contributed to the overall flexibility. These companies maintained competition between their subcontractors and encouraged them to make stronger business efforts. At the same time, these companies built up long-term business relations with subcontractors, allowing for positive technological transfers and subcontractor participation in product planning. This close exchange of information served to lower information costs.

In the 1990s, however, business environment changes were witnessed. Those changes include i) efficient information transmission and processing under IT development, ii) both improvements in production know-how in developing countries and iii) standardization of business systems through the globalization.

In such circumstances, some Internet business companies can focus on their core strengths, while outsourcing production, delivery, payment management, etc. Individuals and small groups of people can easily start businesses. This means that various ideas now can be put into practice more easily and that entrepreneurs can choose business location more flexibly.

Some companies from Europe and the United States have positively responded to such business environment changes, shifting priority to external transactions by spinning off part of their divisions. Over the recent years, the Top 100 U.S. companies have increased their share of total assets held by all U.S. companies and reduced that of operating facilities. This indicates that big U.S. companies have increasingly spun off production and marketing divisions and put them under their indirect control through capital participation.

It is suggested that in response to the increasing development of IT, corporate management structure is expected to undergo a large change in the future, focused on, "bottom up transmission of information," "top-down transmission of information," and "corporate flattening" (Figure 28).

New Technologies and Aging Society

The recent IT-related consumption concentrates on the younger-generation. In order to link future technological innovations to economic growth, however, Japan will have to look to older people with greater potential purchasing power. The rate of diffusion among older people, however, is very low, limited to only 5.4% for personal computers and to 0.5% for mobile terminals. Present information technologies do not necessarily promote facility for older people. If IT systems were to become easier to use, older people would take and interest

The fast-aging society may be unfavorable from the viewpoint of productions capacity, but it indicates that several new technologies can be combined to stimulate new demand, such as on-screen health checks using telecommunications services (Figure 29).

References

Economic Planning Agency (2000), *Economic Survey of Japan 1999-2000*
Economic Planning Agency (2000), *Current Status of Japanese Economy 2000*
Economic Planning Agency (2000), *The Effect of IT (Information Technology) on Productivity: In search of Japan's "New Economy"*
        http://www5.cao.go.jp/2000/f/1031f-seisakukoka4-e/main.html
Economic & Social Research Institute, Cabinet Office (2001), *Questionnaire Concerning Corporate Activities 2000* (available in Japanese only)
Ministry of Post and Telecommunications (1998), *White Paper on Telecommunications 1998*

Figure 1 Contribution of IT-Related Industries

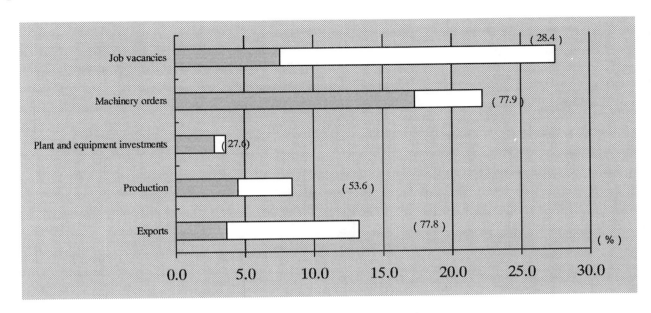

Source: Economic Planning Agency   *Current Status of Japanese Economy 2000*

Notes: 1. Figures given in brackets are the percentage of the IT-related contribution (= IT-related growth)

2. In regards to the plant and equipment investments, the ratio of the first half of 2000 to the same period in year before, and regarding the others, a comparison of the April-June '99 period to the July-September period.

3. In this analysis, the IT-related sectors are defined as

(Exports)	The total of "Electronic parts such as semi-conductors" "Office "Telecommunications apparatus" "Scientific and optical
(Production)	The total of "Telecommunications apparatus" · electronic parts" "Semi-conductor devices" "Accumulation circuit" "Semi-conductor "Electronic computers"
(Plant and equipment investments)	The annual investment amount was found by taking the domestic consumption account and calculating the computerization investment amount every five differentiating by the investment entity of the total investment amount and manufacturers (general machinery, electric machinery), IT-user industries (foods, textiles, paper/pulp, chemicals, petroleum/coal), and clay, steel, non-ferrous metals, metals, transportation equipment, machinery, other manufacturing industries), IT-user non-manufacturing (construction, electricity/gas, wholesale, financing and insurance, real transport, services), and IT infrastructures (communication, radio and broadcasting). (Calculated based on the Inter-Industry Relations Management and Coordination
(Job vacancies)	"Electronic machinery manufacturing industry" "Information services

Figure 2 Contribution of IT Investments to the Business Investment

(Compared to the same period of the
previous year, %)

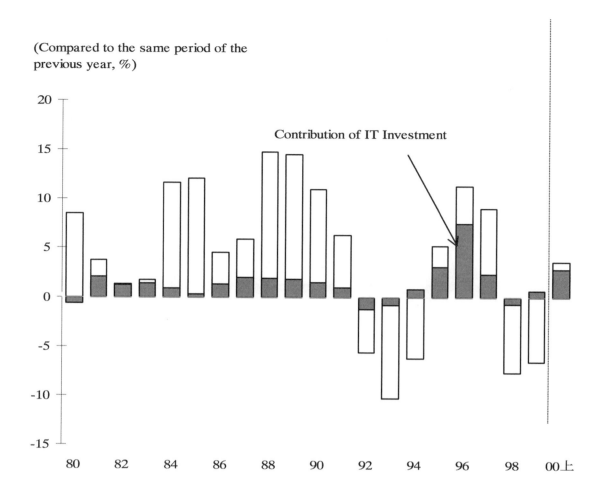

Notes:

1. Sources: *National Accounts*, Economic Planning Agency; *Inter-Industry Relations* Table, Management and Coordination Agency; *Census of Manufacturers, Monthly Statistics on Machinery*, Ministry of International Trade and Industry and the *Monthly Trade Table*, Japan Tariff Association.

2. The annual investment amount was found by taking the domestic consumption into account and calculating the computerization investment amount every five years, differentiating by the investment entity of the total investment amount and IT manufacturers (general machinery, electric machinery), IT-user manufacturing industries (foods, textiles, paper/pulp, chemicals, petroleum/coal), ceramics/stone and clay, steel, non-ferrous metals, metals, transportation equipment, precision machinery, other manufacturing industries), IT-user non-manufacturing industries (construction, electricity/gas, wholesale, financing and insurance, real estate, transport, services), and IT infrastructures (communication, radio and television broadcasting). (Calculated based on the Inter-Industry Relations Table, Management and Coordination Agency)

3. For the year 2000, the estimation was made with the data for only the first half of the year.

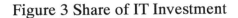

Figure 3 Share of IT Investment

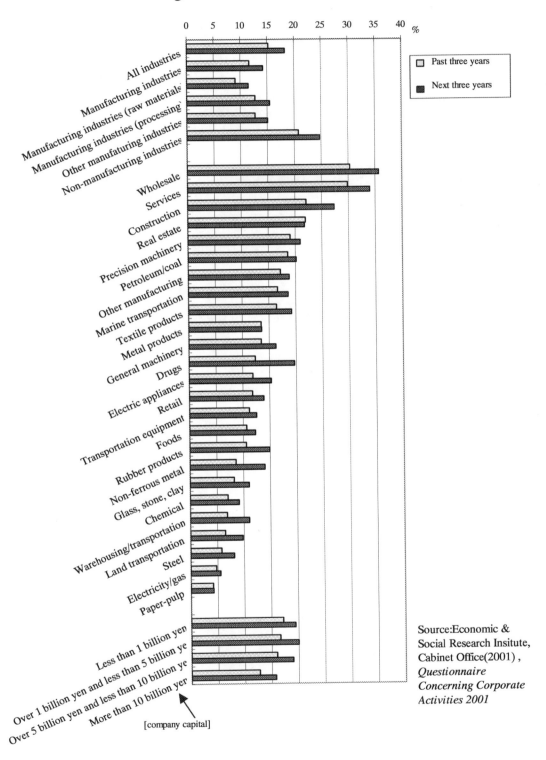

Source:Economic &
Social Research Insitute,
Cabinet Office(2001) ,
Questionnaire
Concerning Corporate
Activities 2001

Figure 4 Contents of IT Investment

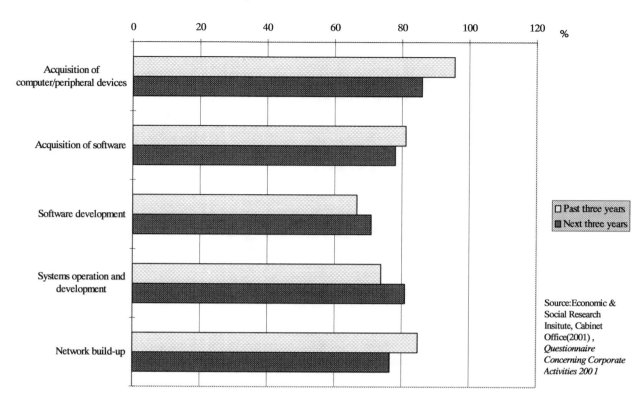

Source:Economic & Social Research Insitute, Cabinet Office(2001) , *Questionnaire Concerning Corporate Activities 200 1*

Figure 5

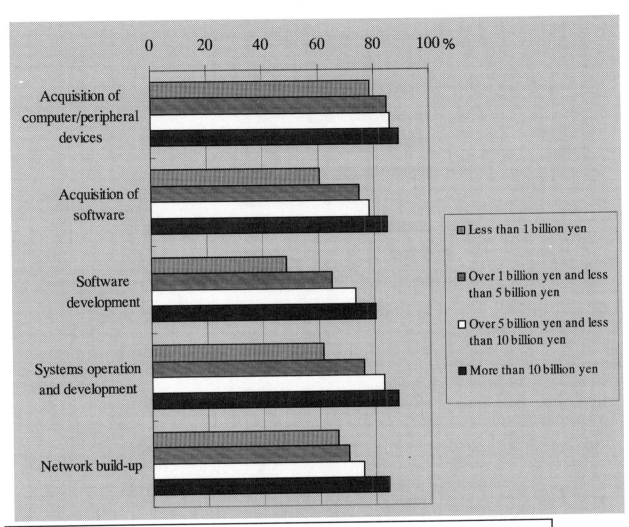

Source: Economic & Social Research Insitute, Cabinet Office (2001) , Questionnaire Concerning Corporate Activities 2001

Figure 6 Status of Introduction of IT-Related Equipment

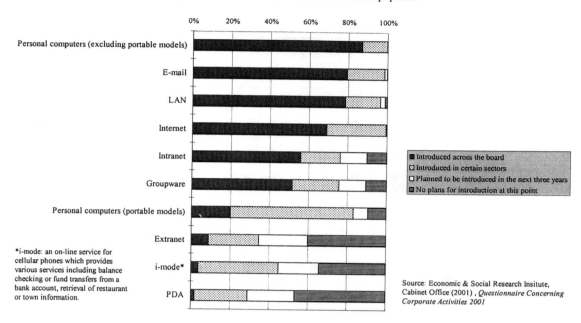

*i-mode: an on-line service for cellular phones which provides various services including balance checking or fund transfers from a bank account, retrieval of restaurant or town information.

Source: Economic & Social Research Insitute, Cabinet Office (2001) , *Questionnaire Concerning Corporate Activities 2001*

Figure 7 Status of Introduction of IT-Related Equipment (by scale of company capital)

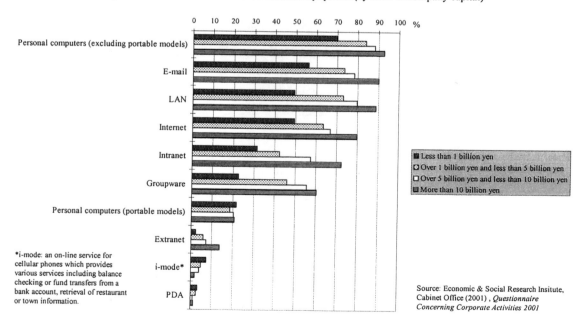

*i-mode: an on-line service for cellular phones which provides various services including balance checking or fund transfers from a bank account, retrieval of restaurant or town information.

Source: Economic & Social Research Insitute, Cabinet Office (2001) , *Questionnaire Concerning Corporate Activities 2001*

178

Figure 8 Targeted Areas of IT Investments

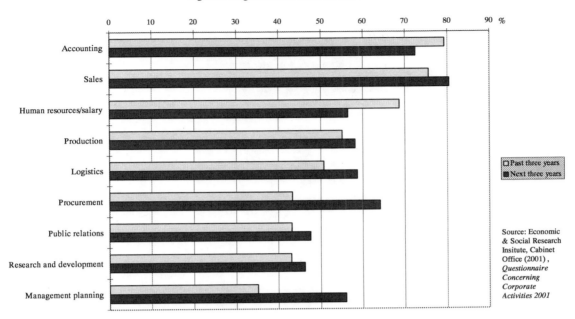

Source: Economic & Social Research Insitute, Cabinet Office (2001), *Questionnaire Concerning Corporate Activities 2001*

Figure 9 Ojective of IT Investments

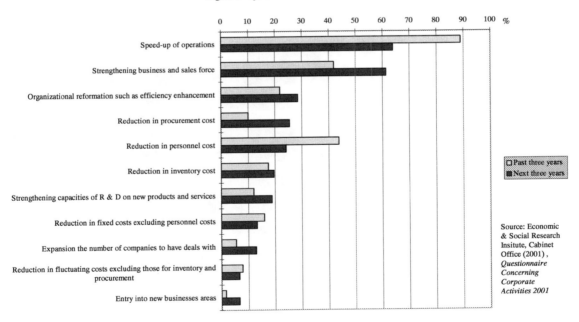

Source: Economic & Social Research Insitute, Cabinet Office (2001), *Questionnaire Concerning Corporate Activities 2001*

Figure 10 Effects of Increased Use of Computers and IT

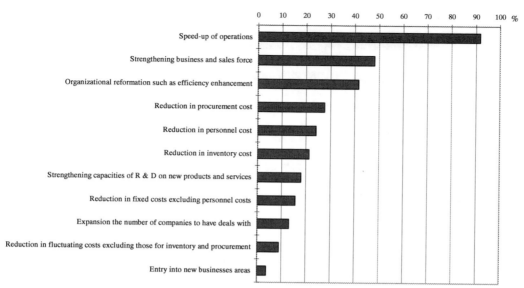

Source: Economic & Social Research Insitute, Cabinet Office (2001) , *Questionnaire Concerning Corporate Activities 2001*

Figure 11 Problems of Proceeding with IT Investments

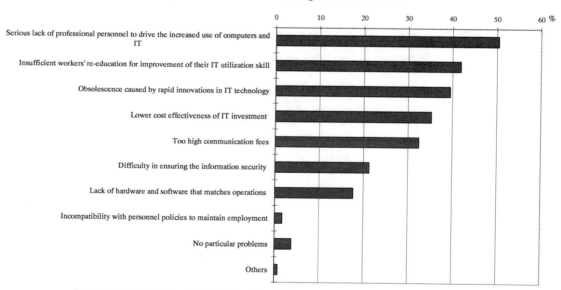

Source: Economic & Social Research Insitute, Cabinet Office (2001) , *Questionnaire Concerning Corporate Activities 2001*

Figure 12 Measures to Solve Problems

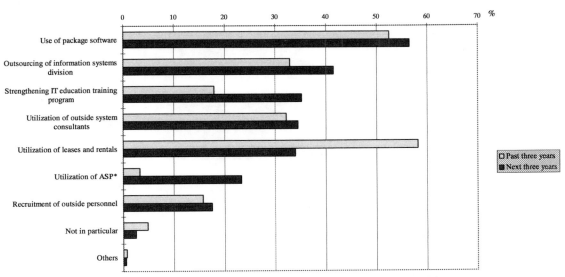

*ASP   Application Service Provider   : a company that provides an environment
such as servers or settlement system and conducts its maintainance.

Source: Economic & Social Research Insitute, Cabinet Office
(2001) , *Questionnaire Concerning Corporate Activities*
2001

Figure 15 Introduction Status and Plans of B to C

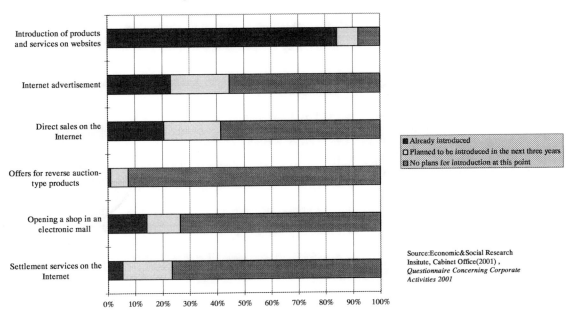

Source:Economic&Social Research
Insitute, Cabinet Office(2001) ,
*Questionnaire Concerning Corporate
Activities 2001*

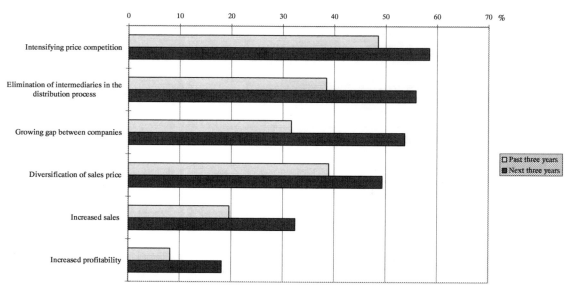

Figure 16 Effects of Growth in B to C E-commerce

Source:Economic&Social Research Insitute, Cabinet Office(2001) , *Questionnaire Concerning Corporate Activities 2001*

Figure 17 Advantages of Internet Shopping

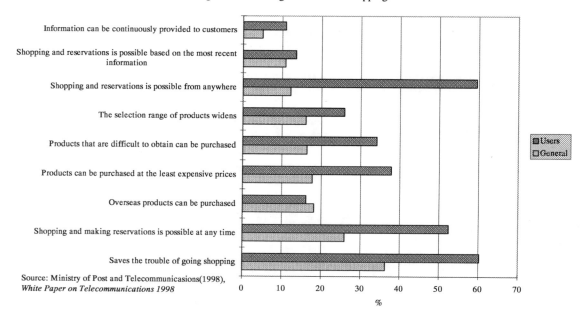

Source: Ministry of Post and Telecommunicasions(1998), *White Paper on Telecommunications 1998*

Figure 18 Product Purchased or Wanted through Internet Shopping

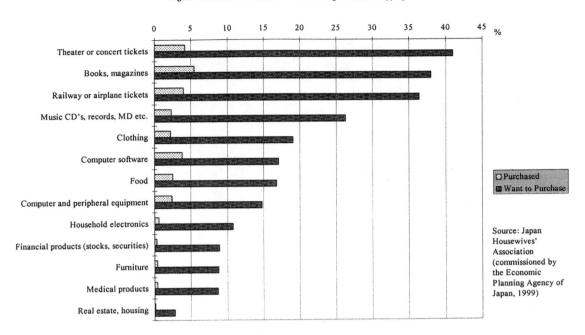

Source: Japan Housewives' Association (commissioned by the Economic Planning Agency of Japan, 1999)

Figure19 Preconditions for Promotion of Internet Shopping

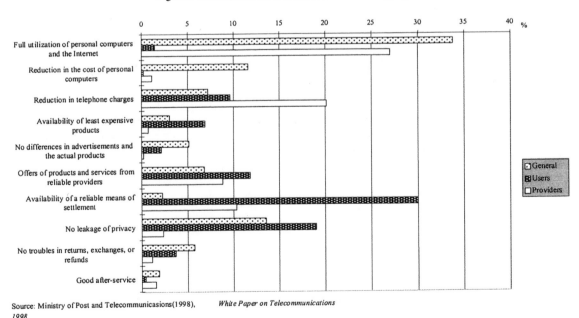

Source: Ministry of Post and Telecommunicasions(1998),   *White Paper on Telecommunications*
1998

Figure 20 Factor-by-Factor Breakdown of Labor Productivity

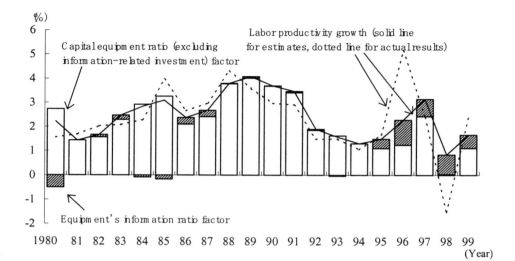

	Labor productivity growth	Capital equipment ratio (excluding information-related investment) factor	Equipment's information ratio factor	Others
1980-1984	1.93	2.19	-0.06	-0.19
1985-1989	3.51	3.11	0.09	0.30
1990-1995	1.98	2.37	0.01	-0.39
1996-1999	2.03	1.18	0.70	0.14

Sources: Inter-Industry Relations Table, Management and Coordination Agency;
Census of Manufactures, Ministry of International Trade and Industry, *National Accoun*

Statistics on Gross Capital Stock of Private Enterprises, Economic Planning Agency

Note: The change in labor productivity was broken into changes in the capital equipment ratio (excluding IT-related equipment) and in the IT equipment ratio.

Its estimation was carried out according to the Cochrane-Orcutt method, using data on Real GDP, net capital stock, IT-related capital stock, Regular employment index, Gross real working hour index, and Capacity utilization ratio index.

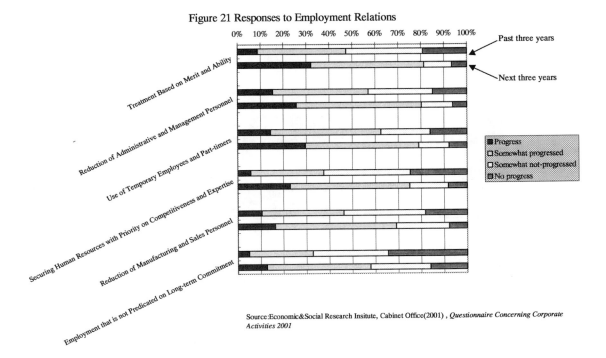

Figure 21 Responses to Employment Relations

Source:Economic&Social Research Insitute, Cabinet Office(2001) , *Questionnaire Concerning Corporate Activities 2001*

Figure 23 Status of Sharing Information Using IT

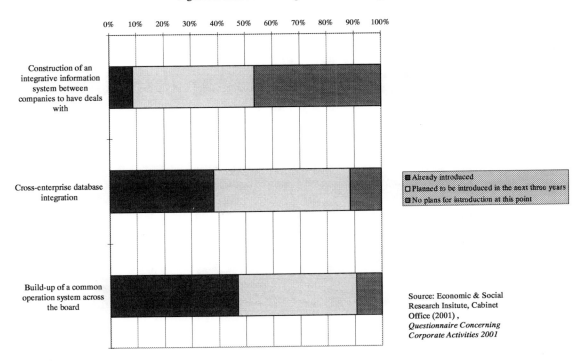

Source: Economic & Social Research Insitute, Cabinet Office (2001) , *Questionnaire Concerning Corporate Activities 2001*

Figure 24 Information Sharing Using IT

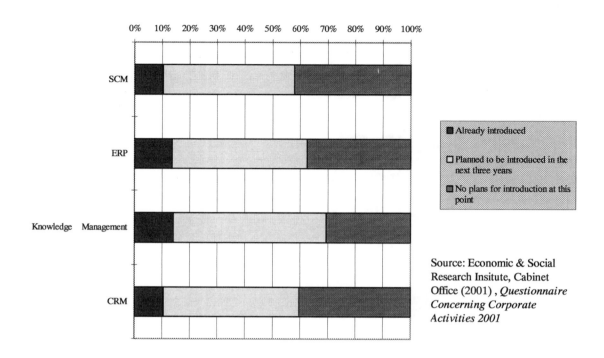

Source: Economic & Social Research Insitute, Cabinet Office (2001) , *Questionnaire Concerning Corporate Activities 2001*

Figure 25 Information Exchange Between Businesses

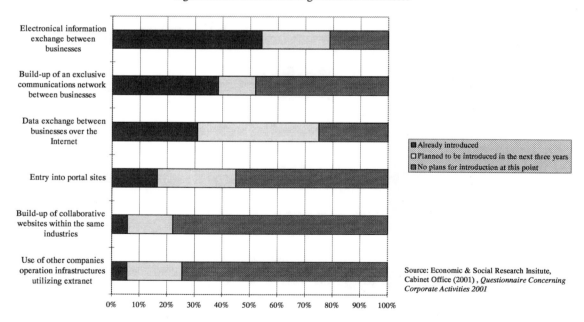

Source: Economic & Social Research Insitute, Cabinet Office (2001) , *Questionnaire Concerning Corporate Activities 2001*

Figure 26 Effects of Growth in B-toB E-commerce

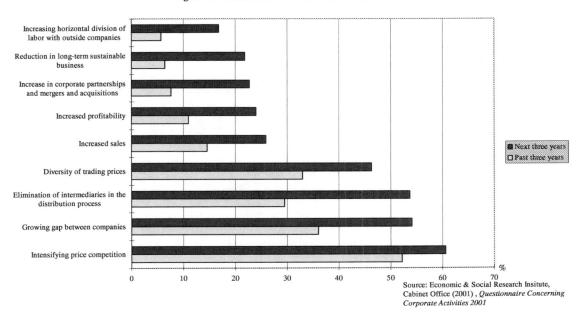

Source: Economic & Social Research Insitute,
Cabinet Office (2001) , *Questionnaire Concerning
Corporate Activities 2001*

Figure 28 Changes in Management Organization

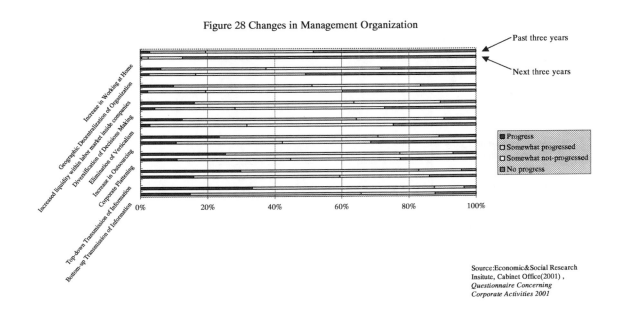

Source:Economic&Social Research
Insitute, Cabinet Office(2001) ,
*Questionnaire Concerning
Corporate Activities 2001*

Figure 29 Older People's Views on Information and Communications Systems

i) Problems with Word Processors and Personal Computers

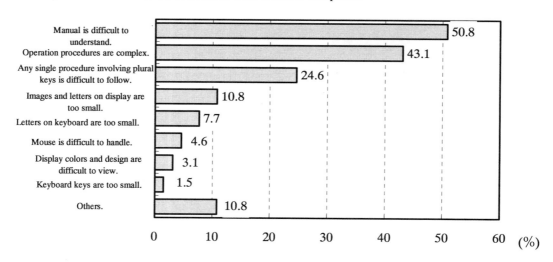

ii) Preconditions for Use of Internet

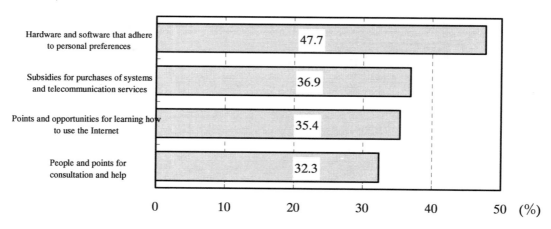

Source: *Research Report on Life-Supporting Information and Communications Systems*,
Ministries of Posts and Telecommunications, and Health and Welfare
Note: Respondents were allowed to choose plural alternatives.

CASE STUDY OF SAMSUNG- TESCO, KOREA

Korea Institute For International Economic Policy

1. Introduction

1) Description of Retail Business in Korea

Retail business is emerging as one of the most promising businesses in Korea due to what Samsung-Tesco calls a 'powershift' from manufacturing to distribution. Indeed, it is especially true in Korea; while the retail business of U.S. and Japan took 32% of GDP on average, that of Korea's took only 21% in year 2000. Samsung-Tesco conservatively forecasts that the average growth of retail business, between 2000 and 2005, would be 8.6%.

Currently, the 'big five' – Homeplus (Samsung-Tesco), E-Mart, Carrefour, Magnet, Wal-mart - consists 52% of the market. As small retail businesses are increasingly being absorbed to big retailers, department store, and supermarket, the competition among the 'big five' is becoming fierce to take advantage of high growth market, which also possesses the strategic advantage of a spearhead for entering Chinese market.

2) This Case Study and the Timeframe

This case study describes the implementation of new economy paradigm, which took place during and after the merger of Samsung Corporation and Tesco PLC. Although the major target of the merger was not exactly on uptaking new economy paradigm, the merger process has played critical role in implementing new economy paradigm in Samsung-Tesco. The case study timeframe stretches from early 1994 to the present while many of the important issues in this case unfolded from 1997 to present. Information in this case was gathered through an interview and questionnaires along with direct observations.

3) Background

In March 1994, after separating out from Samsung group (*chaebol*), Samsung Corporation entered into retail business. There was little doubt that Samsung Corporation would be very competitive because of its well-recognized management skills and capital. However, when it opened its first three retail stores (Homeplus Taegu, Samsung Plaza Bundang, Samsung Plaza Seoul) in 1997, the financial crisis broke out. Plummeting consumer confidence and viciously high cost of financing inevitably placed Samsung Corporation into financial status of literally a step away from bankruptcy; accumulated loss during 1998 was KRW 249 billion (approximately US$200 million)[16]. To overcome this unprecedented difficulty, Samsung Corporation began to restructure its business and downsized the organization while searching

---

[16] Calculated in KRW 1,200 per US$. It should be much higher if it was calculated by exchange rate of that time (Approximately KRW 1,800 per US$).

for the breakthrough strategy. Recognizing that retail business is too attractive to give up, Samsung Corporation decided to seek for foreign investment[17].

At the same time, after successfully establishing its business in Thailand, Tesco PLC was also looking for partner that could provide strong local background as well as capability of creating synergy for Tesco's regional network. As the need of both parties met, Samsung-Tesco was established in May 1, 1999. Through the merger, and initial investment of US$ 220 million from Tesco PLC, Samsung-Tesco was able to clear out all debts and rehire all of 1,137 workers who were laid off during 1998. Strategy and Planning Division of now Samsung-Tesco evaluates the merger a success for two reasons. First advantage was financial. The merger not only saved Samsung-Tesco from bankruptcy but also guaranteed Samsung-Tesco a subsequent investment of $170 million (KRW200 billion) to dominate the market. Second advantage was access to the advanced management skills and IT technology to compete with other world class rivals such as Wal-mart, Carrefour, Costco, *etc.* <Table 1> shows visible improvements of Samsung-Tesco after the merger.

Table 1 Trend of Sales Growth Rate and the Market Rank of Samsung-Tesco

	1999	2000	2001*
Sales	US$363 milllion (KRW 435 billion)	US$516 million (KRW619 billion)	US$1.2 billion (KRW 1.4 trillion)
Growth Rate	-	42.3%	126.1%
Market Rank	5th	4th	3rd**

* Estimated

** First and second rankers are E-Mart and Carrefour

While the 'catching up' of Samsung-Tesco since the merger in Korean retail market is impressive, these figures shown in <Table 1> are not the sole factor for increased attention that Samsung-Tesco receive from the media, the competitors, and the business analysts. In fact, Samsung-Tesco's critical success factor lied in its effective management of the new trend that influenced every industrial nations including Korea – the new economy paradigm.

2. New Economy Narratives

As it was shown in the case of U.S., new economy benefits cannot be fully exploited unless it is supported by infrastructures including human resources capabilities and organizational (socio-cultural) capacity. And it is obvious that, depending on the stages of the development, each recipient of new economy paradigm (business, civil society, government agency *etc.*) will have different degrees of impact and will show different reactions to the new economy paradigm.

Samsung-Tesco's situation was unique in that it had already had IT hardware prepared but it had to adopt global standard IT hardware as well as software (infrastructures such as readiness of workers to adopt new system and culture) for heightened competitiveness. If we

---

[17] Since the financial crisis of 1997, Korean government actively promoted foreign investments and deregulated related laws. It would have been much difficult or impossible if the regulation that existed before the financial crisis still existed.

define[18] new economy paradigm narrowly and limit to just IT hardware, Samsung Corporation had already established its own IT system independently. The IT industry of Korea was quite competitive and the very nature of retail business required intensive IT system throughout its entire value chain. However, after the merger, the requirements on the system have expanded to cover global network, as well as future expansion of logistics system. Samsung Corporation's former system did not meet the requirements of global standards although it worked well on the domestic basis.

Samsung-Tesco faced dilemma of either just modifying the former system or changing the entire system to Lotus system that has been used in Thailand[19]. The Lotus system was more desirable for it was a global standard and flexible enough to take into account a rapid expansion; the former system was consistent with Korean currency, language, practices, and most importantly, people were used to it. The former system was operated in Windows system while the Lotus system was operated in DOS system[20].

Samsung-Tesco decided to partly adopt Lotus system: for retail system, Samsung-Tesco fully adopted Lotus system, and for finance, Samsung-Tesco adopted Oracle financial. However, for personnel management and groupware, Samsung-Tesco decided to stay with the former system. The Lotus system was chosen for retail system – the backbone of the entire value chain in retail business – because of following reasons. First, the former system does not reflect characteristics of multiple stores network – the multiple stores network requires simplification, standardization, and specification of the system. This problem will inevitably be intensified as Samsung-Tesco expands its business. Second, it is clear that, in the near future, global supply chain system will be developed and it will require global standard that the former system is lacking of[21]. It is highly probable that future competitiveness of Samsung-Tesco will be built around its global network; one of Samsung-Tesco's tough competitor – Wal-mart – already introduced its global EDI system. Third and the most important reason was reliability of the Lotus system. Because the Lotus system has already proven its performance in practice, Samsung-Tesco did not have to risk reliability of the system in the situation where the competition is already intensifying.

The principle in adopting the Lotus system in Samsung-Tesco was glocalization (globalization + localization), which is one of the business motto introduced by Seung Han Lee, the CEO of Samsung-Tesco. Glocalization basically pursues, as far as possible, the global standard while recognizing that global standard is not the panacea and therefore business environment of Korea should also be respected. The transition process took three stages as shown in <Table 2>. Note that it took almost one year (10 months) to adopt new IT system.

---

[18] In this case study we define new economy as economic model which any networked two-way information and data communication devices facilitate better decision making of the organization and lead to higher performance.
[19] Samsung-Tesco has chosen the Lotus Thailand system because the Thai environment was most similar to that of Korea's among Tesco's global network.
[20] It does not necessarily mean that DOS system is global standard.
[21] Samsung-Tesco plans to increase global sourcing by 4% of total sales in 2002, 6% in 2003, 8% in 2004 and 11% in 2005

Table 2 Stages of IT System Transition

Stages	Content
1. Survey '99.7– 12	• 30 managers from product/operation/accounting/IT were sent to Thailand to review the Lotus system. • Korean version of Lotus was established and Korean manual was developed.
2. Education '99.12–'00. 2	• 60 trainers were sent to Thailand to experience actual operation of the system
3. Adoption '00.1-5	• Change management project was launched to minimize the friction from the transition

Samsung-Tesco's case implies some insights for the nature of new economy paradigm. *First*, the merger enabled Samsung-Tesco to tap into networked information resources that Tesco PLC has developed around the global network. Samsung-Tesco, without taking risk of developing and testing IT system in the battlefield (competitive retail market of Korea), adopted global standard IT system along with related experiences and business know-hows that were developed in Thailand. It is consistent with the existing theory that drafting in behind the global technology leaders or becoming part of the global technology leaders can be more beneficial than starting from the scratch. *Second*, as international operability of the system gains its importance, so is the importance of localization. This paradoxical statement implies that, to garner the maximum network benefits, the one-way flow of information will not be enough. While pursuing global standard, there should be a continued supply (feedback) of local information to increase the network effect. If Thailand's experiences (which had similar environment to that of Korea's) were not accumulated in the knowledge pool of Tesco, Samsung-Tesco would not have benefited as much from the network. *Third* implication is the importance of infrastructure, especially the human resources infrastructure. Samsung-Tesco accredited that IT workforces who were trained in government institutions and hired by Samsung-Tesco have played an important role in adopting and adjusting the Lotus system to Korean environment. Samsung-Tesco was very satisfied with their skills and appreciated the effort made by the Korean government. However, as will be described later, Samsung-Tesco emphasized post-hiring education and corporate culture as more important aspect. Samsung-Tesco also noted that quality of non-IT workforces is important as well[22]. As the boundary of management has increased and routine works were done by IT system, the quality and impact of decision making by workers (IT and non-IT) became much more important than before.

3. New Economy and Policy

1) Macroeconomic Policy

Macroeconomic environment of Korea played a unique role in promoting new economy. The financial crisis of 1997 had both negative and positive impacts on Korea. Although the crisis led many Korean companies to go bankrupt, it also drove out many inefficient companies out

---

[22] They asserted that, at least in retail business, there is no distinction between IT and non-IT because so many decision making processes are dependent on IT technology.

of business and forced the companies to be competitive to survive in harsh macroeconomic conditions. Had the macroeconomic conditions been favorable, Samsung Corporation would never have considered a merger with Tesco PLC and the result would not have been as good as now. Strategy and Planning department of Samsung-Tesco pointed out that while favorable macroeconomic condition is important and much more preferred, it is also the case that the unfavorable macroeconomic condition sometimes boosts restructuring and creates an environment for what Samsung-Tesco calls a 'step change'[23]. When the organization does not have capability of conducting 'creative destruction', unfavorable macroeconomic conditions could stimulate the innovation process, but it should not be (and cannot be) deliberately created for its risk is too big.

2) Services Infrastructures

Service infrastructures such as physical distribution network, communication network indicates national competitiveness and plays critical role in determining the success or failure of the businesses. Samsung-Tesco, while satisfied with the communication infrastructure of Korea, evaluates Korea's logistics network as insufficient. According to Samsung-Tesco, the ratio of logistics cost to sales was 12.9%, which is far behind that of U.S. (9.0%), Japan (6.4%), and Great Britain (4.7%). However, Samsung-Tesco commented that the Korean government's current effort[24] to enhance logistics network in Korea will have positive effects and show improvement in the near future.

3) Business Environments

Despite the continuous deregulation efforts of the government after the financial crisis of 1997, there still is more room to be filled. Samsung-Tesco finds following problem with government regulations on business. Samsung-Tesco focuses on three core businesses: Homeplus Hypermarket, Homeplus Internet Shopping mall, Homeplus Retail Banking. In fact, this was basic strategy of Tesco's global business. While other two businesses were successfully launched, Homplus Retail Banking was not permitted by the Korean government. However, Samsung-Tesco was optimistic about the financial liberalization of Korea and expects to launch Retail Banking unit in a near future[25].

4) Human Resources Capability

According to Samsung-Tesco, human resources management has two different aspects. While universities and institutions play important role in supplying qualified human resources, the maintenance and improving of human resources should be facilitated by Samsung-Tesco (or other organizations such as government agency, private firms, etc). Samsung-Tesco emphasized its role in further developing human resources after hiring. The basic philosophy of its training programs such as English learning programs, computer classes, capability

---

[23] A breakthrough, or innovative change as opposed to incremental change.

[24] Currently there are six logistics centers in Korea. But it is expected to be twenty-nine by year 2002

[25] The Korean government's hesitance was quite natural after facing severe financial crisis due to lack of supervision on financial sector.

developing programs were to establish glocalized corporate culture that unifies Tesco PLC and Samsung Corporation together.

Samsung-Tesco faced difficulties in 1999, right after the merger. The morale of the employees was quite low due to cultural difference caused by merger, language barriers, and communication difficluties. The major conflict was that employees perceived the new management process of Samsung-Tesco to be too rational and lacking humanity. To make reconciliation of the conflict between Tesco PLC's corporate culture and Samsung Corporation's, Shinbaration Task Forces was launched by the CEO, Seung Han Lee. Shinbaration is a concept that consist of 'Shinbaram' and rationality. Shinbaram is emotional reaction that allows people to achieve more than their limit. This very Korean culture is somewhat too emotional and lacks rationality, which Tesco PLC has been emphasizing in management. The object of Shinbaration Campaign was to encourage teamwork and create working environment where employees can surpass their limit while not letting it develops to cronyism.

While the Shinbaration Campaign is still on progress, Samsung-Tesco's personnel management team finds that there are some signs of two different business cultures getting balanced out. Personnel management team added that the next step is to develop a philosophy that binds two different cultures together.

What Samsung-Tesco emphasized in human resource capability development was well-balanced management of different cultures that cannot be evaluated as which one is good or bad. Samsung-Tesco's case implied that, in developing human resources capability under new economy paradigm, the cultural glocalization concept should be emphasized as a basis for functional skill training programs (e.g. English, Computer skills, *etc.*)

4. Summing-up and Looking Forward

To Samsung-Tesco, the new economy meant more than just adopting IT hardware. It is relatively easy to adopt just the new hardware and train employees the new skills that are required by new technology. The harder part is the balancing of different culture (in this case, British and Korean) to create glocalized culture of management. As new economy thrives on network and the network connects different regions and cultures, the balanced (globalized but also localized) mindset of the workers plays critical role in utilizing the benefits of global network.

Samsung-Tesco plans to anchor on Shinbaration Campaign until they could concretely define Samsung-Tesco culture (unique but conforms to global standard) because it is philosophy and culture, rather than functional adoption of new economy technology, that decides the success or failure in adopting new economy paradigm.

Although Samsung-Tesco recognizes current reform efforts of the government and benefited from it, there exists room for improvements. Samsung-Tesco recommended following suggestions. First, while the second stage foreign exchange liberalization act of 2001 allowed repatriation of proceeds if the management desires, Samsung-Tesco still feels that the process was still too complicated. Second, public-private sector partnership in developing logistics network in Korea will be profitable for both parties. Third, to develop global supply chain, the customs clearance procedures should be enhanced to shorten the lead-time.

MINI-CASE STUDY: MALAYSIA*

Karim Raslan
Kuala Lumpur-based Lawyer and Regionally Syndicated Columnist

Short Overview of Client:

The client is a Malaysia-based, privately owned trading and distribution company involved in the import and export of industrial products. Owned and controlled by a what is commonly dubbed an 'overseas Chinese family', the firm has thirty employees and offices in three countries (Singapore, Hong Kong and Malaysia). The firm's turnover is approximately US$12.5 million per annum. Founded in 1945, the business was acquired by the present owners over 35 years ago.

'New Economy' Narrative:

By their own admission the client firm is conservatively run and extremely cautious. However it became clear in 1998 that the client could cut costs by using information technology (IT) especially vis-à-vis international communication. Initiating the move themselves they invested in the networking facilities in order to remain competitive.

There is no doubt that the reduced costs have been a direct benefit to the bottom line. Furthermore the accelerated operation times has reduced inventory costs. However the internet has not resulted in an expansion of either the customer or supplier base. The clients stressed that in the industrial supply business the element of personal relationship remains crucial: "we want to know who we're dealing with. There has to be a 'face to face' meeting before we can proceed to business." Clients were adamant that a good track record of service, reliability and a strong market reputation helped them maintain their competitive edge. They doubted that a web-site – without the personal touch – could help them.

Clients explained that in their business, customers often had very specific, customised orders and requests. For example a customer might order a semi-finished product such as brass rod. Even if the order volume is low, in the event of a hitch, clients were expected to visit the workplace and rectify the problem. Clients understood that by maintaining close ties and regular site-visits that they would be able to track customer preferences as well as head-off any future problems.

In the case of the brass rods, clients would be expected to examine the problem and make an immediate assessment of the damage and means of rectification. "We have to know our customers inside-out, the processes they use, the workers, their skill-level and the machinery in situ". Having made the investment in time and effort they say 'there is a lot of give and take in the business relationship: we work together'.

---

* This case study was edited at the request of the Government of Malaysia.

Our clients - especially new accounts - refuse to negotiate over the internet. "Discussing terms over the telephone and via fax and email somehow undermines the legitimacy of the company and the perception of our seriousness. It's just too impersonal. We are not paper-shufflers. We have to meet clients face-to-face to give them the comfort." As a consequence clients were very skeptical of the likely success of B2B exchanges in their business.

New Economy and policy:

Since most of the new technology and software is imported and/or assembled with foreign inputs the pricing tends to follow the movement of the US$. Exchange rate volatility can impact on whether or not clients chose to implement a new round of investment in technology. Of course, when as now industrial activity appears to be slowing, clients put off investments in new technology.

Services infrastructures, policy and environment:

Telephone lines within Malaysia are according to clients always congested and the Internet Service Providers (ISP) are insufficient. "When it fails, you're dead". They also voiced concerns about occasional fluctuations in electricity supply and the detrimental impact on stored data, saying "often we make non-electronic duplicates of data which is expensive and time-consuming".

But clients were much more unhappy with what they saw as the software suppliers' attempts to generate more sales by introducing software with only marginal increases in terms of efficiency and costs. As they say "there should be to be tax write-off provisions." They were unhappy about the way the hardware and software suppliers are determined to gouge buyers. "We are not wealthy multinationals and yet we are expected to pay exorbitant costs to protect our data base. Large companies have entire teams manning their systems, we can't afford that."

Furthermore with the advent of email, clients have discovered that their "extremely expensive data" is also vulnerable to external viruses. "In the past faxes and telephone calls wouldn't corrupt our data. This has meant a further duplication of effort as emails are often backed up by faxes This is a 'dead cost' in our eyes." Clients felt that instead of spending the time 'mining the data' for value, valuable management time was devoted to monitoring the data systems and their protection from external corruption and viruses.

When asked about financial intermediaries and distribution, clients were of the view that efficiencies depended on the quality of management and supervision. "We are concerned about the calibre of the people inputting data and supervising the process." Given the amount of information now made available through the internet, they were also worried about security provisions.

Micro business and labour environment including rule of law:

Clients felt that the regulatory environment created price controls. They doubted the openness of the markets, the transparency of price-setting mechanisms. {...} As far as clients were concerned there were, at least in late 1999 and early 2000 very high expectations about the internet and its ability to cut business costs. However, they have found that many apparent advantages have not been applicable in their service-driven business: "we still have to deal with our clients the old way, by calling them up and seeing them on site. That's what they like and want."

Clients felt that clearer overall policy management would assist them in their business. Improvements in physical infrastructure were important but often the soft-infrastructure had been neglected. They were not aware of any cyber laws but professed not to have followed the developments in this field in any way.

Human resource capability:

Clients felt that the best manpower (foreign-trained) was cherry-picked by the MNCs. "We are left with the second tier." Moreover they were consider that there was a major difference between the skilled and unskilled and that the pool of IT-trained workers was not large enough: "there just aren't enough people to go around." As a result it was often difficult to explore new ways of doing business and evolving new products and services. Clients conceded that the government was investing time and energy in upgrading worker skills: but as they said in exasperation, "it's still not enough. Though we do see a much more IT savvy younger generation of workers emerging."

Clients also observed another new development that troubled them. The language on the net is a new challenge. "At first we thought is was a question of whether or not we'll be using Bahasa Malaysia, Mandarin or English. However now we see the emergence of a new net-based language that uses abbreviations and icons. This is fine for people who are familiar with it. Most of our clients and the operational people on the factory line don't have the time or experience to learn what these icons mean. They want solutions and answers not more confusion."

Conclusion and Policy suggestions:

Clients were skeptical – especially after the deflation of the internet bubble of the value of new technologies – to their business. "We still have to service clients the old way." Whilst they acknowledged they were cautious, they were relieved that they didn't over invest in new software when everyone thought it was the thing to do: "that saved us a ton of money, since most of the software and hardware is obsolete within six months." Clients considered education and human resource development as the key to improving the business environment.

MINI-CASE STUDY: PERU

Christian Rodríguez Ramos
Peruvian Institute For Electronic Commerce

1. Short Overview of the Client

The Peruvian Institute for Electronic Commerce (IPCE in Spanish) is a unique non-profit organization based in Lima, Peru. IPCE's mission is to promote and to spread the knowledge on topics like electronic commerce (e-commerce) and e-business, counting with the commitment from the private sector as well as the Government. Besides, IPCE's contribution will improve the performance of local companies from using the latest technologies for being more competitive and recommending the use of both national and international best practices, under the appropriate legal framework.

Many companies and governmental agencies are associated to IPCE and take decisions through a representative Board of Directors. These companies are leaders in their respective businesses, mostly Information and Communication Technologies (ICTs), while the Government Agencies are the governmental institutions most compromised with the use and spread of ICT. With more than two years of existence, IPCE has positioned itself as an organization in charge of recollecting and analyzing the information regarding the growing e-commerce sector in the country, because there weren't any concrete statistics about the real situation of e-commerce in Peru. IPCE currently has 15 employees distributed on four areas: management, research and projects, communications and legal affairs.

2. "New Economy" Narrative

As an organization completely dedicated to promote and analyze the e-commerce and e-business industry in Peru, the new economy forces influence directly over this institute, since it was created precisely around these forces and the growth perspective they create. The Internet is IPCE's field of analysis and at the same time, it's IPCE's main tool to achieve its goals. The IPCE is an intensive user of ICTs, and owns a local computer network, a web site and all the necessary elements to allow a good performance in a new economy context. The IPCE publishes a daily e-commerce news bulletin (distributed via e-mail) and many industry-related market reports; in both, appropriate software is used to analyze, write and publish the outcomes. The IPCE, as an information generator, is an office software heavy user.

Since it's creation, it was considered absolutely imperative counting with the necessary infrastructure capable to offer IPCE's employees the necessary means to complete their information-generating labor. Companies and government agencies involved in IPCE's foundation decide to contribute with those elements according with their own possibilities, so the project could be carried out. Then, private companies, mostly from the ICT industry, gave the necessary hardware and software, while the government agencies contributed with their influence and the required contacts with multinational entities such as APEC. It was precisely

APEC who has given IPCE some international positioning, considering its already achieved goals related to ICT.

ICTs from the new economy have made possible for IPCE to create a unique labor in this country, such as the specific analysis of the Peruvian ICT, e-commerce and e-business industries, the organization of seminars and events regarding those themes, as well as conferences and forums, constituting some of IPCE's main income sources. Likewise, another of IPCE's main goals is to provide accurate information for the internal market as well as the international one, so they could have an exact idea of the actual situation of these sectors in Peru, generally relegated from international statistics.

As an example of actual IPCE research, it was determined that Business to Consumer (B2C) e-commerce in Peru generated approximately US$10,9 millions on 2000. An even more interesting statistic is that almost 80% of this type of e-commerce was made by Peruvian citizens abroad; according to a report by the Inter-American Development Bank (IADB) the 1,5 million of Peruvians living abroad send back to their families in Peru approximately US$800 millions each year. IPCE concluded that the main market segment to boost B2C e-commerce in Peru would be the ever-growing communities of Peruvians living abroad, who have discovered in e-commerce a way to securely send assorted products, specially groceries, for their relatives, by buying on Peruvian e-tailers and sending the products all over the country with relatively low prices.

Additionally, IPCE was able to determine, evaluate and analyze two new economy phenomena produced solely in Peru, including both of them high amounts of creativity and talent for making accessible some of the new economy benefits to the masses. These ideas are so good that their schemes have been imitated in other countries with similar technology and economic characteristics as Peru's. These two phenomena of approaching Internet and its benefits to the population sectors with lower incomes are the "public Internet rooms" ("cabinas públicas") and the "Internet prepaid credit cards". Both solutions have contributed a lot to boost the e-commerce development and Internet utilization across Peru.

Public Internet rooms are small Internet access areas open to the entire population. The business model is essentially a computer Internet access rent at extremely low prices (approximately US$0.70 an hour), due to the ever-growing competition, in a small area for around 5 to 20 computers. This access phenomenon comes from 1995 and now there are around 1500 public Internet rooms across Peru, giving Internet access for the vast majority of the Peruvian Internet users, which are approximately 1 million people.

The other phenomenon is the Internet prepaid credit cards, which have turned to be the fastest growing and preferred payment method for those who can't afford or meet the requirements to get a credit card, mainly because of the high requirements established by the financial system. This is why most Peruvians were excluded from purchasing products over the web, whether from one of the approximately 50 Peruvian e-tailers or from another e-tailer around the world. Currently only half million Peruvians have a credit card. An Internet prepaid card is no more than an actual physically existing card or a virtual one, based on a credit card number that is related to a bank account, where the owner makes a deposit to "load" the card enabling it to buy goods or services on the Internet. These cards have the support from the main credit card companies, and they work just like any international credit card, allowing the owner to buy on any e-tailer on the web. This way, those steep requirements are reduced, allowing many people to buy products on the Internet. Right now, there are three Internet prepaid credit cards in Peru supported by the three biggest banks in Peru, respectively. There are small differences between each one, but the basic characteristics are identical; there is a healthy competition environment in this sector. There are 83% Peruvian Internet users willing to acquire an Internet prepaid credit card at this very moment. This contributes greatly for the development of the country as well as spreading the Internet for business purposes.

Additional IPCE achievements are: obtaining the Vice-presidency of the E-Commerce Experts Committee for the Free Trade Area of the Americas (FTAA) composed by members of both private and government sectors; development of the APEC Readiness Guide on May 2000 as the only country to do so; being member of the Multi-sectorial Commission for Internet Access Broadening, created by the Peruvian Government; and creation of the suggested agenda for the new government for Internet Access Broadening and Development of ICTs in Peru.

3. New Economy and Policy

Despite inflation is not very high in Peru, the main problem IPCE has found is the economic recession that inflicts serious damage in the country since 1999, caused mainly by external factors. Albeit Peruvian economy has grown just 3,6% last year, the e-commerce and e-business industries in Peru showed an important growth over the last few years, as well as a growth on the Internet users in Peru. Nevertheless, some projects and important investments related mainly to Business-to-Business (B2B) e-commerce and e-business have been delayed, waiting for a clear political scenario and economic reactivation to happen.

IPCE has determined that a sector showing great advances in a short term is the Peruvian Government, through the use of the e-Government policies, implicating the use of ICT that the new economy offers to improve its relationship with the people. During a first phase, the offer of e-Government services was limited for businesses, but now the Government is paying attention to its citizens as well, mainly because there are now enough people with web access to justify these new policies. These technologies mainly provide official information and e-services based on considering the Internet as an interactive communication media. The new batch of e-Government policies being carried out is reflected on the recent creation of the Peruvian Government Portal.

In its constant duty of analyzing the actual situation of e-commerce in Peru, IPCE has found that Internet access costs for people and companies have been greatly reduced in the last couple of years, mainly because of the competition environment that exists nowadays; nevertheless, there is a long way due to follow: the access must reach every single person across the country. Now, most access is found in Lima, the capital city, limiting the reach of the benefits brought by the new economy.

On the financial area, many projects to build Internet focused SMEs have been halted because of the high interest rates in the Peruvian financial system. On the logistics area, some advances have been made in the past few years, even considering Peru has a very tough geography. The biggest logistic companies now have a shipment tracking web-based systems that allow customers knowing where exactly is their cargo. Additionally, Customs Authorities are developing great efforts to improve their processes by using the Internet and ITC. Peruvian Customs are going toward a paperless customs process, and will be exclusively web based on a medium term.

On the legal area, IPCE has been an important player in the whole legal e-commerce framework establishment, since it is an organization in charge of making proposals about e-commerce so that the business sector as well as the whole society result favored from an agile legal system specially focused on these new technologies. Peru has one of the most advanced legal systems in Latin America, and IPCE has actively participated in the making of cyber laws such as those for digital signatures and certificates, cyber crimes and contracts among absent people. Other cyber laws include e-mail legal notifications and tax-free importing of end consumer goods, which favors the foreign trade made by natural people through e-commerce.

Referring to the law on digital signature and certificates, it's waiting for the publishing of its respective regulations, so it can be applied on e-commerce, especially B2B. These laws will ease electronic transactions, making them more secure and more efficient. Over the past few months, the environment of competition on these new legal faces for e-commerce have been significantly developed, and it is becoming a very attractive sector.

Finally, IPCE is composed of young professionals deeply involved in the use of new technologies to achieve the organization's goals. Being an organization completely focused on new economy matters has required a highly trained staff compromised with the efficient use and application of these new technologies. The use of IPCE human resources is also important to apply this knowledge to directly help society. IPCE organizes different events to promote the use of these new technologies as well as giving general advice to anyone interested in this knowledge branch, especially for students and potential entrepreneurs. Likewise, IPCE is now developing educational projects to spread this knowledge to SMEs entrepreneurs, so they can use these technological tools from the new economy to raise their productivity, increase their efficiency and enter new global markets, improving the performance of this enormous business sector in Peru.

4. Summing-Up and Looking Forward

Summarizing, IPCE´s vision is to promote and facilitate the development of electronic businesses throughout the country, spreading knowledge, promoting projects and watching for the establishment of a legal framework that promotes its development in Peru. The new economy represents for IPCE an excellent opportunity to achieve the development for the country, giving the necessary spread and promotion in the use of these technologies and benefits. In the near future, IPCE plans to continue its contribution and compromise with Peru, so that both people and companies could reach their complete insertion in the new economy; additionally, IPCE will be focused on B2B and e-Government tendencies, which are very promising uses of the ITC brought by the new economy. Three recommendations IPCE would give as policy changes are:

- Improve people education, especially on the youth and children, so they can make a better use of the technological resources at their reach.
- Improve Internet access for the masses across the country, making possible that more people could have better and cheaper connections.
- Reduce the barriers that stop technological development, such as high tariffs for technological assets.

CASE STUDY: SINGAPORE e-GOVERNMENT

E-Government Planning And Management Division
Government Chief Information Office
Infocomm Development Authority Of Singapore

Introduction

Globalisation and the explosive entry of infocomm technology (ICT) into every facet of life have changed how people live and work, how companies do business and in particular, redefined the nature of government and its relationship with citizens. We have seen the remarkable changes that have taken place in the business sector with the advent of e-commerce. Similar changes are taking place in governments, spurred by the rising expectations of citizens and global competition.

To survive the fundamental transformations taking place today, all governments need to become e-Governments. For Singapore, e-Government is not simply about adding an "e" to government. It covers more than investments in infocomm equipment or setting up a website to publish information. e-Government requires that we fundamentally re-think all aspects of governance to see how we can leverage on technology and new business models to improve efficiency of internal processes as well as change the nature and quality of government interactions with both individuals and businesses.

In June 2000, Singapore launched its S$1.5 billion e-Government Action Plan. Championed by both the Ministry of Finance and the Infocomm Development Authority of Singapore, and involving all ministries and agencies, it addresses issues that spans across all aspects of the public sector from leadership, delivery of electronic public services, internal government operations and ultimately economic competitiveness. With this plan, the Singapore Public Service is working towards the e-Government vision of becoming a leading e-Government to better serve the nation in the Digital Economy.

Route to E-Government - Government Computerisation

Singapore is one of few countries in the world with an integrated and coherent approach to computerisation in the public sector–thanks to an all encompassing Civil Service Computerisation Programme (CSCP) that aims to turn the entire Civil Service into a world-class exploiter of Information Technology (IT).

Since its launch in 1981, the CSCP has brought about many exciting changes to the way the Singapore government works, interacts and serves the public. Singapore's move towards e-Government is built on the solid foundation of the CSCP, of which the progress and key strategies can be grouped into 4 main development stages:

First Wave (early 1980s): The National Computerisation Plan

It was clear that right from the start, national computerisation was high on the government's agenda. Singapore broke new grounds when the CSCP was launched in 1981 to spearhead the national computerisation effort, directed at improving public administration through the effective use of IT.

The first wave was directed at the automation of traditional work functions, reducing paperwork and clerical staff, and creating demand for the new IT industry. The implementation strategy was to start small and scale fast. The programme, started with the involvement of 12 ministries/departments and 150 IT staff, is extended service-wide today. The National Computer Board (NCB), set up as a central authority to promote and implement IT in 1981, played a key role in co-ordinating the implementation of the programme across the civil service.

The first phase of the CSCP has resulted in significant manpower savings. A cost-benefit review by the Ministry of Finance in 1985 showed that CSCP had generated an impressive 171% return on investment. This was in additional to the many intangible benefits such as operational efficiency improvement, better information support for decision making and new services for the public. These achievements have driven the civil service on, in its quest for organisational excellence through IT.

Second Wave (mid 1980s): The National IT Plan

In the second wave, CSCP strategies have matured over the years from improving internal operational efficiency and effectiveness to providing integrated services to the public through cross-agency linkages. This era of inter-organisational communication and co-ordination saw to the creation of three Data Hubs (Land, People and Establishment) to cut down redundancy in data capturing and promote cross-agency data sharing within the government.

An increasing number of public services were developed in the direction of "one-stop non-stop services" for the public and businesses. Some of the award-winning applications include the School Links, Integrated Land Use System (ILUS), One-stop Change of Address Reporting Services (OSCARS), and the various networks such as TradeNet, LawNet and MediNet.

Third Wave (early 1990s): IT2000

The opportunity for further improvement would be limited if the policies were confined to the domestic IT market. The government met the challenges head on and formulated strategic thrusts to develop Singapore into a global IT hub, improve quality of life, boost the economic engine, link communities locally and globally as well as to enhance the potential of individuals. This plan, unveiled in April 1992, is commonly known as IT2000 – The Intelligent Island Vision.

For the CSCP, IT2000 gave greater emphasis to the trend that has already begun - the integration of computing resources in the civil service, through the consolidation of computing facilities in a data centre and through the setting up of a civil service-wide network. At the national level, one of the key deliverables was the creation of an advanced National Information Infrastructure (NII) which comprises the infrastructure level of networks and the value-added applications such as National Contact Information Service (NCIS), Electronic Commerce (EC) applications, Infrastructure for Electronic Identification (IEI), and content hosting.

Fourth Wave (late 1990s onwards) – Infocomm 21

In the late 1990s, the focus was quite clearly on the possibilities brought about by proliferation of the internet technology and the convergence of IT with telecommunication. Singapore's internet-based e-filing system for individual taxpayers stood out among many widely-acclaimed applications as the world's first when it was launched in 1998.

More importantly, the Infocomm Technology revolution requires a paradigm shift. Strategies that have worked well in the past may no longer be as relevant for this new economy paradigm. Competition is global. Infocomm 21, a five-year plan for infocomm in the New Economy, is Singapore's strategic response to this challenge. At its heart is a vision to develop Singapore into a vibrant and dynamic global Infocomm Capital with a thriving and prosperous e-Economy and a pervasive and infocomm-savvy e-Society.

Singapore's move towards e-Government resides within Infocomm 21, as a strategic thrust aiming to better serve Singaporeans in the New Economy.

Singapore E-Government Action Plan

The Singapore Government intends to be one of the best e-Governments in the world with the innovative and efficient delivery of high quality services to the public, private and people sectors of the new digital economy. Whenever feasible, government services and transactions will be delivered and conducted through electronic means. "Citizen-centric" services will provide seamless end-to-end services to all constituencies.

To realise Singapore's e-Government vision, an e-Government Action Plan was drawn up after wide consultation with all levels of public sector officers. It charts the strategic thrusts and programmes that guide the public service in realising the e-Government vision, while retaining the flexibility to adapt to changing needs.

Strategies and Programmes

The Action Plan presents five strategic thrusts for our e-Government activities.

S1: Re-inventing Government in the Digital Economy
Governance in the Digital Economy requires a clear understanding of the impact of ICT on both internal processes in the public sector and transactions with citizens and businesses. The Digital Economy demands reviews of policies, regulations and processes to align them with the rapid developments in the economy and to meet rising expectations from the public. Public officers must therefore be prepared to change their tried and tested ways in transforming government.

S2: Delivering Integrated Electronic Services
Increasingly, citizens are demanding public services to be delivered online, anytime and anywhere, at their convenience. Greater value will be created for the public if electronic services are integrated and centred around customers' needs. The Singapore Government has set an ambitious goal for its Public Service with the end objective of providing a convenient one-stop, non-stop service for the public.

S3: Being Proactive and Responsive
As "time to market" for new services becomes an important consideration, government agencies are expected to adopt the same "sense and respond" approach as the private sector in anticipating citizens' needs and delivering responsive systems and services with speed. Existing services and processes also need to be fine-tuned to meet customers' changing needs and in line with new technological possibilities.

S4: Using ICT to Build New Capabilities and Capacities
ICT offer tremendous opportunities to create new value; to tap the power of collaborative knowledge management; and to provide instant knowledge and processing capability to make quantum leaps in service delivery. The public sector will go beyond using infocomm technologies as a system, but also to radically re-engineer government processes to benefit from the new business models of the Internet era.

S5: Innovating with Infocomm Technologies
To be a leading e-Government, innovation and experimentation are primordial. Public officers are encouraged to be enterprising and be accustomed to situations whereby there is no one to learn from, simply because they are the first ones there.

Where We Are Today

At the core of government IT infrastructure is the GovII, a multi-layered IT infrastructure, that links public sector agencies to facilitate communication between the civil service as well as with external bodies and the public. It enables a "Connected Government" through which people communicate and work together more effectively and where services are delivered to users in an accessible and timely manner.

Singapore ONE (One Network for Everyone), the first nation-wide broadband information structure in the world, is available islandwide. All the universities and polytechnics are wired with sophisticated campus-wide networks. At primary and secondary schools, we are on target to equip every two students with one personal computer and for 30% of the school curricula to be IT-based by 2002. 59% of Singapore households own PCs while 58% of the residential population subscribe to the internet.

Government-to-Employee

Within the civil service, among the infrastructure and suite of applications delivered over the GovII are the Public Sector (PS) Smart Card, Government Electronic Mail System (GEMS) and the Government Intranet. These enable better communication and sharing of information within and between government departments, allowing public officers to work together more effectively.

The government email system, which has a base of 31,000 users from ministries and statutory boards is now handling 12 million mails per month between civil servants, and five million email exchanges between the government and the public annually.

Government-to-Customer

The eCitizen portal heralds a new era for the Singapore Public Service. The concept requires agencies to work across boundaries to integrate information, processes and systems so as to provide a seamless online experience to the public. It adopts the metaphor of a citizen journeying through life, who along the way goes through certain events and is required to complete certain tasks. Government information and services are integrated into multi-agency packages (called "Service Packages") in a way that every person on the street can relate to, such as "Move House", "Attend Primary School", or "Look for a Job". Service Packages are as far as possible chronologically ordered, reflecting a typical Singaporean's life from birth to death, in order to cover all aspects and events in the citizen's life.

To date, more than 680 eServices have been made available online by the various government agencies with 50 eService Packages and 170 eServices in the eCitizen portal. For 2001, we are targeting a total of 200 eCitizen online services and 60 service packages to be made available to the public.

Government-to-Business

On the G-to-B front, we are looking at GeBiz (Government Electronic Business), which is an integrated, end-to-end, web-based system to facilitate online procurement within the civil service. GeBiz offer individual departments and the government as a whole, sophisticated procurement information management, detailed tender statistics and reduced manual data-entry. For suppliers, it will be a one-stop, round the clock web-site for electronic submission of quotations, offers and invoices.

The Threaded Path

Singapore has travelled a long way in its efforts of government computerisation and has collected numerous accolades that marked our commitment and belief in IT. The eCitizen initiative is rated as one of the best public service delivery platforms in the US Federal Government's survey on Integrated Services Delivery in 1999. Singapore was rated one of the five leaders in eGovernment, after US in Accenture 2000 survey and again in 2001, after the Canadians.

While the path is never always smooth and glamorous, there are several contributing factors which have brought us this far.

Singapore's experience in CSCP has proved once again that foresight and leadership are critical to the success and sustainability of such large-scale projects. Right from the start when the ministerial Committee for National Computerisation (CNC) put forward the CSCP in 1980, it was never intended to be a stand alone project, but subsumed under a greater national goal of building a software centre in Singapore. Such a two-prong mandate of increasing government productivity and developing the demand side of the software industry has enabled the CSCP to garner the required attention and resources for its successful implementation.

The commitment of the public service towards organisation excellence is also an equally important factor. From the productivity campaigns in the early 1980s to the current Public Service 21 vision, the Singapore public service has always strived to improve itself to better serve the public. It is this common goal towards excellence which has propelled us to new heights through the use of technology.

TradeNet, launched in 1989, provides traders, freight forwarders and shipping businesses with a single point of access to exchange trade documentation electronically with more than ten government controlling agencies, including the Trade Development Board, the Customs and Excise Department. The OSCARS benefited the public by linking the National Registration Department (NRD) to relevant agencies such as the Public Utilities Board and the Work Permit Office. Notification of change of address at NRD would activate changes in all relevant agencies automatically.

Cross-agency applications such as these were developed long before integrated services become the catch-phrase of the day. This service-wide vision towards excellence and the buy-in on technology as a key tool have brought ministries and agencies out of their silos and built the foundation of inter-organisational co-operation for integrated service delivery.

The pace of technology is rapid and one has to be in step in order to reap the greatest benefits. Singapore recognises the need to be quick in "time to market" and has made concerted efforts to review its plans and strategies regularly to ensure relevance and flexibility in the ever-evolving technology landscape. Government agencies are expected to be nimble and adaptive to change; the National Computer Board (NCB) being a good example. Formed in 1980 as a statutory board under the Ministry of Finance, it became under the purview of the Ministry of

Trade and Industry in 1997 to create better synergies among economic development and industry-promoting agencies. Within this period, 1996 was another year of corporate transformation for NCB. A wholly owned subsidiary was spun off from NCB to look into the development function of CSCP and the remaining reconstituted to become the Government Chief Information Office. The key milestone of NCB evolution is its merger with the Telecom Authority of Singapore (TAS) in December 1999 to become the present Infocomm Development Authority of Singapore (IDA), following the convergence of telecommunications and the information technology.

What We Are Working Towards

Six programmes have been identified to drive the strategic thrusts in the e-Government Action Plan. These will be our main focus for 2000-2003.

P1: Knowledge-Based Workplace
Public officers will be empowered to be knowledge workers who engage in active and collaborative learning and knowledge-sharing as part of a culture of continuous learning. Learning itself will increasingly be performed online, i.e. e-learning.

P2: Electronic Services Delivery
With the public's growing acceptance and usage of the Internet, the Singapore Government has been working towards electronic delivery as the key delivery channel for public services. The eCitizen portal (www.ecitizen.gov.sg) is the main Government-to-Customer initiative, which aims to provide one-stop, non-stop on-line services and information to the public with the public in mind. It requires government agencies to work across boundaries to integrate information, processes and systems so as to provide a seamless online experience.

P3: Technology Experimentation
Public sector agencies will be encouraged to experiment with new technologies that could potentially revamp the way they work. Agencies can pioneer initiatives, which are "first-of-its-kind" or "first-in-its-series" in the public sector, on a trial or pilot basis to better understand what new capabilities these technologies can offer and how they can benefit their organisations and customers.

P4: Operational Efficiency Improvement
The public sector will continue to identify and invest in new systems that improve operational efficiency. In doing so, public officers should however actively ask radical and fundamental questions to review the relevance and usefulness of functions and processes, and whether these could be streamlined to take advantage of the new capabilities made possible by the Internet age.

P5: Adaptive and Robust Infocomm Infrastructure
Infocomm infrastructure investment in the public sector will be channeled to enable the advent of a knowledge-based workplace and the delivery of integrated electronic services, in addition to improving operational efficiency. These include both agency-specific projects as

well as service-wide infrastructure projects where the emphasis is on scalability, robustness and cost-efficiency.

<u>P6: Infocomm Education</u>
The infocomm education programme will target all levels of the public sector. It extends beyond traditional IT literacy, skills and application systems training to focus on managers' capacity to take advantage of growth in infocomm capability to revamp internal processes and external service delivery. This will facilitate the participation of public officers in the process of "re-inventing government" by making meaningful policy decisions in all aspects of governance in the Digital Economy.

The Road Ahead

Singapore has progressed well so far, but the road to eGovernment has just begun. There remains much to be achieved and it will not be easy. Before the dotcom hype, we were committed to IT; as the era come and go, we are still as committed. We believe that it is this long-term belief and commitment in the innovative use of technology that will see us through this exciting and challenging journey.

CASE STUDY ON BUSINESS-TO-BUSINESS E-COMMERCE AT TAIWAN SEMICONDUCTOR MANUFACTURING CORPORATION

Dr. Chen Shin-Horng, Research Fellow and Deputy Director
International Economics Department of Chung-Hua Institution for Economic Research.

Over the past two decades, the integrated circuit (hereafter IC) semiconductor industry has undergone profound structural change characterized by a process of increasing disintegration (see Figure 1; all figures are at the end of the case study). Within this process, alongside the vertically-integrated integrated device manufacturers (IDMs), pure-play foundries have emerged with the aim of carrying out contract work for external customers, which in turn has facilitated the proliferation of fabless design houses. Moreover, the emergence of the System-on-a-Chip (SOC) has induced the modularization of various design technologies, known as silicon intellectual property (IP), which can be used repetitively as the main building block for SOC. This trend has given rise to 'chipless' IC firms, acting as pure providers of IP without owning a fab or even a chip, leading to further disintegration of the industry.

Taiwan Semiconductor Manufacturing Company (TSMC) may be regarded as a major catalyst in the above-mentioned evolution of the industry. The company was founded in 1987 in Taiwan's Hsinchu Science-based Industrial Park, and was listed first of all on the Taiwan Stock Exchange (TSE) in 1994, and subsequently on the New York Stock Exchange (NYSE) in 1997 under the trading symbol of TSM. The company currently employs 14,500 people worldwide, and posted annual sales of US$5.3 billion in 2000.

TSMC was created to function as a dedicated foundry service provider, but in so doing, it is not involved in IC design and does not have any own-brand products. It simply carries out contract fabrication work for global customers ranging from start-up ventures to world-leading IDMs. Therefore, customer relationship management, as well as fabrication capability and capacity, are central to TSMC's operations, in which e-commerce has come to play an increasingly important role.

E-business in TSMC started in 1995 with the introduction of Total Order Management (TOM) as a tool for bridging supply and demand in fabrication, and for order and production scheduling. TSMC has also formed electronic links with its suppliers by implementing continuous replenishment programming (CRP) in order to minimize its inventory costs; however, these can only be considered as the most basic elements of TSMC's 'extended' supply chain management.

In the 'arms-length' relationship between foundries and fabless design houses, it is essential to manage the flow of knowledge so as to facilitate a smooth and efficient transfer of new designs into production. This has been made possible by the design firm's adherence to 'design rules' laid out by the foundry, namely restrictions on the type of designs that will be manufactured in the foundry on a specific delivery schedule. These design rules are determined by the foundry's manufacturing capability and capacity. In light of this, foundries such as TSMC have become part of the network of innovation of new IC designs, which entails close knowledge interactions between foundries and their customers. As a result, TSMC initiated the concept of the 'virtual fab' in 1996 in order to promote virtual integration with its customers by means of business-to-business (B2B) applications, thus rendering TSMC as the facilitator of its customers' supply chain management.

Apart from online regular business transactions, TSMC's B2B, under a total package of 'eFoundry' covers three major aspects: logistics, engineering and design (see Figure 2). The eFoundry consists of a suite of Internet-based applications that provide TSMC's customers with real-time support in wafer design, engineering and logistics, functioning as the master tool for the concept of the virtual fab. It currently supports five online services, including TSMC-Online (updated to version 3.0), TSMC-Direct, TSMC-YES (Yield Enhancement System), TSMC-ILV (Internet Layout Viewer) and eJobView (see Table 1). Amongst these, TSMC's customers have shown a preference for TSMC-Online as a one-stop tape-out service. This also features the Webex Internet conference forum capability for customer engineering and other communications and collaborative views of charts, screenshots, and SEM pictures.

In terms of collaboration in logistics, TSMC-Online provides access to real-time production and logistics information updates in areas such as the status of wafer fabrication, assembly and testing, and in order handling and shipping. As for engineering collaboration, TSMC-Online provides a variety of engineering capabilities, including interactive views of prototyping, lot status, yield analysis and quality reliability data. It is also empowered with design collaboration capabilities in support of customer access to important information needed during the design process. Aided by Design Service Alliance, to which we shall return later, TSMC-Online provides selected blocks of IP owned by third parties – these are robust design solutions that conform to the production technologies of TSMC – which are then made available to designers. According to Lawrence Chen, TSMC's E-Commerce marketing manager, "[customers] using TSMC-Online 3.0 now have a personalized window into the foundry ...... this advances the concept of a Virtual Fab to new levels by providing the power to select the exact production information to monitor wafers in both engineering and mass production stages".

In terms of service coverage, TSMC-Direct is similar to TSMC-Online, but the former is a system-to-system method of integration between TSMC and its business partners which uses specific software to link mission-critical business processes, whilst the latter is open to wider access, since it is Internet-based. TSMC-Direct acts as an extension of customers' own internal systems enabling collaborative planning, work in progress tracking, engineering data sharing, real-time order placement, confirmation and other important business control features.

Through the use of TSMC-YES, TSMC's customers can perform yield enhancement analysis remotely from their workstations or PCs using exactly the same tools, data and models as those employed by TSMC's engineers. This purports to promote engineering collaboration between TSMC and its customers in order to achieve shorter yield analysis cycles, improved yield enhancement efficiencies and faster ramp to production.

In addition, both TSMC-ILW and eJobView are specifically instrumental in design collaboration. TSMC-ILV is a real-time web-based distributed layout information viewing service providing an engineering collaboration platform for communicating on issues relating to layout. Through these means, designers can interactively review, navigate, highlight and discuss layout issues with TSMC's service engineers. As a result, it may be possible to achieve improved design productivity, lower engineering and debugging costs, and faster time-to-market.

TSMC's eJobView is a mask inspection software system – the first of its kind in the foundry industry – which allows external customers to view mask images anytime or anywhere through their favorite web browser. Foundry mask data sign-off previously involved several days of inspection and discussion, and even expensive air travel costs for international customers. In contrast, through the use of eJobView, mask image inspection is immediate, with remote teams now able to discuss critical projects in real time, leading to faster time to tape-out, lower development costs and faster time to volume.

In order to facilitate design collaboration, TSMC has also formed a Design Service Alliance with third parties. As mentioned earlier, the emergence of SOC has spotlighted the importance of silicon IP, and as a result, IC design has come to resemble the assembly of IPs, from both internal and external sources. Design houses are also faced with the challenge of choosing from amongst a variety of library suppliers and Electronic Design Aid (EDA) tools. TSMC previously functioned as a pure-play foundry with limited design service capacity, but with Design Service Alliance, the company can now mobilize external resources to facilitate the design processes of its customers.
+
Design Service Alliance encompasses the four service areas that make up the IC design process - third party libraries, silicon-verified IPs, experienced IC designers and proven EDA software. A network of leading third party library vendors form the core of the Library Alliance; this enables TSMC's customers to gain access to required technical services, leading edge process-specific technologies and documents on design requirements. IP Alliance encompasses a large category of silicon-verified and production-proven foundry specific IP, which are useful for designers in IP assembly.

Through the Design Center Alliance, TSMC helps its customers to connect to a global network of qualified and experienced IC design centers to gain the necessary design expertise. Similarly, through the EDA Alliance, TSMC's design service engineers work with EDA Alliance members to deliver TSMC-specific technology files and design kits that may simplify its customers' design experience. In essence, the Design Service Alliance as a whole aims to provide TSMC's customers with total IC design solutions to accelerate cycle time from specification, through tape-out, to finished wafers. Both TSMC's customers and the key testing and packaging firms can gain access to the Design Service Alliance using TSMC-Online as the platform.

TSMC's customer services have also been extended to collaboration on prototyping through CyberShuttle. First launched in October 1998, CyberShuttle allows multiple customers to share the costs of a single mask set and prototype in a pilot run. It aims to help customers substantially reduce their non-recurring engineering (NRE) charges for small wafer volumes, providing fast and cost-effective prototyping. According to TSMC, Cybershuttle will launch 93 multi-project wafers during 2001, with the first half alone almost matching the 50 shuttles launched throughout the whole of last year. CyberShuttle has grown in popularity because, according to Mike Pawlik, vice president of marketing at TSMC: "[first], it provides access to state-of-the-art silicon for advanced prototyping at an affordable price …. second, TSMC's ability to assemble these and turn around the working prototypes is exceptional. Designers rightly see the CyberShuttle program as a way of reducing design risk and getting to market faster".

In sum, whilst starting out as a stand-alone OEM foundry, TSMC has come to resemble a provider of integrated service packages covering a wide range of value chain management activities thanks to its extensive application of e-commerce. Basically, through its arms-length relationship with its customers, TSMC is not just a pure manufacturer; it has become the natural place to verify the manufacturability of its customers' designs and to ensure the quality and timely delivery of their finished wafers. The ability of the electronic Internet and e-commerce links to accelerate and broaden information transfer between TSMC and its customers not only helps to simplify their tasks of knowledge management and exchange, but also induces TSMC to widen the scope of its extended supply chain management activities.

In a sense, the method of e-commerce deployed by TSMC, or more specifically TSMC-Online, acts like a portal providing comprehensive support for its customers' major operational tasks, ranging from prototyping and design, to engineering and logistics. In terms of design, aided by B2B Internet applications, TSMC has drawn on a portfolio of design solutions from third parties to help its customers to achieve better designs, more reliable design reuse, and faster time-to-market, leading to virtual integration of a network of firms.

In TSMC's B2B e-commerce model, goods and cash flows are secondary to information flows. As a pure-play foundry, its inventory costs for finished products are not an important issue, whereas in contrast, customer relationship management is regarded as central to TSMC's operations as a means of securing its rates of capacity utilization and profitability. In addition, from their own view, B2B e-commerce is necessary for foundries to come to terms with the trend towards SOC. Therefore, TSMC's e-commerce initiatives aim to meet the across-the-broad needs of its customers, in order to enhance customer loyalty.

Given the importance of information flows, which are first and foremost in TSMC's operations, it is essential for the company to ensure that its customers and partners gain real-time, continuous access to its B2B applications; however, Internet-based applications, such as TSMC-Online, are vulnerable to Internet traffic jams and disruption. To overcome such problems, TSMC recently added 'dual-site' capabilities to its e-commerce systems. For example, an Online 3.0 routing system now automatically switches users to one of two 'mirror sites' – whichever is hosting the least amount of traffic. According to tests performed by an independent consulting firm, Online's dual-site capability has improved the data download time in the US by up to 60 percent. During the Taiwan-to-US cable damage incident in February 2001, the dual-site capability continued to give users around the globe continuous access to TSMC-Online without disruption. In light of this, government efforts need to be geared towards upgrading ICT infrastructure in order to facilitate B2B e-commerce in firms such as TSMC.

Figure 1 Disintegration of the IC Industry

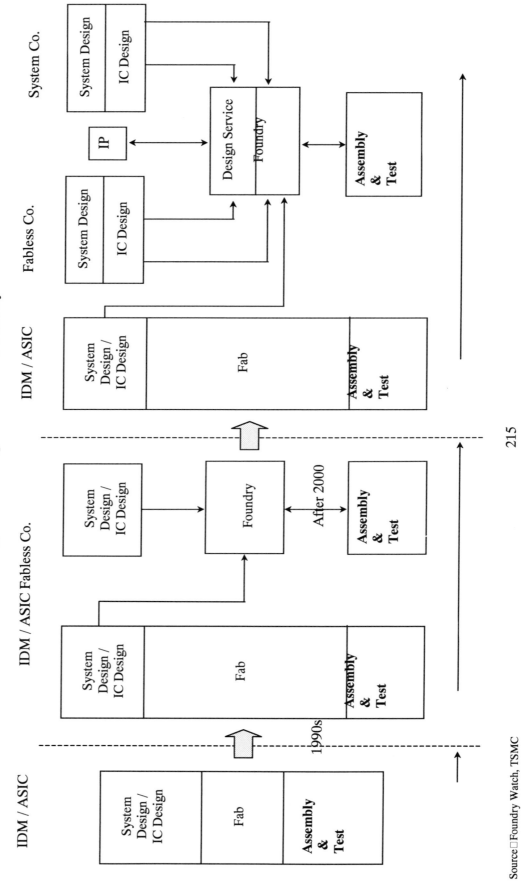

Source⬜Foundry Watch, TSMC

Figure 2   The Framework of TSMC's e-Business

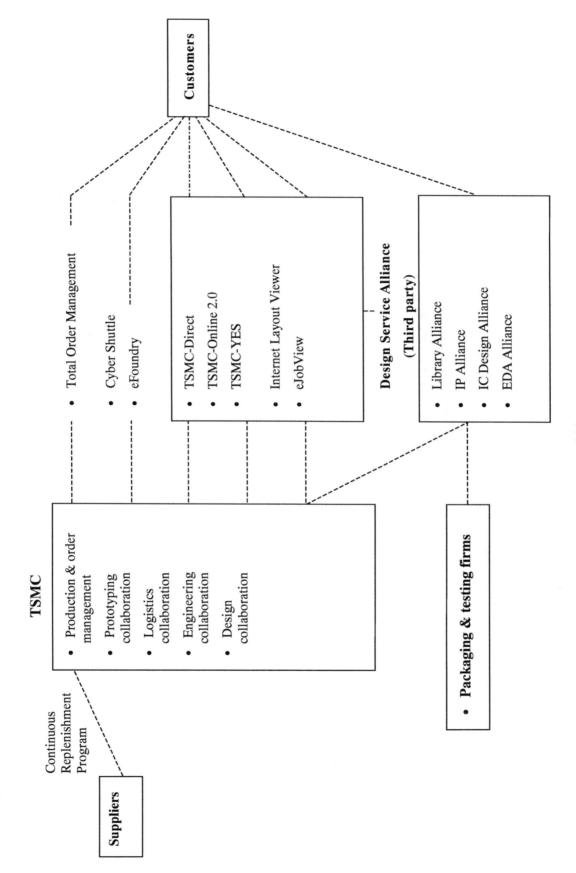

216

Business Cycle	Document	TSMC Online	TSMC Direct	TSMC YES	TSMC ILV	eJobView	How to
Foundry	Company	o	x				
	Foundry service	o	x				Online.tsmc.co
	Technology	o	x				>>TSM-Online
Product	Design	o	x				
	PCM	o	x				
	Process	o	x				
Mask	Design	o	x		o		
	Foundry service request	o	x				Embedded TSMC-Online
	Magnetic tape	o	x				>>TSM-ILV
	Mask data	o	x			o	
	Mask field	o	x				
Wafer Manufacturin	Purchase	o	o				
	Order	o	o				Jobview.tsmc.t
	Shipping	o	o				>>ejobVie
	Shipping	o	o				
	Backlog	o	o				
	Testing		o				
	WAT	o	o				
	Wafer sort	o	o				
	QA	o	o				
	SPC	o	o				
	Process reliability data	o	o				
Engineering Analysis & Yield	Engineer data & Analysis tool	o	o	o			>>TSM-Direct >>TSM-YES
Enhancement Customer Satisfactio	Customer complaint issue & Status	o	o				

Note꞉o = available   x = service per request

THAILAND SCHOOLNET PROJECT

In 1995, as part of the IT promotion activities during Thailand IT Year campaign, NECTEC had extended the ThaiSarn Network (a research and education network connecting universities) to link secondary schools. The project is called Thailand SchoolNet Project, which was started as a demonstration project with 50 public secondary schools in various parts of the country. The aim of the project is to enrich teaching and learning in schools by providing a channel to access the world's "virtual" library, and a channel to exchange information between and among teachers and students, not only within schools, but across the world, through the Internet. The project is run by NECTEC, in collaboration with the Ministry of Education and Ministry of Transport and Communication (through the Telephone Organization of Thailand-TOT and Communications Authority of Thailand-CAT).

During the early phase, a strong boost to the SchoolNet was led by private sector participation where three vendors (i.e., Compaq, Intel, and Powell Computer) joined the project and donated one Pentium computer to 32 schools in the rural areas. Microsoft further donated 50 sets of Windows '95 and utilities to speed up the schools' activities on the Net.

By participating in the project, the school will receive free Internet accounts (three accounts per school), and a space (5 MB) on the central server to put their school's web pages. In addition, the school can join activities such as training courses, and other collaborative projects with other schools.

SchoolNet is the first and only network that **provides universal access to users** (i.e., teachers and students). More specifically, with help from the TOT and CAT, schools all over the country can access SchoolNet via a dial-up mode (using #1509 access No.) and pay only a local telephone charge (i.e., Baht 3 per call). Presently, there are approximately 1,620 schools nationwide connecting to SchoolNet (www.school.net.th), with approximately 500 having their own web sites.

Besides provision of Internet access, NECTEC has also placed emphasis on two other equally important measures, i.e., **training of teachers** and promotion of **content development** in local language (including promotion of Internet activities in the classroom). Teachers training now is run, using the course developed by NECTEC, by 36 Rajabhat Institutes nationwide.

On the issue of content, NECTEC has initiated many pilot projects/activities, such as:
- Classroom 2000
- Digital Library
- Digital Archive

Furthermore, NECTEC also encourages schools to participate in international collaborative projects, such as, GLOBE (Global Learning and Observations to Benefit the Environment), AT&T Virtual Classroom, and Thinkquest Project. Other programs that have been initiated to support SchoolNet are, for example, SchoolNet volunteer program, student camp and web competition on selected subjects, etc., where support came from private or non-governmental sector.

For schools that are ready to run their own server, NECTEC provides a special course on Linux-SIS, its own distribution of Linux, to be used as a School Internet Server. SIS is very popular in Thailand due to its excellent documentation in Thai language, its simple-to-install CD-ROM and web-based server management without the need to know UNIX commands. SIS training courses are always in constant demand from schools looking for a reliable Internet server at the lowest cost.

In October last year (1999), the Cabinet had approved the expansion of SchoolNet to cover 5,000 schools nationwide, as part of the celebrations of His Majesty the King's 6th Cycle Birthday. Once the budget is approved by the budget bureau, implementation can start immediately. It is expected that by the end of 2002, the target of 5,000 schools should be met, where all secondary schools (approx. 3,000) will be connected.

CASE STUDY: VIET NAM
'GREAT BLESSING' POLYCLINIC – A SUCCESS STORY

Dr. Mai Anh

*General Secretary and Vice President: Association of Information Processing
and IT Director, Ministry of Science, Technology and Economy (MOSTE) MOSTE*

In early 1998, an overseas Vietnamese whose name is Le Ngoc Long came home to set up a private limited company trading in apparel. In mid 2000, Long decided to expand his business to health services. He launched a polyclinic called 'Great Blessing' with approximately 30 doctors and nurses in September 2000. The polyclinic located at 42 Ngo Thi Nham, Hanoi, Viet Nam.

As he had exprienced e-mail as an effective tool to communicate with his apparel partners through his personal computer, he made up his mind to select Internet as one of the principle marketing channels for his health services. However, because of the limited knowledge of his staff in doing business on the net, Long co-operated with the Internet Center of The Corporation for Financing and Promoting Technology FPT, the 2nd largest ISP in the country, to develop a website to disseminate information relating to health services to the whole world. FPT acted as the web design and hosting provider for the polyclinic.

In early September 2000, the construction was finished and the website was launched at the http://www.phongkhamhp.com.vn/.

In the initial stage, the website only included static web pages containing introductory information, services description, and price list. The website got over 1,100 visitors after two first months of operation.

However, due to the fact that Internet users not only wanted to get information, they also would like to arrange appointments with doctors and get online health consultany via the website, Long decided to turn his website into a dynamic and interactive one so that he can get online feedbacks and orders from potential Internet clients. After the first week, the polyclinic received 50 orders via the website.

In February 2001, Long put an advertising banner linked to his website on some famous Viet Nam websites such as FPT (http://www.fpt.vn/), Viet Nam Express (vnexpress.net), Viet Nam E-commerce (www.vne.com.vn), etc. to increase the traffic to the website. In addition, the polyclinic also distributed leaflets containing the web address http://www.phongkhamhp.com.vn/ to its clients for reference.

After a very short time, the number of visitors to the website exceeded 6,000 per month, 200 of which made health consultancy request via the net. The average number of clients to the polyclinic increased from 40 patients per day in October 2000 to about 100 patients per day in April 2001.

When asked, Long said, "Internet really helps my clients more satisfied and drives more prospects to the polyclinic. But we have to do everything by ourselves."

Really, what Long and his men have gained bases only on their own efforts. They almost get no support from any governmental organization. The only organzation provided them a 'free support' was Vietnam Association for Information Processing (VAIP). With this help, Long could put his advertising banner on VAIP homepage at the http://www.vne.com.vn/ for free. According to Long, he has no information if the country has any project that supports small and medium businesses like his to develop the application of IT into business.

The Internet growth in Viet Nam for the past 4 years has contributed to the development of Long's online health services. With nearly 130,000 dial-up users in the country in June 2001, the Internet market is a good source for Long's business. Long also has worked out some promotions for urban Internet users who have rural relatives in order to attract a great number of rural prospects.

But because of the low speed of data transfer on the local network and high cost of Internet usage, still less-than-expected number of Internet users access his website. Moreover, there is almost no rule of law regulating business activities on the net in Viet Nam. So Long was more cautious in online transactions.

Therefore, if the communication network infrastructure is improved, the cost of Internet usage is lowed down, new Internet business rules of law are released, Long will have more opportunities to take advantages of the digital economy. He said, if the cost reduced, he might double his investment in the industry.

Another big problem is human resource. Although thousands of IT students graduate in Viet Nam every year, Long have found it difficult for him to recruit IT-qualified staff to administer the website. Because the proper administrator must not only be IT-friendly but also business-minded. Viet Nam is in shortage of such human resource. Long consequently will have to buy web and e-commerce solution from FPT, who is his web hosting provider as well. This has cost him a great deal of money.

Anyway he has recruited some graduated students and asked FPT for training the staff. Now Long has 2 administrators who are able to manage the website. They have rights to access FPT Internet servers from remote computers to perform tasks like updating the website.

In the next few months, Long and his men are planning to develop an online health encyclopedia so that his website will become the Number 1 Internet health service portal in Viet Nam. He also intended to launch an e-mail marketing campaign to send advertising e-mails to some tens of thousands of Viet Nam-based Internet users.

According to Long, if a small and medium business in Viet Nam would like to be successful in the digital era, it would get a considerable technical and financial support from a governmental or international organization.

What Long has done is actually only an experiment.